Acknowledgments

W9-APR-414

Primary writer: Daniel Sigward

This publication was made possible by the support of the Richard and Susan Smith Family Foundation.

Developing this guide was a collaborative effort that required the input and expertise of a variety of people. Many Facing History and Ourselves staff members made invaluable contributions. The guidance of Adam Strom was essential from start to finish. Jeremy Nesoff played a critical role through his partnership with Dan Sigward and, along with Denny Conklin and Jocelyn Stanton, helped to shape the curriculum by providing feedback on numerous drafts. Margot Stern Strom, Marc Skvirsky, and Marty Sleeper served as a thoughtful editorial team. Anika Bachhuber, Brooke Harvey, and Samantha Landry kept the writing and production process moving forward. Catherine O'Keefe and Ariel Perry attended to countless details and transformed the manuscript into this beautiful and polished publication. Erin Kernen carefully managed to secure all license contracts. Rob Tokanel, Alexia Prichard, Wilkie Cook, and Liz Kelleher creatively adapted and extended this resource as they developed the companion videos and website.

We also benefited greatly from the experience and advice of the ninth-grade history teachers in the Boston Public Schools—under the leadership of Robert Chisholm and James Liou—who piloted two versions of this curriculum in successive years. Additional feedback from Facing History staff members and teachers who conducted pilots in Cleveland, Memphis, Denver, and San Francisco helped us fine-tune the curriculum before final publication.

Finally, we are grateful to have received guidance and feedback from distinguished historians and experts in history education. We owe special thanks to Eric Foner, Chad Williams, Steven Cohen, Chandra Manning, and Heather Cox Richardson.

FACING
HISTORY
AND
OURSELVES

The Reconstruction Era

AND The Fragility of Democracy

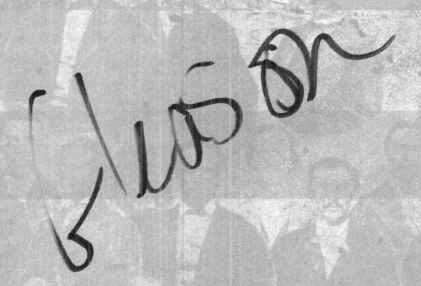

A FACING HISTORY AND OURSELVES PUBLICATION

Facing History and Ourselves is an international educational and professional development organization whose mission is to engage students of diverse backgrounds in an examination of racism, prejudice, and antisemitism in order to promote the development of a more humane and informed citizenry. By studying the historical development of the Holocaust and other examples of genocide, students make the essential connection between history and the moral choices they confront in their own lives. For more information about Facing History and Ourselves, please visit our website at www.facinghistory.org.

The photograph used in the background of our front cover depicts the African American and Radical Republican members of the South Carolina legislature in the 1870s. South Carolina had the first state legislature with a black majority. This photo was created by opponents of Radical Reconstruction, and intended to scare the white population. See Lesson 8, "Interracial Democracy" for suggestions about how to use this image in the classroom.
Photo credit: Library of Congress (1876).

ISBN: 978-1-940457-10-9

Table of Contents

INTRODUCTION   The Fragility of Democracy

by Marty Sleeper, Associate Executive Director, Facing History and Ourselves

In Facing History and Ourselves classrooms, students learn that democracy, among the most fragile of human enterprises, is always a work in progress and can only remain vital through the active, thoughtful, and responsible participation of its citizens. Its ideals of freedom, equality, and justice require constant vigilance and sustenance. Those moments in history when these ideals were assaulted and democracy was put at risk, if not destroyed, need close and rigorous examination in the school curriculum. This unit provides teachers and students with opportunities to look closely at one such moment in American history: the era of Reconstruction after the Civil War.

The core Facing History resource, *Facing History and Ourselves: Holocaust and Human Behavior*, explores the failure of democracy in Germany in the 1920s and 1930s, when such institutions as law, education, and civil legislation collapsed in the face of deep-seated prejudice, hatred, and violence. While Facing History rejects simple comparisons in history, the parallels between the Weimar Republic in Germany and the Reconstruction era in America are striking in their illumination of the fragility of democracy as both a means of governance and a set of societal ideals. The question of how a society heals and rebuilds after extraordinary division and trauma, when the ideals and values of democracy may be most vulnerable, can be explored in histories addressed by other Facing History resources as well, such as the history of South Africa after apartheid, the struggles in Cambodia, Bosnia, or Rwanda after genocides, and the writing of the Universal Declaration of Human Rights after World War II. But this unit on Reconstruction in America reveals how memory and history are themselves vulnerable and can be used by leaders in later generations to unleash racial hatred, justify discrimination, and deny liberty and equality to racial or religious minorities.

New scholarship and perspectives on the past must constantly be brought to bear on how we understand the present. Examining the era of Reconstruction is a prime example. Few would deny that this history has been poorly and insufficiently taught. Its dilemmas deserve the close and rigorous attention that this unit offers. Moreover, themes of identity, membership, individual and group choice, responsibility, and denial—all components of human behavior that Facing History uses as a conceptual framework and vocabulary to help students enter into the past—permeate the era of Reconstruction, and their elaboration in this unit will assist students in understanding Reconstruction's legacy today. Exploring this history in all its complexity offers young people a critical opportunity to exercise their capacity for emotional growth and ethical judgment as they connect its lessons to the issues and the choices faced in their own world and the world of the future.

Teaching This Unit

This curriculum is designed to guide you and your students through a Facing History and Ourselves unit about the Reconstruction era of American history. In this unit, students will investigate the challenges of creating a just democracy in a time of deep division. The resources included here have been selected and sequenced in order to deepen students' ethical and moral reasoning, challenge their critical thinking and literacy skills, and engage them in a rigorous study of history.

This unit unfolds over 16 lessons sequenced according to the scope and sequence that shapes every Facing History and Ourselves course of study. Students begin with an examination of the relationship between the individual and society, reflect on the way that humans divide themselves into "in" groups and "out" groups throughout history, dive deep into a case study on the history of Reconstruction, and then explore the way that history is remembered and the impact of its various legacies in contemporary society. Each lesson includes essential questions, pedagogical rationales, historical overviews, resources to use in your classroom (documents, images, videos, websites, etc.), and activity suggestions.

FOSTERING A REFLECTIVE CLASSROOM

While this curriculum offers a wealth of resources to support a deep exploration of the Reconstruction era, it is missing a crucial ingredient in any Facing History unit: the unique voices of your students and you, the teacher. We cannot predict how the particular students in your classroom will respond to the ideas, history, resources, and activities that comprise this course. We trust and respect your ability to make wise choices based on careful attention to your students' questions and ideas. The roles of the teacher in a successful Facing History classroom are both numerous and essential. It will be your job not only to listen but also, at times, to be directive. It will be your job to carefully guide class discussions, providing accurate answers to clarify points of confusion and enforcing rules and guidelines to safeguard a reflective respectful learning environment.

We believe that two ways in which you can create a strong foundation for a reflective classroom are through the use of student journals and classroom contracts. Journals help students develop their voices and clarify their ideas as they keep a record of their thinking and learning throughout the unit. Engaging students in the process of creating a classroom contract demonstrates to them that both the teacher and their classmates will respect their voices. Even if you already incorporate both of these elements into your instruction, we encourage you to review the appendix sections "Fostering a Reflective Classroom" and "Journals in a Facing History Classroom" for detailed suggestions for guiding and honoring the voices of your students.

USING THESE MATERIALS

The following overview outlines the organization of these materials.

Sections

The lessons in this unit are grouped into six sections. These sections follow the Facing History and Ourselves scope and sequence, and they provide logical thematic divisions for the historical content.

Lessons

Every section in this unit contains one or more lessons. Lessons are divided into the following components:

ESSENTIAL QUESTIONS

Each lesson begins with one or more essential questions. These questions are designed to provide a framework for the lesson by probing the big ideas and important themes that arise from the historical content of the lesson. Our essential questions do not specifically or explicitly probe the historical content of the lesson, and we do not expect that students will fully answer them by the end of the lesson or the unit as a whole.

According to Grant Wiggins, an essential question

- causes genuine and relevant inquiry into the big ideas and core content;

- provokes deep thought, lively discussion, sustained inquiry, and new understanding as well as more questions;

- requires students to consider alternatives, weigh evidence, support their ideas, and justify their answers;

- stimulates vital, ongoing rethinking of big ideas, assumptions, and prior lessons;

- sparks meaningful connections with prior learning and personal experiences; and

- naturally recurs, creating opportunities for transfer to other situations and subjects.[1]

TRANSITION

This short paragraph will help orient you as to how this lesson fits into the unit's sequence of themes and topics. The language included here can help you introduce the lesson to the class, explaining how it relates to lessons that the class has already completed as well as those that will follow.

RATIONALE

The rationale for each lesson is designed to answer the following questions:

- What do we hope students will learn in this lesson?

---

1 Grant Wiggins, "What Is an Essential Question?" from *Big Ideas* (e-journal), Nov. 15, 2007, http://www.authenticeducation.org/ae_bigideas/article.lasso?artid=53 (accessed Jan. 23, 2014).

- Why is this material important?

- What additional background knowledge do you, the teacher, need to understand in order to teach this lesson effectively and answer questions that might arise from the class?

We encourage you to read the rationale for each section carefully in order to glean important information and guidance about how to frame central ideas and present challenging and complicated historical events for your students in ways that best support intellectual and emotional growth. The rationale will provide historical information that will help you better understand and articulate the goals of each lesson to the class.

Our hope is that actively reading our rationale helps you articulate your own goals for teaching this material. As you read each rationale, consider the following questions:

- What parts of the history will resonate most with your students?

- What details and nuances in the history can you share with the class to help them better understand the lesson's documents and think more deeply about the moral and ethical dilemmas they encounter?

LEARNING GOALS

The learning goals for each lesson are divided into *understanding goals* and *knowledge goals*.

Understanding goals include broad ideas, concepts, and patterns relating to the themes of human behavior, freedom, justice, and democracy that extend beyond the particulars of the lesson's historical content. These goals are often related to the essential questions for the lesson.

Knowledge goals include key ideas and concepts we expect students to learn that are particular to the topic and content of the lesson, and especially to the history of Reconstruction.

RESOURCE LIST

The resource list includes documents, images, videos, student handouts, and any other materials you will need to teach the lesson. Many of these materials are included in this curriculum and are suitable to photocopy for students or project in your classroom. Others, such as videos, can be borrowed from the Facing History library or streamed online. Teachers may need to make choices about which resources to include in their lessons and which to omit.

LESSON PLANS AND ACTIVITY SUGGESTIONS

The Reconstruction Era and The Fragility of Democracy includes six full lesson plans: one to help you introduce a central question and writing prompt for the entire unit and five to support specific themes and content in the history of Reconstruction. These lesson plans model how we believe these materials can be effectively implemented. We expect that teachers will use and adapt these lesson plans to best suit the needs of their particular classes.

For lessons that do not include a full lesson plan, we have included brief suggestions for teaching strategies that you might use to achieve the goals of the lesson. The "Teaching Strategies" section at facinghistory.org/reconstruction-era/strategies provides more detailed descriptions of many of the teaching strategies suggested here.

LITERACY SKILLS, HISTORICAL THINKING, AND THE COMMON CORE

This resource provides opportunities for students to practice literacy and historical thinking skills that are appropriate and meaningful in any history classroom. The materials in this unit are also grounded in the three instructional shifts required by the Common Core State Standards for English Language Arts:

1. *Building knowledge through content-rich nonfiction*

   This curriculum presents the history of the Reconstruction era through a variety of primary and secondary sources. Students build knowledge through their deep investigation of text and content through discussion, writing, and individual and group activities.

2. *Reading, writing, and speaking grounded in evidence from text*

   Many activities throughout this curriculum require that students explain and defend their responses and analysis using evidence from one or more texts. (One example of this is the culminating writing assignment based on the central question, described in the next section.) In addition, the resource provides a wide variety of opportunities for different forms of writing and discussion.

3. *Regular practice with complex text and academic language*

   Many of the texts included in this resource are indeed complex and highly sophisticated. In their analysis of these texts, students will practice the close reading of texts and the use of academic vocabulary.

While all of the lessons in this resource were designed, in part, with these skills in mind, two parts of this curriculum in particular target literacy skills valued by the Common Core. The first is a series of structured close reading activities, and the second is a set of central questions that provide the basis for an argumentative or informational writing assignment that spans the duration of the unit.

Close Reading Activities

Five lessons in this unit include materials to help you engage your students in a close reading of one of the lesson's documents. Close reading includes careful *rereading* and analysis of a text with special attention to what the author's purpose is, what the words mean, and what the structure of the text tells us.

Each activity includes a carefully sequenced series of text-dependent questions that will also help you address the Common Core State Standards for literacy in history and social studies. These questions will provide students with practice in drawing conclusions from the text and supporting them with specific textual evidence. The close reading questions were created by Dr. David Pook, chair of the history department at the Derryfield School and an educational consultant. Pook was a contributing writer to the Common Core State Standards.

Each close reading activity also includes suggestions for making connections between what students learn from their careful investigation of the text and broader themes in their study of Reconstruction, as well as essential questions about history, human behavior, and ourselves.

Common Core–Aligned Unit Assessment

We have also provided central questions, or writing prompts, below to guide your entire investigation of Reconstruction and also to use as the basis for a unit assessment. They are meant to be introduced at the beginning of the unit and referred to throughout different lessons. As students learn more about Reconstruction and interrogate historical texts, they will gather evidence to help them reflect deeply about these questions. At times it will be useful to stop and hold class discussions, giving students an opportunity to change their opinions, analyze evidence in relation to the prompt, and develop claims for an essay. We have included one question that can serve as an argumentative writing prompt and one that can serve as an informative prompt to honor both types of writing suggested by the Common Core State Standards for the history/social studies classroom.

The section "Introducing the Writing Prompt" after Lesson 1 provides a detailed lesson plan modeling how to introduce the argumentative prompt. You can adapt the plan as needed if you choose to use the informative prompt instead of the argumentative one. We recommend that students use an evidence log to gather and analyze evidence at regular intervals. A sample evidence log is provided after Lesson 3. We also recommend that students begin to develop a claim (or thesis) and organize their evidence around that claim by the end of Lesson 13. They can draft, revise, and publish their essays after the unit's lessons are complete. A resource entitled "Writing Strategies," available at facinghistory.org/reconstruction-era, provides strategies you can use to supplement this unit and support students at every stage of the writing process.

ARGUMENTATIVE WRITING PROMPT

Laws are the most important factor in overcoming discrimination.

Given your study of Reconstruction in the United States following the Civil War, support, refute, or modify the statement above in a formal argumentative essay. Introduce a precise claim and develop it fully, citing relevant and sufficient evidence from historical documents.

INFORMATIVE WRITING PROMPT

Historian Eric Foner calls Reconstruction "America's unfinished revolution." What debates and dilemmas from the Reconstruction era remain unresolved?

After researching informational texts on Reconstruction, write an essay in which you explain one debate that was central to this period that remains unresolved. Explain why the debate was significant to the history of Reconstruction. In your conclusion, discuss the legacy of the debate not being resolved. Support your discussion with evidence from your research.

Examples of debates that were central to Reconstruction include but are not limited to:

- The role of the federal government in protecting the rights of individuals

- The relationship between the force of law and the beliefs of people in determining who belongs in a nation and who doesn't

- The membership and participation of many groups—including African Americans, women, immigrants, workers, and Native Americans—in political and social life

- The use and prevention of violence in our society and politics

Addressing Dehumanizing Language from History

Many of the historical documents in this curriculum include the word "nigger." In these documents, we have chosen to let the word remain as it originally appeared, without any substitution. The dehumanizing power of this term and the ease with which some Americans have used it to describe their fellow human beings is central to understanding the themes of identity and human behavior at the heart of the unit.

It is very difficult to use and discuss the term "nigger" in the classroom, but its use throughout history and its presence in this unit's primary sources make it necessary to acknowledge it and set guidelines for students about whether or not to pronounce it when reading aloud or quoting from the text. Otherwise, this word's presence might distract students from an open discussion of history and human behavior. We believe that the best way to prepare to encounter this language is to create a classroom contract outlining guidelines for respectful, reflective classroom discussion.

We also recommend the following articles to help you determine how to approach the term in your classroom:

- "Exploring the Controversy: The 'N' Word" from *"Huck Finn" in Context: A Teaching Guide* (PBS)

- "Straight Talk about the N-Word" from *Teaching Tolerance* (Southern Poverty Law Center)

- "In Defense of a Loaded Word" by Ta-Nehisi Coates (*New York Times*)

You may also wish to point out the use of the word "Negro" in many of the documents in this unit. In earlier times, this was an acceptable term for referring to African Americans. While not offensive in the past, today the term "Negro" is outdated and inappropriate, unless one is reading aloud directly from a historical document.

SECTION 1
THE INDIVIDUAL AND SOCIETY

This section contains the following lessons:

LESSON 1 The Power of Names

ESSENTIAL QUESTIONS

What do names reveal about a person's identity? What do they suggest about our agency and freedom in society?

RATIONALE

The era of Reconstruction that followed the American Civil War spawned debates—and significant violence—over issues that are intensely relevant in the lives of adolescents and particularly important for democracy: power, respect, fairness, equality, and the meaning of freedom, among others. At the heart of all of these issues is the relationship between the individual and society, a relationship worth exploring at the outset of a study of Reconstruction.

This lesson begins with an examination of one of the most basic forms of connection between the individual and society: names. "It is through names that we first place ourselves in the world," writes Ralph Ellison. He goes on to say that as we act in the world around us, our names are simultaneously masks, shields, and containers of values and traditions. In this lesson, students will reflect on these three functions of names and explore the relationship between our names and our identities. They will consider the following questions:

- What do our names reveal about our identities? What do they hide?

- What do names suggest about the degree of freedom and agency we have in society?

- How can names bestow upon individuals dignity and respect? How can they also be used to deprive individuals of those qualities?

- To what extent do we choose the names and labels others use for us? What parts of our identities do we choose for ourselves? What parts are chosen for us by others, or by society?

The discussion of names is immediately relevant to the history of the Reconstruction era because, as historian Douglas Egerton explains, shortly after Emancipation, "former slaves had to undertake a task unknown to free-born Americans. They had to adopt a surname."[1] As students may have learned in their previous study of American slavery, enslaved people did not officially or legally have surnames (last names); they were grouped by the names of their owners. This fact alone is sufficient to help students consider the dignity and respect that a name provides as a sign of individual identity and personhood. Students will examine this idea further when they read the testimony of Liza Mixom, who was born into slavery in Alabama. During the war, Union soldiers who had recently invaded the area where she lived convinced Mixom that she deserved to be called by her full name rather than by the epithet "nigger." (We recommend

---

1 Douglas R. Egerton, *The Wars of Reconstruction: The Brief, Violent History of America's Most Progressive Era* (New York: Bloomsbury Press, 2014), 84.

reviewing the "Addressing Dehumanizing Language from History" section on page xiv before sharing this story with your students. Her last name, according to the soldiers, was Mixom, the surname of her owner. The violent responses of her owner and her grandmother to her demand to be called "Liza Mixom" reveal the extent to which this conflict over her name was in reality a conflict over power, self-determination, and freedom. If we have control over our names, we have control over one of the most basic representations of our identity in society.

After the Civil War ended and slavery was abolished, freedpeople, as we will refer to formerly enslaved people, needed surnames in order to identify themselves for a variety of fundamental civil procedures such as obtaining a marriage license and, especially, signing an employment contract. But they also recognized the power to choose their names as a symbol of freedom and dignity they had not enjoyed while enslaved. As historian Taylor Branch writes, "Among the most joyous feelings most frequently mentioned by freed or escaped slaves was the freedom to choose a name." In this lesson, students will examine the testimony of several freedpeople explaining how they chose their new surnames. They adopted names from various sources; some simply took the last name of their former owners, while others adopted their names from national leaders, occupational skills, and family histories. By observing the variety of sources from which freedpeople adopted their surnames, students will begin to learn about the values, traditions, and aspirations of emancipated people in the 1860s. Students will also reflect on the ways they choose to identify themselves and the ways in which we all "place ourselves into the world."

LEARNING GOALS

Understanding: Students will understand that:

- Our identities are influenced by a variety of factors, including gender, ethnicity, religion, occupation, physical characteristics, background, values, and beliefs, as well as our experiences, the way others treat us, and the choices we make.

- Some parts of identity are determined by our choices, while other parts are determined by forces we cannot control.

- Names can simultaneously project ideas about our identity to others, conceal parts of our identity from others, and represent values and traditions that have influenced our identity.

- The ability to choose or change one's name represents a level of freedom and agency that has been denied to many oppressed people throughout history.

Knowledge: Students will know that:

- Before Emancipation, enslaved African Americans had no official or legal surnames, but once slavery was abolished, many freedpeople took great care in choosing a surname.

- Through the process of choosing a new surname, freedpeople exercised, in ways both symbolic and practical, the new degree freedom and self-determination they had attained in American society.

- By studying the surnames that freedpeople adopted upon Emancipation, we can draw conclusions about their beliefs, values, and circumstances.

RESOURCE LIST

- "Two Names, Two Worlds" (poem)
- "Family Names" (document)
- "An Enslaved Woman Declares Her Name" (document)
- Levels of Questions for "An Enslaved Woman Declares Her Name" (activity)
- "Names and Freedom" (document)
- "Changing Names" (document)

ACTIVITY SUGGESTIONS

- Begin the unit by reading the poem from **Handout 1.1** ("Two Names, Two Worlds") together. If possible, ask a student or teacher fluent in Spanish to read the poem aloud. After reading the poem together, ask students to read it again individually or in pairs and create an *identity chart* for Jonathan Rodríguez. Throughout this unit, the lesson plans and activity suggestions will recommend using identity charts to explore the identities of individuals and groups and to create working definitions of key concepts. See page 5 for an example of an identity chart for Frederick Douglass.

  After students complete identity charts for Jonathan Rodríguez, give them the opportunity to share some of the key words and descriptions they included on the charts. Then debrief the activity by discussing with the class the following questions:

  - What does Jonathan mean by the phrase "two names, two worlds"? What are the two worlds his name represents?

  - How does he resolve these two worlds? What does he think is the essence of his identity?

  - What parts of Jonathan's identity are reflected in his name? What parts are hidden?

  - What values and traditions are reflected in his name?

- Provide students with an opportunity to reflect on their own identities. Have each student create an identity chart for him or herself. Using the identity chart they created for Jonathan Rodríguez as a model, prompt students to include both the words and phrases they use to describe themselves as well as the attributes and labels others use to define them. Discuss with students the tension that exists in all of our identities between who others say we are and how we define ourselves.

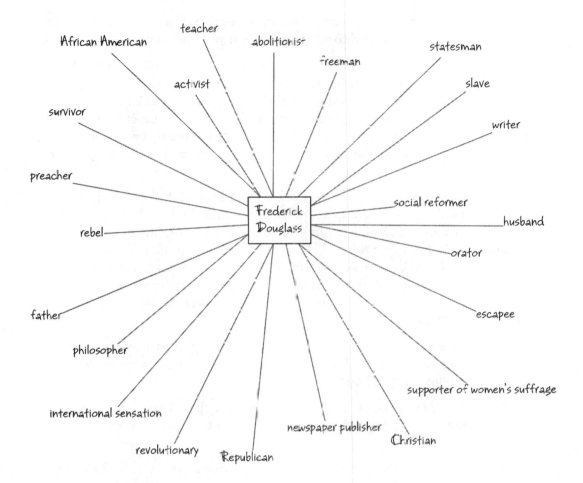

- Read **Handout 1.2** ("Family Names") and ask students to discuss the reading using the "Save the Last Word for Me" strategy (see facinghistory.org/reconstruction-era/strategies for more information). Then give students the opportunity to reflect on their own names and identities in their journals. Finally, encourage students to share a sentence from their reflections with the class. Consider using one or more of the following prompts:

  - What is the relationship between our name and our identity? Would you be the same person if you had a different name? Would others see you in the same way? How does your name place you in the world?

  - How much do you know about the history behind your family name and the way it connects you to the world? If you decided to explore your family and its history, what places would you visit? Whom would you interview? What questions would you ask? How might the answers you get help you place yourself and your family in the world?

- Use **Handout 1.4** ("Levels of Questions") to guide the class's analysis of **Handout 1.3** ("An Enslaved Woman Declares Her Name"). This teaching strategy helps students comprehend and interpret a text by requiring them to answer three types of questions:

  - *Factual questions* (Level 1) can be answered explicitly by facts contained in the text.

  - *Inferential questions* (Level 2) can be answered through analysis and interpretation of specific parts of the text.

- *Universal questions* (Level 3) are open-ended questions that are raised by ideas in the text. They are intended to provoke a discussion of an abstract idea or issue.

Have students answer the questions on the handout individually or in small groups. You might have students choose only one or two questions to answer from each level. Review their responses to the Level 1 and Level 2 questions to make sure everyone understands the text. As you go over the Level 2 questions, encourage students to share different interpretations of the text and use evidence to explain their answers. The universal Level 3 questions make effective prompts for journal entries or a large class discussion.

- Read **Handout 1.5** ("Names and Freedom") together, and then divide the class into small groups. Assign each group one of the three individuals—Martin Jackson, Dick Lewis Barnett, or Mollie (Smith) Russell—whose testimony is included in **Handout 1.6** ("Changing Names"). Have each small group create an identity chart for the individual they were assigned on a piece of chart paper. Encourage students to think deeply about what the testimonies reveal about each person's identity. How does the reasoning behind these individuals' choices for names reveal values and beliefs that can be added to their identity charts?

Post the identity charts in the classroom and give each group the chance to share their thinking with the class. Then debrief the activity with a discussion centered around the following questions:

- What were some of the influences that shaped the choices freedpeople made about their names? How did they use their names to represent their identities to others?

- In what ways does a surname, or last name, provide a person with a sense of dignity?

- What do names reveal about the relationship between the individual and society?

TWO NAMES, TWO WORLDS

In the poem below, Jonathan Rodríguez reflects on his name. How does his name "place him in the world"? How is it a mask, shield, or container?

Hi I'm Jon...........No — Jonathan

Wait — Jonathan Rodríguez

Hold on — Jonathan *Rodríguez*

My Name, Two names, two worlds

The duality of my identity like two sides of the same coin

With two worlds, there should be plenty of room

But where do I fit?

Where can I sit?

Is this seat taken? Or is that seat taken?

There never is quite enough room is there?

Two names, Two worlds

Where do I come from?

Born in the Washington heights of New York City

But raised in good ol' Connecticut

The smell of freshly mowed grass, autumn leaves

a traditional Latin American stew — *Sancocho,* Rice and Beans

The sound from Billy Joel's Piano Keys

a Dominican singer-songwriter — And the rhythm from *Juan Luis Guerra*

I'm from the struggle for broken dreams

Of false promises

Of houses with white picket fences

And 2.5 kids

fields of the Dominican Republic — The mountains and *campos de la Republica Dominicana*

And the mango trees

I'm not the typical kid from suburbia

Nor am I a smooth Latin cat

My head's in the clouds, my nose in a comic book

I get lost in the stories and art

I'm kinda awkward — so talkin' to the ladies is hard

a Dominican merengue singer; a bachata music group — I listen to *Fernando Villalona* and *Aventura* every chance I get,

But don't make me dance *Merengue, Bachata*

styles of dance — Or *Salsa* — I don't know the steps

I've learned throughout these past years

I am a mix of cultures, a mix of races

A race that is black, white and Taino
"Una Raza encendida,

Negra, Blanca y Taina"

A song
You can find me in the parts of a song, *en una cancion*

Percussion instrument used in merengue; percussion instrument used in the Dominican Republic
You can feel my African Roots *en la Tambora*

My *Taino* screams *en la guira*

And the melodies of the lyrics are a reminder of my beautiful Spanish heritage

I am African, Taino and Spanish

A Fanboy, an athlete, a nerd, a student, an introvert

I am Dominican
I'm proud to say: *Yo soy Dominicano*

I'm proud to say, I am me

I am beginning to appreciate that I am

A beautiful blend
Una bella mezcla

I am beginning to see that this world is also a beautiful mix

Of people, ideas and stories.

Is this seat taken?

Or is that seat taken?

Join me and take a seat,

Here we'll write our own stories[1]

---

1 Jonathan Rodríguez, untitled poem.

FAMILY NAMES

Ralph Ellison wrote, "It is through our names that we first place ourselves in the world. Our names, being the gift of others, must be made our own. . . . They must become our masks and our shields and the containers of all those values and traditions which we learn and/or imagine as being the meaning of our familial past."[1] In the documentary Family Name, *filmmaker Macky Alston, who is white, uncovers the history that unites three present-day families that share his last name—two are black and one is white. Alston introduces himself in the film with these words:*

> My grandfather's name was Wallace McPherson Alston and he was a preacher. My father's name is Wallace McPherson Alston, Jr., and he's also a preacher. My name is Wallace McPherson Alston the Third. I dropped out of seminary after two years. Okay, so I rebelled. . . When I was five [my father] put me in a predominately black public school in Durham, North Carolina. It was where I first met black children with the same last name as me. I remember wondering how this could be, but I felt like this was something I couldn't talk about. We moved north when I was eight and the issue never really came up again.

> Recently I asked my dad about our family history and he gave me a book. That's where I discovered that the Alstons were one of the largest slave-owning families in North Carolina.

> Is something a secret if everybody knows it, but nobody talks about it? I want to know the whole story behind my family name.

For many of us, our names can help us learn about our family histories and, ultimately, about ourselves.

Names not only represent our identities but also reflect our relationship to society. Throughout history, names have represented, in a variety of ways, one's degree of power and freedom. In the book Parting the Waters, *historian Taylor Branch writes, "Among the most joyous feelings most frequently mentioned by freed or escaped slaves was the freedom to choose a name. A name was no longer incidental."[2] For most of human history, a man's name was determined at birth and could not be altered. In many societies, however, a woman's name is changed when she marries.*

The belief that one can choose his or her own name and identity is a relatively new idea and a very American notion. Throughout the nation's history, tens of thousands of individuals have changed their names in order to redefine their identities.

At one point in the Family Name *documentary, Macky Alston meets an African American man with the same last name. This man, too, introduces himself through his name:*

> My name is Fred Oliver Alston, Jr. *Fred* comes from the word *Frederick*, which means "peaceful chieftain" or "peaceful ruler." *Oliver* has something to do with peace. And *Alston* has to do with the old village, so technically my name means "peaceful chieftain from the old village." It's also my father's name, so I guess I'm connected with him through that also.[3]

---

1 Ralph Ellison, in *The Collected Essays of Ralph Ellison*, ed. John F. Callahan (Modern Library, 2003), 192.
2 Taylor Branch, *Parting the Waters: America in the King Years 1954–63* (New York: Simon & Schuster, 1988), 45.
3 *Family Name*, directed by Macky Alston (1997, Opelika Pictures).

AN ENSLAVED WOMAN DECLARES HER NAME

We have chosen to include certain racial epithets in this handout in order to honestly communicate the bigoted language of the time. We recommend that teachers review the section "Addressing Dehumanizing Language from History" on page xiv before using this material.

The following is excerpted from the 1937 testimony of a woman born around 1850 as a slave in Alabama. Many words in this document are spelled phonetically to represent her dialect.

Once the Yankee soldiers come. I was big enough to tote pails and piggins then. These soldiers made us chillun tote water to fill their canteens and water their horses. We toted the water on our heads. Another time we heard the Yankees was coming and old Master had about fifteen hundred pounds of meat. They was hauling it off to bury it and hide it when the Yankees caught them. The soldiers ate and wasted every bit of that good meat. We didn't like them a bit.

One time some Yankee soldiers stopped and started talking to me—they asked me what my name was. I say Liza, and they say, "Liza who?" I thought a minute and I shook my head. "Jest Liza, I ain't got no other name."

He say, "Who live up yonder in dat Big House?" I say, "Mr. John Mixon." He say, "You are Liza Mixon." He say, "Do anybody ever call you nigger?" And I say, "Yes Sir." He say, "Next time anybody call you nigger you tell 'em dat you is a Negro and your name is Miss Liza Mixon." The more I thought of that the more I liked it and I made up my mind to do jest what he told me to. . . . One evening I was minding the calves and old Master come along. He say, "What you doin' nigger?" I say real pert like, "I ain't no nigger, I'se a Negro and I'm Miss Liza Mixon." Old Master sho' was surprised and he picks up a switch and starts at me.

Law, but I was skeered! I hadn't never had no whipping so I run fast as I can to Grandma Gracie. I hid behind her . . . 'bout that time Master John got there. He say, "Gracie, dat little nigger sassed me." She say, "Lawsie child, what does ail you?" I told them what the Yankee soldier told me to say and Grandma Gracie took my dress and lift it over my head and pins my hands inside, and Lawsie, how she whipped me . . . I jest said dat to de wrong person.[1]

---

1 Excerpted from William E. Gienapp, ed., *The Civil War and Reconstruction: A Documentary Collection* (New York: W. W. Norton, 2001), 234.

LEVELS OF QUESTIONS FOR "AN ENSLAVED WOMAN DECLARES HER NAME"

After reading the text, answer the following questions. Refer back to the text to help you respond thoughtfully and accurately.

Level 1: Comprehension

1. What do the soldiers tell Liza to say the next time someone calls her "nigger"*?

2. Who is Liza speaking to when she takes the soldiers' advice? What does she say and how does she say it?

3. What are the consequences of Liza taking the soldiers' advice?

Level 2: Inferential

1. Why do the soldiers tell Liza that Mixon is her last name?

2. What was the difference during this time between the labels "Negro" and "nigger"?

3. Why does John respond so negatively when Liza resists the label "nigger"? Why does her grandmother respond so negatively?

4. What does Liza mean when she concludes, 'I jest said dat to de wrong person"?

5. What does the conflict between Liza, her owner, and her grandmother reflect about the amount of power Liza has to define herself and her own identity?

Level 3: Universal

1. Is there a difference between a label and a name? Explain your answer.

2. Do names have an effect on the way others think about our identities? Do they have an effect on the way we think about ourselves? Explain your answers.

3. What is freedom? What parts of one's identity does a free person have the power to determine? What parts are influenced by others or by society?

4. What name do others use for you most often? Who decided it? What does that name reflect about your identity? What does it hide?

---

* We have chosen to include this word in order to honestly communicate the harshness of the bigoted language. We recommend that teachers review "Addressing Dehumanizing Language from History" on page xiv before using this material in class.

NAMES AND FREEDOM

Historian Douglas Egerton explains one of the first tasks freedpeople had to complete once they were emancipated from slavery:

> Former slaves had to undertake a task unknown to free-born Americans. They had to adopt a surname. Although slaves often adopted family names for use among themselves, few masters wished to bestow upon their chattel the sense of dignity a surname implied.[1]

Historian Leon Litwack describes some of the factors freedpeople considered when adopting names:

> In some instances, Federal officials expedited the naming process by furnishing the names themselves, and invariably the name would be the same as that of the freedman's most recent master. But these appear to have been exceptional cases; the ex-slaves themselves usually took the initiative—like the Virginia mother who changed the name of her son from Jeff Davis, which was how the master had known him, to Thomas Grant, which seemed to suggest the freedom she was now exercising. Whatever names the freed slaves adopted, whether that of a previous master, a national leader, an occupational skill, a place of residence, or a color, they were most often making that decision themselves. That was what mattered.[2]

---

1 Douglas R. Egerton, *The Wars of Reconstruction: The Brief, Violent History of America's Most Progressive Era* (New York: Bloomsbury Press, 2014), 40.
2 Leon F. Litwack, *Been in the Storm So Long: The Aftermath of Slavery* (New York: Vintage Books, 1980), 251.

CHANGING NAMES

In the 1930s, ex-slave Martin Jackson explained why he chose his last name after Emancipation:

> The master's name was usually adopted by a slave after he was set free. This was done more because it was the logical thing to do and the easiest way to be identified than it was through affection for the master. Also, the government seemed to be in a almighty hurry to have us get names. We had to register as someone, so we could be citizens. Well, I got to thinking about all us slaves that was going to take the name Fitzpatrick. I made up my mind I'd find me a different one. One of my grandfathers in Africa was called Jeaceo, and so I decided to be Jackson.[1]

Dick Lewis Barnett and Phillip Fry were African American veterans of the Union Army during the Civil War. In 1911, Barnett and Fry's widow, Mollie, both applied for pensions from the government. This financial assistance was available to all Civil War veterans and their families. However, many African Americans faced a problem when they applied for their pensions. After the war ended and slavery was abolished, they exercised their freedom by changing their names. This meant that army records documented their service with their old names instead of their new ones. In order to receive their pensions decades later, these former soldiers and their family members had to demonstrate to the government that they were who they claimed to be. The following documents are excerpts from government records in which Dick Barnett and Mollie (Smith) Russell explain when and why they changed their names.

Testimony of Dick Lewis Barnett, May 17, 1911:

> I am 65 years of age; my post office address is Okmulgee Okla. I am a farmer.

> My full name is Dick Lewis Barnett. I am the applicant for pension on account of having served in Co. B. 77th U.S. Col Inf and Co. D. U.S. Col H Art under the name Lewis Smith which was the name I wore before the days of slavery were over. I am the identical person who served in the said companies under the name of Lewis Smith. I am the identical person who was named called and known as Dick Lewis Smith before the Civil War and during the Civil War and until I returned home after my military service . . .

> I was born in Montgomery County, Ala. the child of Phillis Houston, slave of Sol Smith. When I was born my mother was known as Phillis Smith and I took the name of Smith too. I was called mostly Lewis Smith till after the war, although I was named Dick Lewis Smith—Dick was the brother of John Barnett whom I learned was my father . . .

> When I got home after the war, I was wearing the name of Lewis Smith, but I found that the negroes after freedom, were taking the names of their father like the white folks. So I asked my mother and she told me my father [was] John Barnett, a white man, and I took up the name of Barnett . . .[2]

Testimony of Mollie Russell (widow of Phillip Fry), September 19, 1911:

> **Q.** Tell me the name you were called before you met Phillip Fry?

> **A.** Lottie Smith was my name and what they called me before I met Phillip and was married to him.

> **Q.** Who called you by that name and where was it done?

> **A.** I was first called by that name in the family of Col. Morrow in whose service I was in Louisville, Ky.,

---

1 Norman R. Yetman, ed., *Voices from Slavery: 100 Authentic Slave Narratives* (Dover Publications, 2012), 175.
2 Civil War Pension File of Lewis Smith (alias Dick Lewis Barnett), Co. B, 77th US Colored Infantry, and Co. D, 10th US Colored Heavy Artillery, Record Group 15, Records of the Department of Veterans Affairs, National Archives, Washington, D.C.

just after the war. I worked for him as nurse for his children, and my full and correct name was OCTAVIA, but the family could not "catch on" to that long name and called me "LOTTIE" for short. LOTTIE had been the name of the nurse before me and so they just continued that same name. I was called by that name all the time I was with the Morrows. . . .

Q. Besides the Morrows, whom else did you live with in Louisville?

A. Mr. Thomas Jefferson of Louisville, bought me when I was three years of age from Mr. Dearing. I belonged to him until emancipation. They called me "OCK". They cut it off from OCTAVIA. It was after emancipation on that I went back to work for Col. Morrow and where I got the name "Lottie," as already explained. I liked the name better than Octavia, and so I took it with me to Danville, and was never called anything else there than that name. . . .

Q. How did you ever come by the name of "Mollie"?

A. After I had returned to Louisville from Danville, My sister, Lizzie White, got to calling me Mollie, and it was with her that the name started.

Q. Where did you get the maiden name of Smith from?

A. My mother's name was Octavia Smith and it was from her that I got it but where the name came from to her I never knew. I was only three years old when she died. No, I don't know to whom she belonged before she was brought from Virginia to Kentucky.[3]

3 Civil War Pension File of Phillip Russell (alias Fry), 114th US Colored Infantry, Record Group 15, Records of the Department of Veterans Affairs, National Archives, Washington, D.C.

Introducing the Writing Prompts

This is an appropriate time to introduce the writing prompt you intend to use as a frame for the unit and a final assessment. This section provides a detailed model for how to introduce the argumentative writing prompt suggested at the beginning of this curriculum. The lesson plan provides suggestions both to help students dissect and understand the meaning of the argumentative prompt and to stake out a preliminary position in response to it. At the end of each subsequent section of this curriculum, you will be prompted to give students the opportunity to gather evidence to help them answer the prompt. At these times, students will also have the opportunity to modify the initial position they articulate in this lesson. An informative writing prompt is also provided on page xii. You can adapt the suggestions in the lesson plan below for the informative prompt if you choose to use it.

LESSON PLAN

ESTIMATED DURATION: 1 CLASS PER CD

SKILLS ADDRESSED:

- **Literacy:** Development of an initial position for an argumentative essay

- **Historical thinking:** Crafting historical arguments from historical evidence

- **Social-emotional:** Self-management—engaging with others who hold different perspectives

I. Introduce and Dissect the Writing Prompts

This unit includes two writing prompts that can serve as essential questions for the unit and as comprehensive assessments at the end of the unit (for more information, see the section "Common Core–Aligned Unit Assessment" on page xii):

- Argumentative prompt: Support, refute, or modify this statement. *Laws are the most important factor in overcoming discrimination.*

- Informative prompt: *Historian Eric Foner calls Reconstruction "America's unfinished revolution." What debates and dilemmas from the Reconstruction era remain unresolved?*

Understanding the prompt is the first step in writing a formal essay. Students need time both to understand what they are being asked to write about and to practice writing about a topic to learn what they think. Dissecting the prompt gives them experience with both thinking about and decoding the question to which they will respond.

PROCEDURE

1. Print out the prompt in a larger font and tape it to the center of a piece of paper.

2. Ask students, in pairs, to dissect the prompt. As they read the prompt, direct them to make the following notations:

   - Circle words you do not know or understand in the context of the prompt.

   - Star words that seem to be the central ideas of the prompt.

- Underline the verbs that represent what you, the writer, are supposed to do.

- Cross out any extra information that does not seem specifically relevant to the writing task.

3. Next, ask students to do a "Think-Pair-Share" activity with the prompt. Individually, students should try to answer the prompt simply based on their "gut reaction" or personal philosophy. If possible, ask students to try to support their current thinking with an example from history or their own lives. After a few minutes, ask each pair to share their thinking with each other. Finally, ask students to share a few opinions or ideas with the larger group.

4. Before moving on, ask students to write the prompt in their journals. As they have new thoughts about it throughout the unit, they can make notes to themselves.

Consider following up this activity by giving students the opportunity to define the term *discrimination*. Use the "Attribute Linking" activity to help the class develop a definition for this term. (More information on both the "Think-Pair-Share" and "Attribute Linking" strategies can be found at facinghistory.org/reconstruction-era/strategies.)

II. Anticipation Guide and "Four Corners" Discussion

Having students share responses to debatable statements can engage them with the writing prompt and help them think about the topic in a nuanced way. Students can return to these same statements after their study of Reconstruction to see how learning this material has reinforced or shifted their earlier beliefs. This activity will focus on the argumentative writing prompt.

PROCEDURE

1. Pass out the Lesson 2 anticipation guide (**Handout 1.7**, "The Power of Laws").

2. Ask students to read the statements and decide if they strongly agree, agree, disagree, or strongly disagree with each one. They should circle their responses and then write a brief explanation for each choice.

3. After students have filled out their guides, organize the room into four "corners." Each corner should have one of the following four signs: "strongly agree," "agree," "disagree," and "strongly disagree."

4. Next, use the "Four Corners" strategy to share ideas. Read each statement aloud and ask students to stand in the corner that best represents their current thinking. After students move, ask them to explain their thinking to others in their corner. (See facinghistory.org/reconstruction-era/strategies for more information on the "Four Corners" strategy.)

5. Next, ask students in each corner to share their ideas with the rest of the class. As one corner disagrees with another, encourage students to respond directly to each other's statements and have a mini-debate about the prompt. If students' ideas change due to the debate, tell them that they are free to switch corners.

III. Return to the Prompt

Close this lesson by returning to the argumentative prompt, introduced earlier: *Laws are the most important factor in overcoming discrimination.* Support, refute, or modify this statement.

Ask students to revise their "gut reaction" to the prompt that they wrote as part of the "Dissecting the Prompt" activity above. In particular, you might have them reflect on how the "Four Corners" activity in this lesson affected their thinking.

Tell students that they will return to these ideas as they learn about the history of Reconstruction. They can keep all their notes about these ideas in their journals.

THE POWER OF LAWS

Read the statement in the left column. Decide if you strongly agree (SA), agree (A), disagree (D), or strongly disagree (SD) with the statement. Circle your response and provide a one- to two-sentence explanation of your opinion. Use separate paper if needed.

Statement	Your Opinion			
1. Laws alone can make freedpeople and their former masters equal members of society.	**SA** Explain:	**A**	**D**	**SD**
2. Laws play an important role in shaping who I am.	**SA** Explain:	**A**	**D**	**SD**
3. It is possible to create a fully equal society.	**SA** Explain:	**A**	**D**	**SD**
4. People are most responsible for creating an equal society, not laws.	**SA** Explain:	**A**	**D**	**SD**
5. Granting new rights to one group threatens the rights of another.	**SA** Explain:	**A**	**D**	**SD**
6. People, not laws, create justice.	**SA** Explain:	**A**	**D**	**SD**
7. People, not laws, create labels attached to individuals or groups.	**SA** Explain:	**A**	**D**	**SD**
8. Fear is the fundamental cause of racism and prejudice.	**SA** Explain:	**A**	**D**	**SD**
9. People create racism, not institutions.	**SA** Explain:	**A**	**D**	**SD**

SECTION 2
WE AND THEY

This section contains the following lessons:

LESSON 2 Differences That Matter

ESSENTIAL QUESTIONS

Why do some types of human difference matter more than others? How does race affect how we see others and ourselves?

TRANSITION

In the previous lesson, students reflected on how the beliefs and expectations of the society we are born into can influence how we think about others and ourselves. This lesson seeks to deepen that reflection by examining the ways that humans respond to differences between individuals and groups. More specifically, this lesson prompts students to consider why some types of difference have little impact on the way that we think about others and ourselves, while other types of difference are the basis around which a society's "in" groups and "out" groups are determined. This lesson focuses primarily on the concept of race, a form of human difference that was central to the debates about freedom and equality throughout American history.

RATIONALE

Legal scholar Martha Minow begins her book on inclusion and exclusion, *Making All the Difference*, with the example of the *Sesame Street* children's song "One of These Things Is Not Like the Others." The song, according to Minow, illustrates how we use vocabulary, perception, and analysis to categorize the people and things around us. Minow suggests that the categories we create to organize the world often have consequences. These categories, indeed, are hardly ever neutral, and they reflect our understanding of the world, which itself is shaped by our identities and our experiences.

Understanding Race

All of these categories—differences with consequences—are worthy of exploration in any historical investigation, but it is essential for students of the Reconstruction era to examine the category of human difference we know as *race*. This is because beliefs about race were critical in shaping the attitudes and beliefs of Americans from both the North and South as well as the laws debated and passed during this era.

This lesson first seeks to explore the ways in which humans sort and categorize their world and the people that inhabit it. It asks students to ponder the myriad characteristics we *could* use as the basis of human classification, and then it asks students to think of the characteristics that society actually *does* use to group people. This exploration will raise several related questions about why different groups organize the world the way they do. What do these organizational categories tell us about the people who use them?

Students will then examine the concept of race. It is important for students to understand that the idea of race was created by society rather than discovered as a significant genetic difference within human biology. By knowing one's race, scientists can predict almost nothing else about an individual's physical or intellectual capacities. Despite this fact, it remains common for people to believe in a connection between race and particular abilities or deficiencies. Society, not science has made race a difference that matters.

In the film *Race: The Power of an Illusion*, professor Evelynn Hammonds states: "Race is a human invention. We created it, and we have used it in ways that have been in many, many respects quite negative and quite harmful." This lesson, and this unit, will explore many ways in which the idea of race was harmful—especially the way in which it undermined the prospect of an inclusive society.

Introducing "Universe of Obligation"

If race is a human invention, when and why was it invented? Discussing this question requires that we reach back into history, including the history of early America and the beginnings of slavery. The goal is not to reteach this history, since your class has likely already studied these topics. Rather, the goal of this lesson is to review pieces of this earlier history to deepen students' understanding of race and to introduce an important concept, *universe of obligation*. Scholar Helen Fein defines *universe of obligation* as the circle of individuals and groups toward whom obligations are owed, to whom rules apply, and whose injuries call for amends. In this unit, we extend Fein's concept and suggest that both nations and individuals can have a universe of obligation. In either case, it consists of those an individual or a society believes are worthy of respect and protection.

The story of Anthony Johnson provides students with an opportunity to reflect on how a society's universe of obligation is defined. Johnson was an African-born resident of Virginia in the seventeenth century who arrived in the New World as an indentured servant. Like many other indentured servants, both white and black, he won his freedom. But unlike many newly freed servants, he became a prominent landowner. During Johnson's lifetime, Virginia's attitudes and laws regarding race and slavery changed. Shortly after his death, slavery became a permanent condition reserved for people with dark skin.

By studying Johnson's story, students can trace the change in Virginia's universe of obligation and see the origins of not only the belief in the existence of different races but also the claim that one race is superior to another. Students will see the seeds of race and racism planted in seventeenth-century Virginia come to fruition in the reading "Are All Men Created Equal?" (included here as an extension). This reading quotes Alexander Stephens's "Corner-Stone Speech," delivered on the eve of the Civil War, in which the Confederate vice president argues that white supremacy is the foundation of Southern society and the new Confederate government. Also quoted in this lesson is a Georgia newspaper editor asserting, in 1865, that because the white and black races are "like different coins at mint," no amount of legislation or education can make them equal. This is a belief and worldview that proved hard to change throughout the Reconstruction era. This lesson, and the history that follows in this unit, underscores the fact that in the United States, race has perhaps been the difference that matters most.

LEARNING GOALS

Understanding: *Students will understand that:*

- While it is part of human behavior to categorize the things and people around us, it becomes problematic when categories are used to justify unequal treatment.

- Beliefs about race have been used to create different groups and provide or deny benefits based on those beliefs.

Knowledge: *Students will know that:*

- Race is a socially constructed concept: it is an idea that evolved over time and was constructed by society to further certain political and economic goals.

- The concept of race developed in tandem with the need to justify the profitable practice of permanent enslavement of Africans in the Americas.

- A society's universe of obligation is the circle of individuals and groups toward whom obligations are owed, to whom rules apply, and whose injuries call for amends.

RESOURCE LIST

- "Which One of These Things Is Not Like the Others?" (activity)

- "Making All the Difference" (excerpt from book by Martha Minow) (document)

- "Circles of Responsibility/Universe of Obligation" (activity)

- *Race: The Power of an Illusion* (note-taking guide)

- *Race: The Power of an Illusion*, Episode 2: "The Story We Tell" (0:43–9:46) (video) (To stream this video, visit facinghistory.org/reconstruction-era/videos.)

- "Anthony Johnson: A Man in Control of His Own" (document)

- "Are All Men Created Equal?" (document)

LESSON PLAN

ESTIMATED DURATION: 2 CLASS PERIODS

SKILLS ADDRESSED:

- **Literacy:** Integrating and evaluating content presented in diverse forms and media

- **Historical thinking:** Contextualization—connecting historical developments to specific circumstances in time and place

- **Social-emotional:** Social awareness—recognizing and appreciating individual and group similarities and differences

I. Opener: One of These Things Is Not Like the Others

This brief opening activity introduces students to the idea that when we sort and categorize the things and people around us, we make judgments about which characteristics are more meaningful than others. Students will be asked to look at four shapes and decide which is not like the others, but in doing so they must also choose which category (shape or color) they will base their decision on.

PROCEDURE

1. Share with students the **Handout 2.1** ("Which One of These Things Is Not Like the Others?"). If possible, you might simply project the image in the classroom.

2. Ask students to answer the question by identifying the object in the image that is not like the others.

3. Prompt students to share their answers and explain their thinking behind the answer to a classmate using the "Think-Pair-Share" strategy. What criterion did they use to identify one item as different? Why? Did their classmate use the same criterion? (For more information about the "Think-Pair-Share" strategy, visit facinghistory.org/reconstruction-era/strategies.)

4. Explain that while students' choices in this exercise are relatively inconsequential, we make similar choices with great consequence in the ways that we define and categorize people in society. While there are many categories we might use to describe differences between people, society has given more meaning to some types of difference (such as skin color and gender) than others (such as eye and hair color). You might ask students to brainstorm some of the categories of difference that are meaningful in our society.

5. Share the quotation by Martha Minow in **Handout 2.2** ("Making All the Difference") to reinforce the goal and central idea of this opening discussion: societies collectively decide that some differences between people are more important than others, and those differences we deem important often have social, political, and economic consequences.

II. Introduce "Universe of Obligation"

One approach to helping students understand the ways in which some differences are more consequential than others in a society is by introducing the concept of *universe of obligation*. First, students will think about the levels of responsibility and caring that they themselves feel for others. Then they will apply the same idea to nations.

PROCEDURE

1. Explain to students that this activity will help them think about the ways that some differences matter more than others when it comes to the rights and respect individuals receive in a society.

2. Pass out **Handout 2.3** ("Circles of Responsibility/Universe of Obligation"). Prompt students to follow the instructions and add the name of at least one group or individual to each concentric circle. If it helps to clarify their thinking, you might ask students to consider those for whom they are most willing to sacrifice their own well-being to help or protect.

3. Ask students to share some of the differences they notice that distinguish those they list in the inner circles from those in the outer circles. Likewise, ask them to describe the differences between people they list in the diagram and those who they do not list at all. Students might answer by mentioning categories such as family, friends, teammates, and neighbors.

4. Explain that where others sit within one's universe of obligation is often fluid, meaning that it can change depending on the circumstances and events of our lives. Ask students to reflect on what types of circumstances and events might cause their universe of obligation to change. Spend a few minutes asking students to share and discuss their thinking.

5. Introduce the idea that one might be able to complete a similar graphic organizer for a nation as a whole, instead of just an individual. Ask students to consider what characteristics a nation might use to determine whose rights and safety deserve to be protected. Explain that a nation might express this explicitly through its laws or more organically through the customs, beliefs, and choices made by individuals in that society.

6. Finally, explain to students that in this exercise, they are exploring the concept of *universe of obligation*. Provide students with the definition:

   > *Universe of obligation*: *The circle of individuals and groups toward whom obligations are owed, to whom rules apply, and whose injuries call for amends. In other words, those that a society believes have rights that are worthy of respect and protection.*

   Explain to students that even though the term *universe of obligation* was originally used to describe nations, we might adapt this concept to describe the levels of responsibility individuals feel toward others.

III. Discuss the Social Construction of Race

A short clip from the documentary *Race: The Power of an Illusion* can introduce students to the idea that race is one category of human difference that has been used throughout history as the basis for including some within a nation's universe of obligation and excluding others. Importantly, this clip will also help students understand what it means for race to be *socially constructed*.

PROCEDURE

1. Distribute the note-taking guide for *Race: The Power of an Illusion* (**Handout 2.4**).

2. Show the clip from *Race: The Power of an Illusion*, Episode 2: "The Story We Tell" (0:43 to 9:46). As students watch the clip, they should answer as many of the questions on the note-taking guide as they can. Because some questions require them to synthesize information from the clip, give students a few extra minutes after the clip ends to complete the note-taking guide.

3. Briefly discuss the questions on the note-taking guide. For some classes, the history and ideas discussed here will be a review of learning from earlier in the course. Provide special focus to the final question about the idea of race as a social construction. If necessary, review the following statement from the video by historian Theda Perdue:

We have the idea that it's somewhere written in stone that there are these fundamental differences between human beings. We don't realize that race is an idea that evolves over time, that it has a history, that it is constructed by society to further certain political and economic goals.

IV. Read and Discuss "Anthony Johnson: A Man in Control of His Own"

Reading and discussing the story of Anthony Johnson, who arrived in Virginia as an indentured servant from Africa in the 1600s and became a landowner, provides students with the opportunity to deepen their reflection on the nature of race and their understanding of the concept of a universe of obligation. Students will use the "S-I-T" ("Surprising, Interesting, Troubling") strategy to discuss Johnson's story.

PROCEDURE

1. Distribute **Handout 2.5** ("Anthony Johnson: A Man in Control of His Own"). Prompt students to read the document individually and answer the questions embedded in the document.

2. After completing the reading and comprehension questions, ask each student to identify the following from the reading:

   - One Surprising fact or idea

   - One Interesting fact or idea

   - One Troubling fact or idea

3. Divide the class into groups to share their "S-I-T" facts and ideas.

4. Lead a whole-group sharing and discussion of their reading and small-group work. Focus the discussion on how Anthony Johnson's story deepens students' understanding of (1) universe of obligation and (2) race as a social construct.

5. Create class definitions for *universe of obligation* and *race*, and post them in the classroom.

V. Extension

The documents in this lesson focus on the creation of the concept of race in North America in the 1600s. If your students need the opportunity to reflect on how the idea of white supremacy manifested itself in the 1860s, you might choose to share **Handout 2.6** ("Are All Men Created Equal?") with the class. The document is followed by a series of comprehension and reflection questions that can form the basis of an activity or assignment.

WHICH ONE OF THESE THINGS IS NOT LIKE THE OTHERS?

MAKING ALL THE DIFFERENCE

Legal scholar Martha Minow writes about the consequences of the way we respond to differences between us:

When we identify one thing as unlike the others, we are dividing the world; we use our language to exclude, to distinguish—to discriminate. . . . Of course, there are "real differences" in the world; each person differs in countless ways from each other person. But when we simplify and sort, we focus on some traits rather than others, and we assign consequences to the presence and absence of the traits we make significant. We ask, "What's the new baby?"—and we expect as an answer, boy or girl. That answer, for most of history, has spelled consequences for the roles and opportunities available to that individual. And when we respond to persons' traits rather than their conduct, we may treat a given trait as a justification for excluding someone we think is "different." We feel no need for further justification: we attribute the consequences to the differences we see. We neglect other traits that may be shared. And we neglect how each of us, too, may be "different."[1]

---

1 Martha Minow, *Making All the Difference* (Ithaca, NY: Cornell University Press, 1990), 3–4.

CIRCLES OF RESPONSIBILITY/UNIVERSE OF OBLIGATION

- In **Circle 1**, write your name.

- In **Circle 2**, write the name of people to whom you feel the greatest obligation—for example, people for whom you'd be willing to take a great risk or put yourself in peril (you don't have to write actual names; you could refer to a group of people, such as "my family").

- In **Circle 3**, write the names of the people on the next level—that is, people to whom you feel some responsibility, but not as great as for those in Circle 2.

- In **Circle 4**, write the names of the people on the next level—people to whom you feel some responsibility, but not as great as for those in Circle 3.

- To whom do you feel no sense of responsibility? List these groups outside Circle 4.

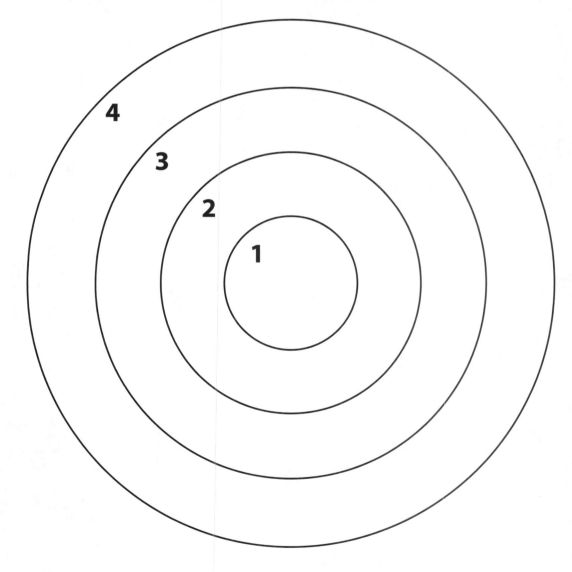

RACE: THE POWER OF AN ILLUSION

Note how the film answers these questions as you watch the clip from Episode 2: "The Story We Tell" of the film Race: The Power of an Illusion.

1. According to the video, how did the Founding Fathers explain the contradiction between their ideals of freedom and liberty and the existence of slavery in early America?

2. In 1619, when the first Africans arrived in Virginia, what defined social status? What types of differences had the most meaning?

3. Why did planters eventually identify Africans as the ideal labor source to enslave—better than indentured servants from Europe or Native Americans?

4. Why did whiteness become important to the identity of many Virginians? Why did being white become a more important characteristic than being Christian or English?

5. What gave white Americans the idea that Africans were "a different kind of people"?

6. What do we mean when we say that the idea of race is "socially constructed"?

ANTHONY JOHNSON: A MAN IN CONTROL OF HIS OWN

In Virginia in the 1620s, slavery and indentured servitude existed, but there were both white and black servants and slaves. No one was a slave for life; rather, many immigrants to North America agreed to work for a planter for a specific period of time in exchange for their passage to the New World and food and shelter once they arrived. In 1622, a black indentured servant named Anthony Johnson appeared in the historical record. Charles Johnson and Patricia Smith tell his story.

PART ONE

Antonio may have arrived at the colony from Angola [Africa] the year before aboard the *James*. Sold into bondage to toil in the tobacco fields, "Antonio, a Negro" is listed as a "servant" in the 1625 census. Virginia had no rules for slaves. So it was possible that Antonio knew hope. Perhaps he felt that redemption was possible, that opportunities existed for him even as a servant . . .

"Mary a Negro woman" had sailed to the New World aboard the *Margret and John*. Soon she became Antonio's wife.

"Antonio the Negro" became the landowner Anthony Johnson . . .

Although it is not known exactly how or when the Johnsons became free, court records in 1641 indicate that Anthony was master to a black servant, John Casor. During that time, the couple lived on a comfortable but modest estate and Anthony began raising livestock. In 1645, a man identified as "Anthony the Negro" stated in court records, "Now I know myne owne ground and I will work when I please and play when I please."

It cannot be proved that it was actually Anthony Johnson who spoke those words. But if he did not speak them, he felt them, felt them as surely as he felt the land beneath his feet. The words didn't reflect his state of ownership as much as they reflected his state of mind. He owned land. He could till the soil whenever he wished and plant whatever he wished, sell the land to someone else, let it lie fallow, walk away from its troubles. He could sit in his house—*his* house—and ignore the land altogether. Anthony was a man in control of his own.

Comprehension Questions

1. In the census documents and court records described in this passage, how is Anthony identified? Does the way he is described appear to have any consequences so far in his story?

2. What detail suggests to historians that Anthony became free in 1641 or before?

3. According to the authors, what did Anthony think it means to be free? What are the benefits of freedom?

PART TWO

By 1650, the Johnsons owned 250 acres of land stretched along the Pungoteague Creek on the eastern shore of Virginia, acquired through the headright system, which allowed planters to claim acreage for each servant brought to the colony. Anthony claimed five headrights . . .

No matter how he amassed his acreage, Anthony's "owne ground" was now formidable.

The couple was living a seventeenth-century version of the American dream. Anthony and Mary had no reason not to believe in a system that certainly seemed to be working for them, a system that equated ownership with achievement. If not for the color of their skin, they could have been English.

Very few people who had inked their signatures on indenture forms received the promise of those contracts. At the end of their periods of servitude, many were denied the land they needed to begin their lives again. Anthony Johnson was one of a select few able to consider a piece of the world his own.

In 1653, a consuming blaze swept through the Johnson plantation. After the fire, court justices stated that the Johnsons "have bine inhabitants in Virginia above thirty years" and were respected for their "hard labor and known service." When the couple requested relief, the court agreed to exempt Mary and the couple's two daughters from county taxation for the rest of their lives. This not only helped Anthony save money to rebuild, it was in direct defiance of a statute that required *all* free Negro men and women to pay taxes.

The following year, white planter Robert Parker secured the freedom of Anthony Johnson's servant John Casor, who had convinced Parker and his brother George that he was an illegally detained indentured servant. Anthony later fought the decision. After lengthy court proceedings, Casor was returned to the Johnson family in 1655.

These two favorable and quite public decisions speak volumes about Anthony's standing in Northampton County. The very fact that Johnson, a Negro, was allowed to testify in court attests to his position in the community. In the case of the community benevolence following the fire, the fact that Anthony was a Negro never really seemed part of the picture. He was a capable planter, a good neighbor, and a dedicated family man who deserved a break after his fiery misfortune. In the case of his legal battle for Casor, Anthony's vision of property and the value accorded it mirrored that of his white neighbors and the gentlemen of the court. Anthony Johnson had learned to work the system. It was a system that seemed to work for him . . .

Comprehension Questions

4. Based on what the authors imply, what did an inhabitant of Virginia need in order to be considered English?

5. What phrase in the third paragraph best summarizes what the authors mean by "a seventeenth-century version of the American dream"?

6. What evidence can you find in this passage that suggests whether or not the Johnsons were part of Virginia's universe of obligation?

PART THREE

[I]n the spring of 1670 . . . "Antonio, a Negro"—respected because he had managed to live so long on his own terms—met the end of his life. He was still a free man when the shackles binding him to this world were unlocked.

. . . In August of that year, however, an all-white jury ruled that Anthony's original land in Virginia could be seized [from his surviving family] by the state "because he was a Negroe and by consequence an alien." And fifty acres that Anthony had given to his son Richard wound up in the hands of wealthy white neighbor George Parker. It didn't matter that Richard, a free man, had lived on the land with his wife and children for five years.

The "hard labor and knowne service" that had served the family so well in the New World was now secondary to the color of their skin. The world that allowed captive slave "Antonio, a Negro," to grow confident as Anthony Johnson, landowner and freeman, ceased to exist. The Virginians no longer needed to lure workers to their plantations. Now they could buy them and chain them there.[1]

Comprehension Questions

7. Were the Johnsons included within Virginia's universe of obligation after Anthony's death? What evidence from this passage supports your answer?

8. According to Virginia officials, what did it mean to be a "Negro" in the 1670s? How is this meaning different from the meaning that prevailed earlier in Anthony's life?

9. According to the last paragraph, how did the criteria by which Anthony's status in Virginia society was judged change?

---

1 Excerpted from Charles Johnson and Patricia Smith, *Africans in America: America's Journey through Slavery* (San Diego: Harcourt & Brace, 1999), 37–43.

ARE ALL MEN CREATED EQUAL?

As Anthony Johnson's story illustrates, the concept of race had not fully developed before the beginning of African slavery in the Americas. Yet, after permanently enslaving people of African descent proved profitable and popular, many white Americans not only considered people of the "Negro race" alien but also began to claim that they were naturally inferior to the "white race." Claiming that those of African descent were from a naturally inferior race made it easier to justify their permanent enslavement and their status as property. Nearly 200 years after Anthony Johnson's death, the concept of race and the idea that black people are naturally inferior to whites was commonly accepted among most white Americans from both the North and the South, despite the words enshrined in the Declaration of Independence that "all men are created equal." In fact, several of the founders who endorsed these words were aware of the contradiction, but they were not sure what to do about it.

On the eve of the Civil War, Confederate vice president Alexander Stephens gave a speech asserting that the new Confederate government was founded upon "exactly the opposite idea" from the equality asserted in the Declaration of Independence:

> [I]ts foundations are laid, its corner-stone rests, upon the great truth that the negro is not equal to the white man; that slavery subordination to the superior race is his natural and normal condition. This, our new government, is the first, in the history of the world, based upon this great physical, philosophical, and moral truth . . .

> Many governments have been founded upon the principle of the subordination and serfdom of certain classes of the same race; such were and are in violation of the laws of nature. Our system commits no such violation of nature's laws. With us, all of the white race, however high or low, rich or poor, are equal in the eye of the law. Not so with the negro. Subordination is his place. He, by nature, or by the curse against Canaan, is fitted for that condition which he occupies in our system.[1]

Two months after Stephens's Confederate government was defeated in the Civil War, the editor of a Georgia newspaper wrote:

> The different races of man, like different coins at mint, were stamped at their true value by the Almighty in the beginning. No contact with each other—no amount of legislation or education—can convert the negro into a white man. Until that can be done—until you can take the kinks out of his wool and make his skull thinner—until all of these things and abundantly more have been done, the negro cannot claim equality with the white race.[2]

Slavery was abolished as a result of the war, but the belief of many Americans in white supremacy did not change.

Comprehension Questions

1. Does Alexander Stephens agree with the statement in the Declaration of Independence that "all men are created equal"?

---

1 Excerpted from Alexander Stephens's "Corner-Stone Speech," in Henry Cleveland, *Alexander H. Stephens, in Public and Private: With Letters and Speeches, Before, During, and Since the War* (Philadelphia, 1886), 717–729, available at http://teachingamericanhistory.org/library/document/cornerstone-speech/ (accessed Jan. 23, 2014).

2 E. Merton Coulter, "Slavery and Freedom in Athens, Georgia, 1860–1866," in *The Georgia Historical Quarterly* 49, No. 3 (September 1965), Georgia Historical Society, 264–293, http://www.jstor.org/stable/40578502.

2. What evidence does Alexander Stephens present to justify his claim that slavery of African Americans is "natural"? Why might his arguments appeal to white Southerners at the time? How would you respond to his comments?

3. How does the word choice of the Georgia editor support his claim that blacks and whites are not equal? How do his words dehumanize African Americans?

4. How do you think Stephens and the editor might respond to attempts to provide freedpeople with new rights and opportunities to create a more equal society?

LESSON 3 Defining Freedom

ESSENTIAL QUESTIONS

What is freedom? What does it mean to be free?

TRANSITION

In the last lesson, students explored the socially constructed meaning of race and reflected on how that concept has been used to justify "in" groups and "out" groups in society. In this lesson, they will consider the frequently used but rarely defined concept of freedom. By learning about the choices and aspirations of freedpeople immediately after Emancipation, students will consider what it means to be free, and they will consider what role freedom plays in their own lives. They will also begin to reflect on the question of whether or not one who is excluded from full and equal membership in society is truly free.

RATIONALE

While the Civil War and Thirteenth Amendment ended the enslavement of four million people in the United States, they did not determine what would replace it. As historian Leon Litwack explains, the question on the minds of many Americans regarding the status of formerly enslaved people was, "How free is free?" While news of Emancipation caused celebration among millions of formerly enslaved Americans and their supporters, the lack of definition to their freedom tempered some of the jubilation with realism about American society. George G. King, born into slavery in South Carolina, reflected on this reality when he learned that he was no longer enslaved: "The Master he says we are all free . . . but it don't mean we is white. And it don't mean we is equal."[1]

In this lesson, students will learn about the variety of ways that black Americans sought to define freedom in their lives immediately after Emancipation. In particular, they will examine how such Americans attempted to give meaning to freedom through (1) the ways in which they thought about themselves and their lives, (2) the actions and choices they made in their day-to-day lives immediately after Emancipation, and (3) their longer-term political, economic, and social aspirations to be full and equal members of American society.

For many freedpeople, Emancipation brought immediate and drastic changes to their lives, while for others day-to-day life remained largely the same. Regardless, according to Litwack's analysis, nearly all freedpeople experienced a profound change in how they thought about themselves and their lives: "Nearly all of them could subscribe to the underlying principle that emancipation had enabled them to become their own masters."[2] Four million Americans were no longer the property of another person, subject to another's will. Even when freedpeople chose to stay and work on the plantations where they had been enslaved, at this point in time it was often *their* choice.

---

1 Leon Litwack, *Been in the Storm So Long: The Aftermath of Slavery* (Vintage Books, 1980), 224.
2 Ibid., 226.

This shift in the way that freedpeople thought about their identities empowered them with a new sense of agency and possibility. They now perceived choices in their lives that they did not have before, even if some of the choices would once again be taken away in the months and years to come.

These choices inspired many to begin to test their freedom. To know how it felt to be free, Litwack explains, "demanded that the ex-slave begin to act like a free man, that he test his freedom, that he make some kind of exploratory move, that he prove to himself (as well as to others) by some concrete act that he was truly free."[3] Such concrete actions that freedpeople took to define their freedom and demonstrate control over their own lives included:

- leaving the plantation

- negotiating wages and work conditions

- changing employers

- reuniting families split apart when some were sold away under slavery

- getting married

- changing their names

- learning to read

- establishing churches

- claiming land as their own

These day-to-day choices of freedpeople were met with opposition by some white Americans and support by others. According to Litwack, "To those accustomed to absolute control, even the smallest exercise of personal freedom by a former slave, no matter how innocently intended, could have an unsettling effect."[4] Throughout the Reconstruction era and for many decades after, white supremacists attempted through laws, intimidation, and violence to reestablish control over the black laboring class in the South, reasserting severe restrictions on their ability to exercise many of the types of choices listed above. The resistance of many white Americans to the way freedpeople and their allies defined freedom will be explored in several lessons later in this unit.

Yet, in this unsettled environment, other Americans supported many of the ways in which ex-slaves sought to define their freedom. Perhaps no greater effort was made in support of freedpeople than that of the Freedmen's Bureau. In *The Souls of Black Folk*, W. E. B. Du Bois called the Freedmen's Bureau "one of the most singular and interesting of the attempts made by a great nation to grapple with vast problems of race and social condition."[5] Created by Congress in March 1865, the Bureau of Refugees, Freedmen, and Abandoned Lands represented the first significant postwar attempt by the federal government to define freedom for black Americans. Involved in the daily local affairs of communities across the South, the bureau represented a significant expansion of the reach of the federal government. The Freedmen's Bureau's most immediate job was to provide government aid to penniless freedpeople and destitute refugees from the war. The bureau also oversaw land abandoned and confiscated during the war, the status

---

3 Litwack, *Been in the Storm So Long*, 226–227.
4 Ibid., 227.
5 W. E. B. Du Bois, "Of the Dawn of Freedom" (Chapter 2), in *The Souls of Black Folk* (public domain), available at http://www.gutenberg.org/files/408/408-h/408-h.htm#chap02.

of which would prove to be a particularly contentious issue. In addition, the bureau's mission included helping blacks transition from slavery to freedom by educating them about their new rights and responsibilities. One of those responsibilities, according to the bureau, was to resume working in the Southern fields as quickly as possible, but now as wage laborers instead of slaves. The resumption of labor, according to assistant bureau commissioner Rufus Saxton, would disprove their former masters' arguments that African Americans were lazy and worked only when under threat of the lash.[6] By quickly returning to the fields, the freedpeople would also help the postwar national economy get back on its feet. To that end, the bureau agents played an essential role by helping to negotiate labor contracts between former slaves and planters and resolving disputes by acting as a court of law in areas where the local courts did not recognize blacks. The Freedmen's Bureau also played an important role in reconstructing the postwar South through its work in education. The schools that the bureau created to educate the freedpeople, augmenting schools created by Northern missionaries and the freedpeople themselves, constituted the first public school systems the region had ever seen and established a legacy of public education enjoyed by all children in the South.[7]

Beyond the freedom to be "their own masters" in matters of work, family, and church, African Americans expressed even more robust political, economic, and social aspirations for their lives as free people. In this lesson, students will explore four documents in which black Americans define what they believe they need in order to be both free and equal members of American society. To Garrison Frazier, a minister and leader of the Savannah, Georgia, community of freedpeople, the bases of freedom and equality for black Americans were economic rights, including land of their own, and the ability to live apart from the prejudice of white Americans. In addition to land, Frederick Douglass also demanded voting rights and civil equality for freedpeople. Once government action secured these rights for freedpeople, Douglass believed blacks would be placed on the footing where they could exist on their own without further outside assistance. To Jourdon Anderson, a former slave writing in response to his former master's request that he return to work on the plantation, to be free and equal meant safety for his family, education for his children, and compensation for the labor his family performed as slaves. Yet, as students may conclude from the sarcastic tone of Anderson's writing, he also believed that freedom provided him the dignity to be able to address his former master as his equal in social status.[8] Finally, a convention of freedmen who convened in Charleston, South Carolina, demanded education for their children, arguing that "an educated and intelligent people can neither be held in, nor reduced to slavery."[9] By exploring these four documents, students will begin their reflection on key issues at the core of the debates and struggles of the Reconstruction era—voting rights, land distribution, and education, but also dignity, safety, and the nature of equality.

---

6 United States Congress Joint Committee on Reconstruction, *Report of the Joint Committee on Reconstruction, at the First Session, Thirty-ninth Congress,* vol. 3 (US Government Printing Office, 1866).

7 John Hope Franklin, *Reconstruction After the Civil War*, 2nd ed. (University of Chicago Press, 1994), 36–39.

8 Allen G. Breed and Hillel Italie, "Origins of Famous Note Revealed," *The Memphis Commercial Appeal*, July 15, 2012.

9 *Proceedings of the Colored People's Convention of the State of South Carolina, Held in Zion Church, Charleston, November 1865* (Charleston: South Carolina Leader Office, 1865).

LEARNING GOALS

Understanding: Students will understand that:

- Freedom is difficult to capture in a single definition, but individuals often experience it as independence in their daily choices about work, family, and religion, as well as in their exercise of political, economic, and social rights.

- Both laws and customs, as well as the choices of individuals, influence a society's definition of freedom.

Knowledge: Students will know that:

- While the Thirteenth Amendment abolished slavery, it did not define what rights and status freedpeople would have in American society.

- Many Americans during the Civil War and the Reconstruction era believed that different groups of Americans could be free without being equal.

- Immediately after Emancipation, ex-slaves sought to define the freedom in their lives through the daily choices they made about work, family, education, and religion and by expressing their aspirations to be full, equal members of American society.

RESOURCE LIST

- "How Free Is Free?" (document)

- "Savannah Freedpeople Express Their Aspirations for Freedom" (document)

- "What the Black Man Wants" (document)

- "Letter from Jourdon Anderson: A Freedman Writes His Former Master" (document)

- "South Carolina Freedpeople Demand Education" (document)

- "The Freedmen's Bureau Outlines the Duties of Freedpeople" (document)

ACTIVITY SUGGESTIONS

Note that a detailed Common Core–aligned close reading protocol for the document "Letter from Jourdon Anderson: A Freedman Writes His Former Master" (**Handout 3.4**) *follows this lesson. The Common Core standards recommend that students begin a close reading activity with little, if any, prior knowledge of the text at the heart of the activity. Therefore, if you plan to include a close reading of this document in your unit, we recommend that you complete the activity prior to using any of the suggested activities below.*

Consider using the following activity ideas and strategies when you implement this lesson in your classroom.

- Begin the lesson by asking students to reflect in their journals on what they think it means to be free. Consider using the following journal prompt: *What does it mean to be free? What can free people do that people who aren't free cannot? What does freedom look like in your life? What gets in the way of your freedom?*

Use the identity chart format to create a concept map for the term *freedom*. Ask students to share ideas from their journal entries and add them to the map. As students read and discuss the documents in this lesson, continue to add new attributes to the map based on students' ideas. Save the concept map for reference later in the unit.

- **Handout 3.1** ("How Free Is Free?") provides an introduction to some of the initial ways that Emancipation changed the lives of former slaves. Read the document together as a whole group and discuss with the class the attributes of freedom that historian Leon Litwack describes in the document. Add those attributes to the concept map for *freedom* that you started at the beginning of class.

- Use the "Jigsaw" strategy to read the four handouts representing African American voices on the meaning of freedom:

  - "Letter from Jourdon Anderson: A Freedman Writes His Former Master" (**Handout 3.4**)

  - "What the Black Man Wants" (excerpt of speech by Frederick Douglass) (**Handout 3.3**)

  - "Savannah Freedpeople Express Their Aspirations for Freedom" (the testimony of Garrison Frazier) (**Handout 3.2**)

  - "South Carolina Freedpeople Demand Education" (a resolution from an 1865 convention of freedmen) (**Handout 3.5**)

For more information on the "Jigsaw" strategy, visit facinghistory.org/reconstruction-era/strategies.

Students will work in "expert" groups to read one of these four documents and determine the attributes of freedom discussed by the primary source's author. Each group should focus its discussion on the following questions:

- According to the author, what can free people do that people who aren't free cannot?

- What do people need in order to sustain and protect their freedom?

- What does the document suggest about the meaning of freedom? Do you agree or disagree with that perspective? Why?

Students will next reshuffle into "teaching" groups, in which they will share the findings of their "expert" group with their new group members. In their "teaching" groups, students can use evidence from all four documents to discuss the questions above. As you debrief this activity as a whole group, add the new ideas that come up about the meaning of freedom to the concept map you started at the beginning of class.

- **Handout 3.6** ("The Freedmen's Bureau Outlines the Duties of Freedpeople") represents another perspective on the meaning of freedom. Writing to the freedpeople, Rufus Saxton, an assistant commissioner of the Freedmen's Bureau, outlines what he perceives as the new rights and responsibilities of freedpeople as well as his bureau's role in supporting emancipated Americans.

It is important to note that this document also reflects assumptions by Saxton that are rooted in widely held biases about black life at the time. In particular, Saxton shares the assumption held by many white Americans, from both the North and South, that freedpeople had no sense of family ties or values, when an abundance of historical evidence proves that assumption false. Therefore, it is important to encourage students to read this document critically.

One way to facilitate such a critical reading is by conducting an activity in which students write a letter from the perspective of Garrison Frazier, Frederick Douglass, or Jourdon Anderson in response to Rufus Saxton of the Freedmen's Bureau. What parts of Saxton's letter would Frazier, Douglass, or Anderson agree with? What might they disagree with? What might they find insulting? What else might they wish Saxton had said?

HOW FREE IS FREE?

The following is an excerpt from historian Leon Litwack's book Been in the Storm So Long.

Although former slaves chose to manifest their freedom in many different ways, with each individual acting on his or her own set of priorities, nearly all of them could subscribe to the underlying principle that emancipation had enabled them to become their own masters. And those were precisely the terms they most often deployed to define their freedom. When the earliest contrabands reached Fortress Monroe, they testified that the most compelling idea in their minds had been to "belong to ourselves." . . .

By enlarging the freedman's sense of what was attainable, desirable, and tolerable, emancipation encouraged a degree of independence and assertiveness which bondage had sharply contained. To leave the plantation without a pass, to slow the pace of work, to haggle over wages and conditions, to refuse punishment, or to violate racial etiquette were all ways of testing the limits of freedom. No doubt a Mississippi freedman derived considerable satisfaction from refusing to remove his hat when ordered to do so in the presence of a white man, as did a Richmond black who turned down the request of a white man to help him lift a barrel, telling him at the same time, "No, you white people think you can order black people around as you please." To those long accustomed to absolute control, even the smallest exercise of personal freedom by a former slave, no matter how innocently intended, could have an unsettling effect. . . .

To determine the "one difference" between freedom and bondage, the ex-slaves found themselves driven in many directions at the same time. But the distance placed between themselves and their old status could not be measured by how far they traveled or even if they left the old plantation. That "difference" could most often be perceived in the choices now available to them, in the securing of families and the location of loved ones who had been sold away, in the sanctification of marital ties, in the taking of a new surname or the revelation of an old one, in the opportunity to achieve literacy, in the chance to move their religious services from "down in the hollow" to their own churches, in sitting where they pleased in public places, in working where the rewards were commensurate with their labor. What emancipation introduced into the lives of many black people was not only the element of choice but a leap of confidence in the ability to effect changes in their own lives without deferring to whites. "What I likes bes, to be slave or free?" Margrett Nillin, a former Texas slave, pondered over that question many decades after her emancipation. "Well, it's dis way," she answered. "In slavery I owns nothin' and never owns nothin'. In freedom I's own de home and raise de family. All dat cause me worriment and in slavery I has no worriment, but I takes freedom."[1]

---

1 Leon Litwack, *Been in the Storm So Long: The Aftermath of Slavery* (Vintage Books, 1980), 226–229.

SAVANNAH FREEDPEOPLE EXPRESS THEIR ASPIRATIONS FOR FREEDOM

In January 1865, after Union general William T. Sherman's army arrived in Savannah, Georgia, followed by thousands of newly emancipated people, the secretary of war Edwin Stanton joined Sherman at a meeting with representatives of Savannah's black community. The black community chose Garrison Frazier, a minister who was formerly enslaved, to represent their views before Sherman and Stanton. What follows is an excerpt from the transcript of this meeting, known as the Savannah Colloquy. Following the meeting, Sherman ordered 400,000 acres of land along the coasts of South Carolina, Georgia, and Florida to be divided into 40-acre plots and given to freedpeople and their families.

1. **State what your understanding is in regard to the acts of Congress, and President Lincoln's proclamation, touching the condition of the colored people in the rebel States.**

   Answer. So far as I understand President Lincoln's proclamation to the rebellious States, it is, that if they would lay down their arms and submit to the laws of the United States before the 1st of January, 1863, all should be well; but if they did not, then all the slaves in the rebel States should be free, henceforth and forever: that is what I understood.

2. **State what you understand by slavery, and the freedom that was to be given by the President's Proclamation.**

   Answer. Slavery is receiving by irresistible power the work of another man, and not by his consent. The freedom, as I understand it, promised by the proclamation, is taking us from under the yoke of bondage and placing us where we could reap the fruit of our own labor, and take care of ourselves, and assist the Government in maintaining our freedom.

3. **State in what manner you think you can take care of yourselves, and how can you best assist the Government in maintaining your freedom.**

   Answer. The way we can best take care of ourselves is to have land, and turn it and till it by our labor—that is, by the labor of the women, and children, and old men—and we can soon maintain ourselves and have something to spare . . . We want to be placed on land until we are able to buy it and make it our own.

4. **State in what manner you would rather live, whether scattered among the whites, or in colonies by yourselves.**

   Answer. I would prefer to live by ourselves, for there is a prejudice against us in the South that will take years to get over; but I do not know that I can answer for my brethren.

   [Mr. Lynch says he thinks they should not be separated, but live together. All the other persons present being questioned, one by one, answer that they agree with 'brother Frazier.']

5. **Do you think that there is intelligence enough among the slaves of the South to maintain themselves under the Government of the United States, and the equal protection of its laws, and maintain good and peaceable relations among yourselves and with your neighbors?**

   Answer. I think there is sufficient intelligence among us to do so.[1]

---

1 "Sherman Meets the Colored Ministers in Savannah," O.R. Series I, Vol. XLVII/2 [S# 99], Union Correspondence, Orders, and Returns Relating to Operations in North Carolina (from February 1), South Carolina, Southern Georgia, and East Florida, from January 1, 1865, to March 23, 1865, #2.

WHAT THE BLACK MAN WANTS

During the Reconstruction era, Frederick Douglass demanded government action to secure land, voting rights, and civil equality for black Americans. The following passage is excerpted from a speech given by Douglass to the Massachusetts Anti-Slavery Society in April 1865.

We may be asked, I say, why we want it [the right to vote]. I will tell you why we want it. We want it because it is our *right*, first of all. No class of men can, without insulting their own nature, be content with any deprivation of their rights. We want it again, as a means for educating our race. Men are so constituted that they derive their conviction of their own possibilities largely from the estimate formed of them by others. If nothing is expected of a people, that people will find it diffi-cult to contradict that expectation. By depriving us of suffrage, you affirm our incapacity to form an intelligent judgment respecting public men and public measures; you declare before the world that we are unfit to exercise the elective franchise, and by this means lead us to undervalue ourselves, to put a low estimate upon ourselves, and to feel that we have no possibilities like other men . . .

What I ask for the Negro is not benevolence, not pity, not sympathy, but simply *justice*. [Applause.] The American people have always been anxious to know what they shall do with us . . . Everybody has asked the question, and they learned to ask it early of the abolitionists, "What shall we do with the Negro?" I have had but one answer from the beginning. Do nothing with us! . . . All I ask is, give him a chance to stand on his own legs! Let him alone! If you see him on his way to school, let him alone, don't disturb him! If you see him going to the dinner-table at a hotel, let him go! If you see him going to the ballot-box, let him alone, don't disturb him! . . .[1]

---

1 Frederick Douglass, "What the Black Man Wants" (speech before the Massachusetts Anti-Slavery Society, April 1865), available at http://teachingamericanhistory.org/library/index.asp?document=495 (accessed Apr. 25 2013).

LETTER FROM JOURDON ANDERSON: A FREEDMAN WRITES HIS FORMER MASTER

Dayton, Ohio, August 7, 1865.

To my old Master, Colonel P. H. Anderson, Big Spring, Tennessee.

Sir:

I got your letter, and was glad to find that you had not forgotten Jourdon, and that you wanted me to come back and live with you again, promising to do better for me than anybody else can. I have often felt uneasy about you. I thought the Yankees would have hung you long before this, for harboring Rebs they found at your house. I suppose they never heard about your going to Colonel Martin's to kill the Union soldier that was left by his company in their stable. Although you shot at me twice before I left you, I did not want to hear of your being hurt, and am glad you are still living. It would do me good to go back to the dear old home again, and see Miss Mary and Miss Martha and Allen, Esther, Green, and Lee. Give my love to them all, and tell them I hope we will meet in the better world, if not in this. I would have gone back to see you all when I was working in the Nashville Hospital, but one of the neighbors told me that Henry intended to shoot me if he ever got a chance.

I want to know particularly what the good chance is you propose to give me. I am doing tolerably well here. I get $25 a month, with victuals and clothing; have a comfortable home for Mandy (the folks call her Mrs. Anderson), and the children, Milly, Jane, and Grundy, go to school and are learning well. The teacher says Grundy has a head for a preacher. They go to Sunday school, and Mandy and me attend church regularly. We are kindly treated. Sometimes we overhear others saying, "Them colored people were slaves" down in Tennessee. The children feel hurt when they hear such remarks; but I tell them it was no disgrace in Tennessee to belong to Colonel Anderson. Many darkeys would have been proud, as I used to be, to call you master. Now if you will write and say what wages you will give me, I will be better able to decide whether it would be to my advantage to move back again.

As to my freedom, which you say I can have, there is nothing to be gained on that score, as I got my free papers in 1864 from the Provost-Marshal-General of the Department of Nashville. Mandy says she would be afraid to go back without some proof that you were disposed to treat us justly and kindly; and we have concluded to test your sincerity by asking you to send us our wages for the time we served you. This will make us forget and forgive old scores, and rely on your justice and friendship in the future. I served you faithfully for thirty-two years, and Mandy twenty years. At $25 a month for me, and $2 a week for Mandy, our earnings would amount to $11,680. Add to this the interest for the time our wages have been kept back, and deduct what you paid for our clothing, and three doctor's visits to me, and pulling a tooth for Mandy, and the balance will show what we are in justice entitled to. Please send the money by Adams Express, in care of V. Winters, Esq., Dayton, Ohio. If you fail to pay us for faithful labors in the past, we can have little faith in your promises in the future. We trust the good Maker has opened your eyes to the wrongs which you and your fathers have done to me and my fathers, in making us toil for you for generations without recompense. Here I draw my wages every Saturday night; but in Tennessee there was never any payday for the negroes any more than for the horses and cows. Surely there will be a day of reckoning for those who defraud the laborer of his hire.

In answering this letter, please state if there would be any safety for my Milly and Jane, who are now grown up, and both good-looking girls. You know how it was with poor Matilda and Catherine. I would rather stay here and starve and die, if it come to that, than have my girls brought to shame by the violence and wickedness of their young masters. You will also please state if there has been any schools opened for the colored children in your neighborhood. The great desire of my life now is to give my children an education, and have them form virtuous habits.

From your old servant,

Jourcon Anderson

P.S.— Say howdy to George Carter, and thank him for taking the pistol from you when you were shooting at me.[1]

---

1 Excerpted from William E. Gienapp, ed., *The Civil War and Reconstruction: A Documentary Collection* (New York: W. W. Norton, 2001), 380.

SOUTH CAROLINA FREEDPEOPLE DEMAND EDUCATION

In November 1865, a convention of freedmen met in Charleston, South Carolina, to demand new rights for African Americans. Foremost among their demands was education for their children. The convention issued the following resolution:

> *Whereas*, "Knowledge is power," and an educated and intelligent people can neither be held in, nor reduced to slavery; Therefore [be it] Resolved, That we will insist upon the establishment of good schools for the thorough education of our children throughout the State; that, to this end, we will contribute freely and liberally of our means, and will earnestly and persistently urge forward every measure calculated to elevate us to the rank of a wise, enlightened and Christian people. Resolved, That we solemnly urge the parents and guardians of the young and rising generation, by the sad recollection of our *forced* ignorance and degradation in the past, and by the bright and inspiring hopes of the future, to see that schools are at once established in every neighborhood; and when so established, to see to it that every child of proper age, is kept in regular attendance upon the same.[1]

---

1 *Proceedings of the Colored People's Convention of the State of South Carolina, Held in Zion Church, Charleston, November 1865* (Charleston: South Carolina Leader Office, 1865), (accessed Sept. 18, 2014). http://fax.libs.uga.edu/e185x93xg4xs7x1865/1f/State_Convention_of-the_Colored_People_of_South_Carolina_1865.pdf.

THE FREEDMEN'S BUREAU OUTLINES THE DUTIES OF FREEDPEOPLE

Rufus Saxton, the assistant commissioner of the Freedmen's Bureau, wrote the following letter to the freedpeople of South Carolina, Georgia, and Florida.

HEADQUARTERS ASS'T COMMISSIONER BUREAU REFUGEES, FREEDMEN,
AND ABANDONED LANDS, SOUTH CAROLINA, GEORGIA, AND FLORIDA,
Beaufort, S. C., August 16, 1865.

To the Freedmen of South Carolina, Georgia, and Florida :

. . . By the emancipation proclamation of President Lincoln, the laws of Congress, and the will of God, you have been declared "forever free." At the outset of your new career it is important that you should understand some of the duties and responsibilities of freemen. Your first duty is to go to work at whatever honest labor your hands can find to do, and provide food, clothing, and shelter for your families. Bear in mind that a man who will not work should not be allowed to eat. Labor is ennobling to the character, and, if rightly directed, brings to the laborer all the comforts and luxuries of life. The only argument left to those who would keep you in slavery is, that in freedom you will not work; that the lash is necessary to drive you to the cotton and rice fields; that these fair lands which you have cultivated so many years in slavery will now be left desolate. On the sea-islands of South Carolina, Georgia, and Florida, where your brethren have been free for three years, they have nobly shown how much better they can work in freedom. Over forty thousand are now engaged in cultivating the soil, their children are being educated, and they are self-sustaining, happy, and free. Some are working for wages, others are cultivating the land on shares, giving one-half to the owner.

The agents of the Freedmen's Bureau will aid you in making contracts to work for fair wages for your former masters or others who may desire to hire you, or will locate you on small farms of forty acres, which you can hire at an easy rent, with an opportunity to purchase at low rates any time within three years. These are splendid opportunities. Freedmen, let not a day pass ere you find some work for your hands to do, and do it with all your might. Plough and plant, dig and hoe, cut and gather in the harvest. Let it be seen that where in slavery there was raised a blade of corn or a pound of cotton, in freedom there will be *two*. Be peaceful and honest. Falsehood and theft should not be found in freedom; they are the vices of slavery. Keep in good faith all your contracts and agreements, remembering always that you are a slave no longer. While guarding carefully your own rights, be as careful not to violate your neighbor's. "Do unto others as you would they should do unto you."

In cases where you feel that you have been wronged, it is neither wise nor expedient to take redress into your own hands, but leave the matter to be settled by three impartial friends of both parties. In cases of difficulty between white men and yourselves, you should appeal to one of the agents of this bureau in your vicinity, who may appoint one referee, the other party one, and you should appoint a third, and the decision of the majority should be considered final. By this easy mode of settling difficulties much trouble may be avoided.

In slavery you only thought of to-day. Having nothing to hope for beyond the present, you did not think of the future, but, like the ox and horse, thought only of the food and work for the day. In freedom you must have an eye to the future, and have a plan and object in life. Decide now what you are to do next year—where you are to plant in the spring, and how much—and in the autumn and winter prepare your land and manure for the early spring planting. After being sure that you have planted sufficient corn and potatoes for food, then put in all the cotton and rice you can, for these are the crops which will pay the best. Bear in mind that cotton is a regal plant, and the more carefully it is cultivated the greater will be the crop. Let the world see ere long the fields of South Carolina, Georgia, and Florida white with this important staple cultivated by free labor.

In slavery the domestic relations of man and wife were generally disregarded. Virtue, purity, and honor among men and women were not required or expected. All this must change now that you are free. The domestic altar must be held sacred, and with jealous care must you guard the purity of a wife, a sister, or a daughter; and the betrayer of their honor should be punished and held up to universal condemnation. You are advised to study, in church and out of it, the rules of the marriage relation issued from these headquarters. Colored men and women, prove by your future lives that you can be virtuous and pure.

No people can be truly great or free without education. Upon the education of your children depends in a great degree the measure of your success as a people. Send your children to school whenever you can. Deny yourselves even the necessaries of life to keep your boys and girls at school, and never allow them to be absent a day or an hour while it is in session.

Your liberty is a great blessing which has been vouchsafed to you, and you should be patient and hopeful. The nation, through this bureau, has taken your cause in hand, and will endeavor to do you ample justice. If you do not obtain all your rights this year, be content with part; and if you act rightly, all will come in good time. Try to show by your good conduct that you are worthy of all; and whatever may happen, let no uneasy spirit stir you up to any act of rebellion against the government. Strive to live down by your true and loyal conduct the wicked lie and weak invention of your enemies, that in any event you would rebel against that government and people which have sacrificed so many precious lives and so much treasure in your cause. Could you rise even against those who oppress you, or against a government which has given you a right to yourselves, your wives and children, and taken from you the overseer, the slave trader, the auction block, and broken the driver's whip forever? I have no fears on this point, and trust you to show those who have how groundless they are, and that you are willing to leave your cause in the hands of the government. Ever cherish in your hearts the prayerful spirit, the trusting, childlike faith in God's good providence, which has sustained so many of you in your darkest hour.

The assistant commissioners and agents of this bureau will publish this circular to the freedmen throughout these States, and ministers of the Gospel are requested to have it read in all the churches where the freedmen are assembled.

R. SAXTON,
Brevet Major General, Assistant Commissioner.[1]

1 United States Congress Joint Committee on Reconstruction, *Report of the Joint Committee on Reconstruction, at the First Session, Thirty-ninth Congress,* vol. 3 (US Government Printing Office, 1866), available at http://books.google.com/books?id=edg0AQAAMAAJ&source=gbs_navlinks_s.

Letter from Jourdon Anderson: A Freedman Writes His Former Master

*Close reading is carefully and purposefully **rereading** a text. It's an encounter with the text in which we closely focus on what the author has to say, what the author's purpose is, what the words mean, and what the structure of the text tells us. Close reading ensures that we truly understand what we've read. At Facing History and Ourselves, we use this careful investigation of text to make connections to essential questions about history, human behavior, and ourselves. This protocol can be used to implement a close reading for select documents during the Reconstruction unit. Adapt the following procedure to best meet your goals and the needs of your students.*

FIRST READ: Read aloud. Either the teacher or an extremely fluent student can read the text aloud. Ask students to circle unfamiliar words as they listen. After the read-aloud, as students share these words with the class, decide which words to define immediately to limit confusion and which definitions you want students to uncover through careful reading.

SECOND READ: Individual read. Ask students to read silently to get a feel for the text. They can note specific words or phrases that jump out at them for any number of reasons: because they are interesting, familiar, strange, confusing, funny, troubling, difficult, etc. Share some of these as a class. Particular questions to ask students at this stage of the reading are:

- What can you already infer about the author of this text?

- How is the text structured?

- Does this structure make it easy or difficult to make meaning?

- Does this structure tell us anything about the author's style or purpose?

THIRD READ: Text-dependent questions. In small groups, have students read the text in chunks and answer a set of text-dependent questions. These questions are included with each close reading exemplar. Sample answers are provided to help guide the teacher. See the "Close Reading A: Student Handout" form for a student version of the document; see "Close Reading A: Teacher Guide" for the teacher's version.

FOURTH READ: Visual image. In small groups, have students create a visual image on paper that captures the essence of the text. You may also ask them to include three words or a sentence summary of each section of text. Groups can be assigned either the entire text or sections of text for this portion of the close reading.

FIFTH READ: Gallery read. Ask students to do a "gallery read" of the images that have been created.

TRANSITION TO DISCUSSION

At this point, we recommend organizing a class discussion so that students can make connections beyond the text. This discussion can be informal or can use the format of the "Socratic Seminar" or "Save the Last Word for Me" strategy (see the "Teaching Strategies" section of our website at facinghistory.org/reconstruction-era/strategies for details).

DISCUSSION SUGGESTIONS

As mentioned earlier, this unit includes two writing prompts. Both prompts can be used to launch a discussion after a close reading. Examples include:

- To connect to the argumentative writing prompt (*Support, refute, or modify the statement: Laws are the most important factor in overcoming discrimination*):

  - What is the role of laws in creating a just democracy? How do you think Jourdon Anderson would answer that question? How do you answer that question? What else might we need to create a just democracy?

- To connect to the informative writing prompt: *Historian Eric Foner calls Reconstruction "America's unfinished revolution." What debates and dilemmas from the Reconstruction era remain unresolved? After researching informational texts on Reconstruction, write an essay in which you explain one debate that was central to this period that remained unresolved. Explain why the debate was significant to the history of Reconstruction. In your conclusion, discuss the legacy of the debate not being resolved.*

  - Ask students to consider connections between Anderson's letter and contemporary issues surrounding membership and justice in American society today. What aspects of Anderson's argument remain "unfinished" in the twenty-first century?

- To connect to more general Facing History and Ourselves themes:

  - What does it mean to be free? How does Anderson define freedom?

  - What can you infer about how Anderson is defining justice for freedpeople? How does that connect to how he might be viewing the universe of obligation of former slaveholders?

  - How would you describe the different "universes of obligation" of individuals, groups, institutions, and the government at this point in American history?

- It's also possible to have students themselves create the questions for a discussion. To do this, you might guide students by asking them to find connections between the essential questions and the text or to write questions based on what resonates for them. They might choose to make connections to the author's purpose, the structure of the text, the tone of the text, or the main messages of the text. Alternatively, they may want to make connections to issues related to the individual and society, to examples of discrimination, to the role of government in a democracy, and beyond.

CLOSE READING A   Teacher Guide

Text of Anderson's Letter to His Former Master

Dayton, Ohio, August 7, 1865.

To my old Master, Colonel P. H. Anderson, Big Spring, Tennessee.

Sir:

I got your letter, and was glad to find that you had not forgotten Jourdon, and that you wanted me to come back and live with you again, promising to do better for me than anybody else can. I have often felt uneasy about you. I thought the Yankees would have hung you long before this, for harboring Rebs they found at your house. I suppose they never heard about your going to Colonel Martin's to kill the Union soldier that was left by his company in their stable. Although you shot at me twice before I left you, I did not want to hear of your being hurt, and am glad you are still living. It would do me good to go back to the dear old home again, and see Miss Mary and Miss Martha and Allen, Esther, Green, and Lee. Give my love to them all, and tell them I hope we will meet in the better world, if not in this. I would have gone back to see you all when I was working in the Nashville Hospital, but one of the neighbors told me that Henry intended to shoot me if he ever got a chance.

I want to know particularly what the good chance is you propose to give me. I am doing tolerably well here. I get $25 a month, with victuals and clothing; have a comfortable home for Mandy (the folks call her Mrs. Anderson), and the children, Milly, Jane, and Grundy, go to school and are learning well. The teacher says Grundy has a head for a preacher.

Guided Close Reading
with Text-Dependent Questions

1. **After reading the first paragraph, what can you infer based on the way the writer addresses the letter?**

   A good close reading starts with some "easy wins" for students, and this question should definitely elicit the response that "old" indicates that Colonel Anderson is Jourdan's former master.

2. **What evidence is there in the opening paragraph to support Jourdon's claim that he has "often felt uneasy about" Colonel Anderson?**

   While Jourdon is glad that Anderson hasn't forgotten about him and does not wish Anderson ill (indeed, he is genuinely surprised that Anderson wasn't killed by Union soldiers for harboring rebels), he nonetheless expresses reluctance to return. That caution stems from the fact that the colonel shot him twice before he left, and he has heard word that he might be shot again by someone named Henry should he return.

3. **In the first paragraph, what reasons does Jourdon offer to suggest that he might return to Big Spring? What clues are there that he might not return?**

   He still has many friends there that he would like to visit, and in fact he twice asks Colonel Anderson to give them his regards (once in the opening paragraph and once in the postscript). In asking the colonel to give his friends his love, he mentions that he hopes they will meet in the afterlife if they do not meet in the present—indicating some uncertainty regarding his return.

4. **What information can you gather from the second paragraph about what happened to Jourdon after he left Colonel Anderson?**

   As Jourdon says, he is doing "tolerably well," with a monthly salary as well as food and clothing. While we do not know how he is presently employed, he had been working previously at a hospital in an unknown capacity.

Text of Anderson's Letter to His Former Master

They go to Sunday school, and Mandy and me attend church regularly. We are kindly treated. Sometimes we overhear others saying, "Them colored people were slaves" down in Tennessee. The children feel hurt when they hear such remarks; but I tell them it was no disgrace in Tennessee to belong to Colonel Anderson. Many darkeys would have been proud, as I used to be, to call you master. Now if you will write and say what wages you will give me, I will be better able to decide whether it would be to my advantage to move back again.

As to my freedom, which you say I can have, there is nothing to be gained on that score, as I got my free papers in 1864 from the Provost-Marshal-General of the Department of Nashville. Mandy says she would be afraid to go back without some proof that you were disposed to treat us justly and kindly; and we have concluded to test your sincerity by asking you to send us our wages for the time we served you. This will make us forget and forgive old scores, and rely on your justice and friendship in the future. I served you faithfully for thirty-two years, and Mandy twenty years. At $25 a month for me, and $2 a week for Mandy, our earnings would amount to $11,680. Add to this the interest for the time our wages have been kept back, and deduct what you paid for our clothing, and three doctor's visits to me, and pulling a tooth for Mandy, and the balance will show what we are in justice entitled to.

Questions

5. **What do we learn about Jourdon's family in the second paragraph?**

   Jourdon's family, consisting of his common-law wife, Mandy, and their three children, is well situated, and they live with him in a home of their own. The family goes to church, and the children participate in Sunday school as well as receiving regular schooling, with Jourdon's son receiving special praise from his teacher.

6. **What other evidence is there of the importance Jourdon places on education?**

   Jourdon ends his letter by inquiring about whether there are any schools for colored children nearby, indicating the importance of education to him by stating that "the great desire of my life" is to give not just his son an education but his daughters as well.

7. **What feelings might Jourdon and his family have regarding their status as former slaves?**

   Despite being treated "kindly" by those they associate with, the children are ashamed of their past. Their father tells them (by way of a backhanded compliment to the colonel) that there was "no disgrace" in having been the colonel's slave and that he was even proud of that fact.

8. **Based on what Jourdon says at the beginning of the third paragraph, what can be inferred regarding what the colonel offered Jourdon in his letter to him?**

   It can be deduced from Jourdon's remarks that the colonel "offered" Jourdon his freedom—an offer Jourdon quickly brushes aside here, noting that he has been free for a year already.

9. **What is the sticking point regarding Jourdon's return to work for the colonel?**

   While there are several issues that Jourdon raises over the course of the letter that require resolution (e.g., Henry's threat, what wages he will earn), for him the issue hinges on restitution for past work. If the colonel will not compensate Jourdon and his wife for the decades of work they performed, they can have "little faith" in his future promises to treat them well.

Guided Close Reading
with Text-Dependent Questions

10. **What clues are there in the passage as to the meaning of the word recompense?**

    In his letter to the colonel, Jourdon notes that it is wrong to "defraud the laborer of his hire," or in other words that an injustice has been done in not rewarding the "toil of generations" with compensation in the form of lost wages. Recompense is therefore contextually defined in the letter as payment for one's labor.

11. **What explanation does Jourdon provide for feeling justified in asking his former master for lost wages from when he was a slave?**

    Jourdon bluntly states that God will hold those who held slaves in bondage accountable for their actions, and he "trusts" that "the good Maker has opened your eyes to the wrongs which you and your fathers have done to me and my fathers." He offers a moral argument to justify his demand for payment.

12. **What final worry does Jourdon raise in the last paragraph of the letter? What can you infer about the experience of female slaves prior to Reconstruction?**

    In keeping with the moral theme opened in the previous paragraph, Jourdon notes that his daughters are attractive and "you know how it was" with other girls—so bad that he would rather starve and die than "have my girls brought to shame by the violence and wickedness of their young masters." The implication is that he is worried that upon returning, his daughters would be raped—like the women he names (presumably slaves) who were violated when held in involuntary servitude.

13. **What hints are there in the letter that Jourdon now sees himself as the equal of his former master?**

    There are many indications of Jourdon's evident pride in replying to his master on equal terms, from his demand for restitution for lost wages to something as simple as referring to both his master and himself now as "old," whereas before, he explains, slaves were treated no differently from cattle. Students should be encouraged to explore the different tones that Jourdon might be using over the course of the letter (e.g., ironic, accusatory, matter-of-fact, casual).

Text of Anderson's Letter to His Former Master

Please send the money by Adams Express, in care of V. Winters, Esq., Dayton, Ohio. If you fail to pay us for faithful labors in the past, we can have little faith in your promises in the future. We trust the good Maker has opened your eyes to the wrongs which you and your fathers have done to me and my fathers, in making us toil for you for generations without recompense. Here I draw my wages every Saturday night; but in Tennessee there was never any pay-day for the negroes any more than for the horses and cows. Surely there will be a day of reckoning for those who defraud the laborer of his hire.

In answering this letter, please state if there would be any safety for my Milly and Jane, who are now grown up, and both good-looking girls. You know how it was with poor Matilda and Catherine. I would rather stay here and starve and die, if it come to that, than have my girls brought to shame by the violence and wickedness of their young masters. You will also please state if there has been any schools opened for the colored children in your neighborhood. The great desire of my life now is to give my children an education, and have them form virtuous habits.

From your old servant,

Jourdon Anderson

P.S.— Say howdy to George Carter, and thank him for taking the pistol from you when you were shooting at me.

Text of Anderson's Letter to His Former Master

Dayton, Ohio, August 7, 1865.

To my old Master, Colonel P. H. Anderson, Big Spring, Tennessee.

Sir:

I got your letter, and was glad to find that you had not forgotten Jourdon, and that you wanted me to come back and live with you again, promising to do better for me than anybody else can. I have often felt uneasy about you. I thought the Yankees would have hung you long before this, for harboring Rebs they found at your house. I suppose they never heard about your going to Colonel Martin's to kill the Union soldier that was left by his company in their stable. Although you shot at me twice before I left you, I did not want to hear of your being hurt, and am glad you are still living. It would do me good to go back to the dear old home again, and see Miss Mary and Miss Martha and Allen, Esther, Green, and Lee. Give my love to them all, and tell them I hope we will meet in the better world, if not in this. I would have gone back to see you all when I was working in the Nashville Hospital, but one of the neighbors told me that Henry intended to shoot me if he ever got a chance.

I want to know particularly what the good chance is you propose to give me. I am doing tolerably well here. I get $25 a month, with victuals and clothing; have a comfortable home for Mandy (the folks call her Mrs. Anderson), and the children, Milly, Jane, and Grundy, go to school and are learning well. The teacher says Grundy has a head for a preacher.

Guided Close Reading with Text-Dependent Questions

1. After reading the first paragraph, what can you infer based on the way the writer addresses the letter?

2. What evidence is there in the opening paragraph to support Jourdon's claim that he has "often felt uneasy about" Colonel Anderson?

3. In the first paragraph, what reasons does Jourdon offer to suggest that he might return to Big Spring? What clues are there that he might not return?

4. What information can you gather from the second paragraph about what happened to Jourdon after he left Colonel Anderson?

Guided Close Reading
with Text-Dependent Questions

5. **What do we learn about Jourdon's family in the second paragraph?**

6. **What other evidence is there of the importance Jourdon places on education?**

7. **What feelings might Jourdon and his family have regarding their status as former slaves?**

8. **Based on what Jourdon says at the beginning of the third paragraph, what can be inferred regarding what the colonel offered Jourdon in his letter to him?**

9. **What is the sticking point regarding Jourdon's return to work for the colonel?**

Text of Anderson's Letter to His Former Master

They go to Sunday school, and Mandy and me attend church regularly. We are kindly treated. Sometimes we overhear others saying, "Them colored people were slaves" down in Tennessee. The children feel hurt when they hear such remarks; but I tell them it was no disgrace in Tennessee to belong to Colonel Anderson. Many darkeys would have been proud, as I used to be, to call you master. Now if you will write and say what wages you will give me, I will be better able to decide whether it would be to my advantage to move back again.

As to my freedom, which you say I can have, there is nothing to be gained on that score, as I got my free papers in 1864 from the Provost-Marshal-General of the Department of Nashville. Mandy says she would be afraid to go back without some proof that you were disposed to treat us justly and kindly; and we have concluded to test your sincerity by asking you to send us our wages for the time we served you. This will make us forget and forgive old scores, and rely on your justice and friendship in the future. I served you faithfully for thirty-two years, and Mandy twenty years. At $25 a month for me, and $2 a week for Mandy, our earnings would amount to $11,680. Add to this the interest for the time our wages have been kept back, and deduct what you paid for our clothing, and three doctor's visits to me, and pulling a tooth for Mandy, and the balance will show what we are in justice entitled to.

55

Guided Close Reading
with Text-Dependent Questions

10. **What clues are there in the passage as to the meaning of the word *recompense*?**

11. **What explanation does Jourdon provide for feeling justified in asking his former master for lost wages from when he was a slave?**

12. **What final worry does Jourdon raise in the last paragraph of the letter? What can you infer about the experience of female slaves prior to Reconstruction?**

13. **What hints are there in the letter that Jourdon now sees himself as the equal of his former master?**

Text of Anderson's Letter to His Former Master

Please send the money by Adams Express, in care of V. Winters, Esq., in Dayton, Ohio. If you fail to pay us for faithful labors in the past, we can have little faith in your promises in the future. We trust the good Maker has opened your eyes to the wrongs which you and your fathers have done to me and my fathers, in making us toil for you for generations without recompense. Here I draw my wages every Saturday night; but in Tennessee there was never any pay-day for the negroes any more than for the horses and cows. Surely there will be a day of reckoning for those who defraud the laborer of his hire.

In answering this letter, please state if there would be any safety for my Milly and Jane, who are now grown up, and both good-looking girls. You know how it was with poor Matilda and Catherine. I would rather stay here and starve and die, if it come to that, than have my girls brought to shame by the violence and wickedness of their young masters. You will also please state if there has been any schools opened for the colored children in your neighborhood. The great desire of my life now is to give my children an education, and have them form virtuous habits.

From your old servant,

Jourdon Anderson

P.S.— Say howdy to George Carter, and thank him for taking the pistol from you when you were shooting at me.

Connecting to the Writing Prompt

This is an appropriate time to provide students with the opportunity to review and reflect on the writing prompt you introduced after completing Lesson 1. We recommend that you introduce an evidence log for students to use to collect and analyze information that may be useful in answering the question posed by the prompt. A sample evidence log is provided on the next page (**Handout 3.7**). You might choose to make copies of the log for your students or have them use it as a model for how to set up their journals for collecting evidence. The "Teaching Strategies" section of our website at facinghistory.org/reconstruction-era/strategies provides additional examples that you might choose to adapt.

Now that they have recorded their first pieces of evidence, ask students to revise their thinking about the question posed in the prompt. When they were first introduced to the prompt, students wrote a "gut reaction." Has any of the evidence they have recorded confirmed their initial thinking? Has any conflicted with it? Has what they have learned about the social construction of race and the meaning of freedom changed their thinking about the question posed in the prompt? Have students record their thoughts in their journals.

{EVIDENCE LOG}

WRITING PROMPT:

Citation	Summary—What information from this source addresses the writing prompt?	Information about author/creator	Source rank (1–3)

SECTION 3
HEALING AND JUSTICE AFTER WAR

This section contains the following lessons:

LESSON 4 The Devastation of War

ESSENTIAL QUESTION

What does it take to reunite a nation torn apart by civil war?

TRANSITION

In the previous lesson, students reflected on the meaning of freedom and explored the ideas about freedom expressed by several Americans shortly after Emancipation. In this lesson, students will learn more about the aftermath of the war itself. They will consider information about the immense destruction the Civil War caused in people's lives and for the nation as a whole. They will also read documents written in 1865 by two women, one from the North and the other from the South, and consider the ways that these opposing perspectives provide insight into the difficult task of reuniting the nation.

RATIONALE

The impact of the death, destruction, and upheaval brought about by the Civil War on the Americans who lived through it cannot be overstated. While your class may have explored this impact while learning about the war, it is important to establish the war's upheaval throughout the country as the backdrop to the challenges and conflicts of Reconstruction. While the nation prepared to confront the enormous political, economic, and social challenges of Reconstruction, many Americans were simultaneously mourning the loss of loved ones (many of whose bodies were not able to be recovered for proper burial) and yearning to restore a sense of safety, stability, and belonging in their daily lives. While the devastation of the Civil War is difficult to capture, this lesson includes a series of resources and documents that can help students get a sense of the range and depth of emotions felt by Americans from both the North and South.

Reflecting on the War's Impact

The statistics quoted in this lesson about the war's devastation present a reality that is difficult for contemporary Americans to grasp. Two and a half percent of the population of the United States died in the Civil War. Today, 2.5% of the country's population is roughly seven million people. By comparison, about 8,000 Americans died in the wars in Iraq and Afghanistan combined between the years 2001 and 2013. It was barely possible for Americans in 1865 to go untouched by the loss of at least one, if not many, friends and loved ones who died in the war, especially in the South, where historians estimate that one in five military-eligible men died. In addition, it was not yet customary for governments to tally, identify, and properly bury those who died in war. Therefore, a large proportion of American families who lost loved ones in the Civil War never knew when or where their loved ones died, and they were not able to recover their remains for funeral and burial ceremonies.

The war's upheaval included more than widespread death. The military victory of the Union left large swaths of the South in ruins. Historian Heather Cox Richardson writes that by the end of the war, two-thirds of Southern wealth had been destroyed. Two-fifths of livestock, half the farm machinery, most factories, and nearly all railroads in the South had been destroyed.[1] Depleted resources left a significant part of the population in the former Confederacy suffering from hunger. At the same time, more than four million African Americans had just been emancipated from slavery, a sudden and drastic transformation of American society for whites and blacks, Southerners and Northerners alike. At the end of the Civil War, Americans everywhere were mourning significant losses, enduring significant hardship, and adapting to unfathomable social change. Under these circumstances, they yearned to know that their loved ones did not die in vain. The meaning and the consequences of the war, therefore, were enormously important to those suffering losses as well as those trying to build a new life in freedom.

It is in this context that the diary entries included in this lesson were written. A staunch opponent of slavery, Caroline Barrett White writes triumphantly of Confederate general Robert E. Lee's surrender at Appomattox and hails a new era of liberty "every where, & to all people, of every color." At her home in Massachusetts, White did not experience up close the destruction and upheaval that Kate Stone did. Exiled to Texas from her Louisiana plantation, Stone writes that "our Confederacy will be a Nation no longer, but we will be slaves, yes slaves, of the Yankee Government." Another white Southern woman, Gertrude Clanton Thomas of Georgia, writes about the disruption in her household brought on by Emancipation and the war's end. Thomas struggles to maintain the trappings of status and privilege as many of her former slaves avail themselves of their newfound freedom to simply leave. Historian Thavolia Glymph explains the changes confronting Thomas: "No longer legally bound to the white household after the Civil War, former slaves set out to demolish the residue of that attachment . . . Former mistresses struggled to get along with free laborers whose 'loyalty' they could no longer even pretend to command." Yet as the excerpt in this lesson from Thomas's diary illustrates, some Southerners, such as Thomas's mother, rejected these changes in power and hierarchy and reaffirmed their belief that they had the right to control the lives of African Americans.

All three of these diary entries offer students an indication of the depth of emotion felt in both the North and South as the war ended. Is it possible to reconcile the hearts and minds of individuals such as Kate Stone and Gertrude Thomas with those of Caroline White?

The Challenge of Reuniting the Nation

These two viewpoints also foreshadow the political difficulty of envisioning the future of a nation in which both the North and South were to be members. In 1863, Lincoln offered the first attempt at a Reconstruction policy. A wartime measure designed to provide Unionist footholds in Confederate states, his "Ten-Percent Plan" readmitted Confederate states to the Union when 10 percent of the state's citizens pledged loyalty and accepted Emancipation. Lincoln's plan gave no voice to former slaves in shaping the new Southern governments. While historian Eric Foner asserts that it would be a mistake to assume that Lincoln would have continued his wartime Reconstruction plan after the war, Republicans in Congress at the time criticized the plan as too lenient. In 1864, Congress passed the Wade-Davis Bill, which required a majority of citizens of each

---

1 Heather Cox Richardson, *West from Appomattox: The Reconstruction of America After the Civil War* (Yale University Press, 2007), 17.

state to pledge loyalty to the Union and guaranteed equality before the law for Southern blacks. While the bill was "pocket vetoed" by Lincoln, it was a precursor of Radical Republican efforts to remake Southern society, rather than reunite the nation under the old social order, in the years to come.[2] As the debate over Reconstruction began in the North, however, the war raged on until April of 1865, and in the face of mass desertion from the Confederate army and widespread hunger, Confederate leaders remained as defiant as ever. In February 1865, Confederate president Jefferson Davis declared: "If the power of the enemy were ten times greater, and ours ten times less than it is, there are still some rights of which they could not dispossess us; the right to maintain our personal honor, and the right to fill an honorable grave."[3]

It is in this context that Abraham Lincoln delivered his Second Inaugural Address, one of the most famous and important speeches in American history. In the close reading activity included in this lesson, students will examine this speech carefully, noting the way Lincoln defines the meaning of the war, portrays Northerners and Southerners as a common people, and frames the purpose of Reconstruction. In the address, Lincoln recognizes the end of slavery as fact (the Thirteenth Amendment was well on the way to ratification) and moves beyond this, emphasizing what is common among Americans from the North and South and proposing a reconciliation that would take place "with malice toward none, with charity for all." Students should consider whether or not they think this standard, a plan for Reconstruction built on the ideal of malice for none and charity for all, would be possible to meet. They should also consider whether such a standard would be just for all Americans, including freedpeople. Little more than a month after delivering this address, Lincoln was assassinated in Washington, and Andrew Johnson took center stage in the politics of Reconstruction.

LEARNING GOALS

Understanding: Students will understand that:

- The range of response to both the death and destruction of the Civil War and the reality of Emancipation sharpened the differences between many Americans and complicated the challenges of Reconstruction.

- Lincoln's phrase from his Second Inaugural Address, "with malice toward none, with charity for all," would prove to be a difficult goal to realize given the variety of interests and experiences that emerged from the war.

Knowledge: Students will know that:

- Basic divisions within American society (black/white, North/South, Republican/Democrat) would complicate Reconstruction.

- Lincoln's wartime Reconstruction plan and the Wade-Davis Bill were important early efforts in the struggle to reshape the nation.

---

2 Eric Foner, *Forever Free: The Story of Emancipation and Reconstruction* (Vintage Books, 2006), 62.
3 From Jefferson Davis's "African Church Speech," Richmond, Virginia, Feb. 6, 1865, in *The Papers of Jefferson Davis*, vol. 11, 383–386, available at http://jeffersondavis.rice.edu/Content.aspx?id=102 (accessed Nov. 13, 2013).

RESOURCE LIST

- American Experience: *Death and the Civil War*, Chapter 1 (11 min.) (video)

- Statistics from the War (data)

- "A Day of Triumph" (document)

- "Conquered" (document)

- "What Do You Expect Them to Do?" (document)

- Speech by President Lincoln: Second Inaugural Address (document)

- "Reactions to the Lincoln Assassination" (document)

ACTIVITY SUGGESTIONS

*Note that a detailed Common Core–aligned close-reading protocol for the document "Speech by President Lincoln: Second Inaugural Address" (****Handout 4.5****) follows this lesson. The Common Core standards recommend that students begin a close-reading activity with little, if any, prior knowledge of the text at the heart of the activity. Therefore, if you plan to include a close reading of this document in your unit, we recommend that you complete the activity prior to using any of the suggested activities below.*

Consider using the following activity ideas and strategies when you implement this lesson in your classroom.

- Use the film clip from *Death and the Civil War* and the data document "Statistics from the War" (**Handout 4.1**) to help students gain a sense of the profound personal impact that the Civil War had on most Americans. You might use the same "Two-Column Note-taking" strategy for both resources. As students watch the film and read the document, they will record facts and data representing obstacles to reuniting the country after the war. In the left column, they should simply record each fact or statistic. In the right column, they will explain the challenge to reunion that they think it represents. To view the film, visit facinghistory.org/reconstruction-era/links

- Ask students to work in pairs to imagine a meeting between Caroline Barrett White and either Kate Stone or Gertrude Clanton Thomas. Students can use the following handouts to help them imagine the dialogue: "A Day of Triumph," "Conquered," and "Reactions to the Lincoln Assassination" (**Handouts 4.2**, **4.3**, and **4.6**).

  Have each pair write a dialogue for such a conversation that answers these questions:

  - How would they start a conversation? What would they talk about?

  - What would be the tone of their conversation?

  - What would each woman want the other to know about her experiences and beliefs about the war?

  - How would each woman defend her side of the war? What arguments would they make?

  - What emotions would each woman feel during the discussion? How would they express those emotions?

- Is there anything that the women might have in common that they could discuss?

- What might they share? What might they decide to conceal?

Invite pairs to act out their dialogue for the class. After a few, have students consider what the conversations have in common. What do they add to our understanding of the challenges of reuniting the country after the Civil War?

- Use the "Save the Last Word for Me" strategy to give students the opportunity to analyze **Handout 4.4** ("What Do You Expect Them to Do?") and challenge some of the statements made by Gertrude Clanton Thomas and her mother. (For more information about this strategy, visit facinghistory.org/reconstruction-era/strategies.) Begin by asking students to read the document silently and highlight three sentences that they would like to discuss or challenge. Have students record each sentence on the front of an index card. Each student can then take a turn reading a sentence. First, the other two members of the group have the opportunity to discuss the meaning and significance of the sentence while the student who provided it listens. Finally, the student who read the sentence gets the opportunity to weigh in on the discussion and explain why he or she chose the sentence. The group can then repeat the process until each member has the opportunity to contribute a sentence for discussion.

Conclude the activity by asking each group to summarize its discussion for the whole class. Record on the chalkboard or chart paper the questions each group raises about the document. *If it does not come up in the discussion, it is crucial for the teacher to ask the class to think about the claim of Thomas's mother that slaves were content and happy.* This is an assertion that has been made throughout American history, but it is not supported by the historical record. Ask the class to use evidence they have encountered from this unit so far to refute or respond to this claim.

Finally, guide the class to consider the following questions:

- What does this document reveal about how the end of the Civil War and the abolition of slavery changed the lives of Southern planter families and the black Americans they used to own as slaves?

- What does the document reveal about how power and agency in Southern society began to change in 1865?

- What challenges does this document reveal for the task of reuniting the country after the war?

STATISTICS FROM THE WAR[1]

750,000	Total number of deaths from the Civil War[2]
504	Deaths per day during the Civil War
2.5	Approximate percentage of the American population that died during the Civil War
7,000,000	Number of Americans lost if 2.5% of the American population died in a war today
8,064	Number of American soldiers who died in the wars in Afghanistan and Iraq (as of 3/13/13)[3]
2,100,000	Number of Northerners mobilized to fight for the Union army
880,000	Number of Southerners mobilized to fight for the Confederacy
40+	Estimated percentage of Civil War dead who were never identified
66	Estimated percentage of dead African American Union soldiers who were never identified
2 out of 3	Number of Civil War deaths that occurred from disease rather than battle
68,162	Number of inquiries answered by the Missing Soldiers Office from 1865 to 1868
4,000,000	Number of enslaved persons in the United States in 1860
180,000	Number of African American soldiers that served in the Civil War
1 in 5	Average death rate for all Civil War soldiers
3:1	Ratio of Confederate deaths to Union deaths
9:1	Ratio of African American Civil War troops who died of disease to those that died on the battlefield, largely due to discriminatory medical care
100,000+	Number of Civil War Union corpses found in the South through a federal reinterment program from 1866 to 1869
303,356	Number of Union soldiers who were reinterred in 74 congressionally mandated national cemeteries by 1871
0	Number of Confederate soldiers buried in those national cemeteries

---

1 Except where noted, figures adapted from "The Civil War by the Numbers," American Experience: *Death and the Civil War* companion website, http://www.pbs.org/wgbh/americanexperience/features/general-article/death-numbers/ (accessed April 25, 2013).
2 Guy Gugliotta, "New Estimate Raises Civil War Death Toll," *New York Times*, April 3, 2012, http://www.nytimes.com/2012/04/03/science/civil-war-toll-up-by-20-percent-in-new-estimate.html.
3 Iraq and Afghanistan statistics from http://www.cnn.com/SPECIALS/war.casualties/.

A DAY OF TRIUMPH

The following is an excerpt from the diary of Caroline Barrett White (1828–1915), a resident of Brookline, Massachusetts.

Monday, April 10, 1865

Hurrah! Hurrah! . . . Early this morning our ears were greeted with the sound of bells ringing a joyous peal—& a paper sent home by Frank announced the glad tidings that Gen. Lee had surrendered with his whole Army to Gen. Grant! Surely "This is the Lord's doings, & it is marvelous in our eyes"—The city has been given up to rejoicings all day & this evening there was to have been a great illumination—with music fireworks & such other demonstrations as are usual in a time like this . . . April 9th! Will long be remembered as a day of triumph—just as one week ago came the thrilling intelligence of the Fall of Petersburg & Richmond—& today the greater triumph still of the surrender of Gen. Lee of the Army of Northern Virginia—This crowns a week unparalleled in the annals of this war—& I doubt if a parallel could be found in all history . . . I wish I could be near to join in the general jubilation—it is stupid enough to be sitting alone in a quiet room—where only the faint echoes of a city's burst of joy reach me—Ah! Well! I can be grateful to the Lord who has made bare His Arm to save this people—& who has brought them through great tribulation— through sufferings not to be described—through battle fields, red with the blood of the best of their sons—to see this belled day—step by step has He led this people up even higher & higher— on to the great plans of righteousness—justice & freedom . . . I think we ought to know what patriotism means—and shall realize more fully than ever what it is to have a <u>Country</u>—and our children will have an inheritance greatly to be desired. Let our starry banner wave—from sea to sea and no slave shall look upon its glorious folds—no chains shall clank beneath it—but every where, & to all people, of every color shall it be the loved emblem of liberty.[1]

---

1 Excerpted from *The Caroline Barrett White Papers, 1844–1915*, at the American Antiquarian Society (Worcester, MA).

CONQUERED

The following is an excerpt from the diary of Kate Stone (1841–1907), who fled to Texas from her family's plantation in Louisiana after the Union victory at Vicksburg.

May 15, 1865

Conquered, Submission, Subjugation are words that burn into my heart, and yet I feel that we are doomed to know them in all their bitterness. The war is rushing rapidly to a disastrous close. Another month and our Confederacy will be a Nation no longer, but we will be slaves, yes slaves, of the Yankee Government.

The degradation seems more than we can bear. How can we bend our necks to the tyrants' yoke? Our glorious struggle of the last four years, our hardships, our sacrifices, and worst of all, the torrents of noble blood that have been shed for our loved Country—all, all in vain. The best and bravest of the South sacrificed—and for nothing. Yes, worse than nothing. Only to rivet more firmly the chains that bind us. The bitterness of death is in the thought. We could bear the loss of my brave little brothers when we thought that they had fallen at the post of duty defending their Country, but now to know that those glad, bright spirits suffered and toiled in vain, that the end is overwhelming defeat, the thought is unendurable. And we may never be allowed to raise a monument where their graves sadden the hillside. There is a gloom over all like the shadow of Death. We have given up hope for our beloved Country and all are humiliated, crushed to the earth. A past of grief and hardship, a present of darkness and despair, and a future without hope. Truly our punishment is greater than we can bear.

Since Johnston's surrender the people in this department are hopeless. If we make a stand, it would only delay the inevitable with the loss of many valuable lives. The leaders say the country is too much disheartened to withstand the power of a victorious Yankee army flushed with victory. Still, many hope there will be a rally and one more desperate struggle for freedom. If we cannot gain independence, we might compel better terms.

By the twenty-fourth we will know our fate—Submission to the Union (how we hate the word!), Confiscation, and Negro equality—or a bloody unequal struggle to last we know not how long. God help us, for vain is the help of man.[1]

---

1 Excerpted from John Q. Anderson, ed., *Brokenburn: The Journal of Kate Stone (1861–1868)* (Baton Rouge: Louisiana State University Press, 1955), 339–340. https://archive.org/details/brokenburnthejou008676mbp.

WHAT DO YOU EXPECT THEM TO DO?

The following is an excerpt from the diary of Gertrude Clanton Thomas (1841–1907), the wife of a planter in Augusta, Georgia, in which she discusses the changes that occurred in her black household servants, who were slaves and then paid employees.

Monday, May 29, 1865

Out of all our old house servants not one remains except Patsey and a little boy Frank. We have one of our servants Uncle Jim to take Daniel's place as driver and butler and a much more efficient person he proves to be. Nancy has been cooking since Tamah left. On last Wednesday I hired a woman to do the washing. Thursday I expected Nancy to iron but she was sick. In the same way she was sick the week before when there was ironing to do. I said nothing but told Patsey to get breakfast. After it was over I assisted her in wiping the breakfast dishes, a thing I never remember to have done more than once or twice in my life. I then thoroughly cleaned up the sitting room and parlour. . . . In the afternoon I went in the ironing room and in to see Nancy. The clothes were all piled upon the table, the flies swarming over them. The room looking as if it had not been cleaned up in several weeks. Nancy's room was in just the same state. I asked her "if she was not well enough to sprinkle some of the clothes." "No" she replied "she was not well enough to do anything." Said I, "Nancy do you expect I can afford to pay you wages in your situation, support your two children and then have you sick as much as you are?" She made no reply . . .

The next morning after Patsey had milked the cow & had fire made in the kitchen, she [Nancy] volunteered to cook breakfast— Immediately after breakfast as I was writing by the window Turner directed my attention to Nancy with her two children, Hannah and Jessy, going out of the gate. I told him to enquire "where she was going." She had expected to leave with flying colours but was compelled to tell a falsehood for she replied "I will be back directly" I knew at once that she was taking "french leave" [not coming back] and was not surprised when I went into her room sometime afterwards to find that all her things had been removed. I was again engaged in housework most of the morning. . . .

. . . One day last week she [Nancy] entered Ma's back yard with a Yankee soldier. . . . Hastening to the door of her room Ma saw Nancy going down into the basement followed by a Yankee soldier who was just at the head of the steps. "By what authority do you presume to search my house?" was her indignant inquiry. "I have none" said he. "I came with this woman who says she left some clothes here." . . . Then continuing her conversation with the Yankee Ma added "What do you expect to do with these Negroes you have freed? Before this war our Negroes were a well contented, happy race of people. You have come amongst us have sown seeds of dissension and deprived us of the right to manage them. Now what do you expect them to do?" "Starve I reckon" was his reply. He then proceeded to tell her that his name was Brown, that he had a brother in the Confederate service, and assured her that she would find white labor much cheaper and better. "I am a southern woman" said she "born and raised at the South, accustomed to the service of Negroes and like them better. That Negro has had time enough to get her clothes" she then added. "Take her out of my yard" and addressing Nancy Ma told her "to leave the yard and never dare to come into it again."[1]

---

1 Virginia Ingraham Burr, ed., *The Secret Eye: The Journal of Ella Gertrude Clanton Thomas, 1848–1889* (Chapel Hill: University of North Carolina Press, 1990), 272–274.

SPEECH BY PRESIDENT LINCOLN: SECOND INAUGURAL ADDRESS

March 4, 1865

Fellow-Countrymen:

At this second appearing to take the oath of the Presidential office there is less occasion for an extended address than there was at the first. Then a statement somewhat in detail of a course to be pursued seemed fitting and proper. Now, at the expiration of four years, during which public declarations have been constantly called forth on every point and phase of the great contest which still absorbs the attention and engrosses the energies of the nation, little that is new could be presented. The progress of our arms, upon which all else chiefly depends, is as well known to the public as to myself, and it is, I trust, reasonably satisfactory and encouraging to all. With high hope for the future, no prediction in regard to it is ventured.

On the occasion corresponding to this four years ago all thoughts were anxiously directed to an impending civil war. All dreaded it, all sought to avert it. While the inaugural address was being delivered from this place, devoted altogether to saving the Union without war, insurgent agents were in the city seeking to destroy it without war— seeking to dissolve the Union and divide effects by negotiation. Both parties deprecated war, but one of them would make war rather than let the nation survive, and the other would accept war rather than let it perish, and the war came.

One-eighth of the whole population were colored slaves, not distributed generally over the Union, but localized in the southern part of it. These slaves constituted a peculiar and powerful interest. All knew that this interest was somehow the cause of the war. To strengthen, perpetuate, and extend this interest was the object for which the insurgents would rend the Union even by war, while the Government claimed no right to do more than to restrict the territorial enlargement of it. Neither party expected for the war the magnitude or the duration which it has already attained. Neither anticipated that the cause of the conflict might cease with or even before the conflict itself should cease. Each looked for an easier triumph, and a result less fundamental and astounding. Both read the same Bible and pray to the same God, and each invokes His aid against the other. It may seem strange that any men should dare to ask a just God's assistance in wringing their bread from the sweat of other men's faces, but let us judge not, that we be not judged. The prayers of both could not be answered. That of neither has been answered fully. The Almighty has His own purposes. "Woe unto the world because of offenses; for it must needs be that offenses come, but woe to that man by whom the offense cometh." If we shall suppose that American slavery is one of those offenses which, in the providence of God, must needs come, but which, having continued through His appointed time, He now wills to remove, and that He gives to both North and South this terrible war as the woe due to those by whom the offense came, shall we discern therein any departure from those divine attributes which the believers in a living God always ascribe to Him? Fondly do we hope, fervently do we pray, that this mighty scourge of war may speedily pass away. Yet, if God wills that it continue until all the wealth piled by the bondsman's two hundred and fifty years of unrequited toil shall be sunk, and until every drop of blood drawn with the lash shall be paid by another drawn with the sword, as was said three thousand years ago, so still it must be said "the judgments of the Lord are true and righteous altogether."

With malice toward none, with charity for all, with firmness in the right as God gives us to see the right, let us strive on to finish the work we are in, to bind up the nation's wounds, to care for him who shall have borne the battle and for his widow and his orphan, to do all which may achieve and cherish a just and lasting peace among ourselves and with all nations.[1]

1 Abraham Lincoln, Second Inaugural Address, March 4, 1865, available from "The Avalon Project," Yale Law School Lillian Goldman Law Library, http://avalon.law.yale.edu/19th_century/lincoln2.asp.

REACTIONS TO THE LINCOLN ASSASSINATION

CAROLINE BARRETT WHITE:

Saturday, April 15, 1865

The darkest day I ever remember—This morning the sun rose upon a nation jubilant with victory—but it sets upon one plunged in deepest sorrow . . . midday—came the shocking intelligence that our beloved President Abraham Lincoln was dead—shot by a brutal assassin—last evening—as he was sitting cheerfully chatting with his wife & other friends in a box at the theatre—he lingered unconscious till about eight o'clock this morning—& died without a word or sign . . . Later in the day came rumors of having secured the murderer—who it is affirmed by Miss Laura Keeve to be J. Wilkes Booth; Oh! where will treason end? & What shall we do with such as fall into our hands . . . The rapidity with which events crowd upon one another is perfectly bewildering. Frank is away & it (?) hard to be alone . . . When will our cup of punishments be drunk to the dregs? Merciful Father, help us.[1]

KATE STONE:

April 28, 1865

We hear that Lincoln is dead. There can be no doubt, I suppose, that he has been killed by J. W. Booth. "*Sic semper tyrannis*" as his brave destroyer shouted as he sprang on his horse. All honor to J. Wilkes Booth, who has rid the world of a tyrant and made himself famous for generations. Surratt has also won the love and applause of all Southerners by his daring attack on Seward, whose life is trembling in the balance. How earnestly we hope our two avengers may escape to the South where they will meet with a warm welcome. It is a terrible tragedy, but what is war but one long tragedy? What torrents of blood Lincoln has caused to flow, and how Seward has aided him in his bloody work. I cannot be sorry for their fate. They deserve it. They have reaped their just reward.[2]

---

1 Excerpted from *The Caroline Barrett White Papers*, 1844–1915, at the American Antiquarian Society (Worcester, MA).
2 Excerpted from John Q. Anderson, ed., *Brokenburn: The Journal of Kate Stone (1861–1868)* (Baton Rouge: Louisiana State University Press, 1955), 333. https://archive.org/details/brokenburnthejou008676mbp.

Speech by President Lincoln: Second Inaugural Address

*Close reading is carefully and purposefully **rereading** a text. It's an encounter with the text in which we closely focus on what the author has to say, what the author's purpose is, what the words mean, and what the structure of the text tells us. Close reading ensures that we truly understand what we've read. At Facing History and Ourselves, we use this careful investigation of text to make connections to essential questions about history, human behavior, and ourselves. This protocol can be used to implement a close reading for select documents during the Reconstruction unit. Adapt this procedure to best meet your goals and the needs of your students.*

FIRST READ: Read aloud. Either the teacher or an extremely fluent student can read the text aloud. Ask students to circle unfamiliar words as they listen. After the read-aloud, as students share these words with the class, decide which words to define immediately to limit confusion and which definitions you want students to uncover through careful reading.

SECOND READ: Individual read. Ask students to read silently to get a feel for the text. They can note specific words or phrases that jump out at them for any number of reasons: because they are interesting, familiar, strange, confusing, funny, troubling, difficult, etc. Share some of these as a class. Particular questions to ask students at this stage of the reading are:

- What can you already infer about the author of this text?

- How is the text structured?

- Does this structure make it easy or difficult to make meaning?

- Does this structure tell us anything about the author's style or purpose?

THIRD READ: Text-dependent questions. In small groups, have students read the text in chunks and answer a set of text-dependent questions. These questions are included with each close reading exemplar. Sample answers are provided to help guide the teacher. See the "Close Reading B: Student Handout" form for a student version of the document. See "Close Reading B: Teacher Guide" for the teacher's version.

FOURTH READ: Visual image. In small groups, have students create a visual image on paper that captures the essence of the text. You may also ask them to include three words or a sentence summary of each section of text. Groups can be assigned either the entire text or sections of text for this portion of the close reading.

FIFTH READ: Gallery read. Ask students to do a "gallery read" of the images that have been created.

TRANSITION TO DISCUSSION

At this point, we recommend organizing a class discussion so that students can make connections beyond the text. This discussion can be informal or can use the format of the "Socratic Seminar" or "Save the Last Word for Me" strategy (see the "Teaching Strategies" section of our website at facinghistory.org/reconstruction-era/strategies for details).

DISCUSSION SUGGESTIONS

As mentioned earlier, this unit includes two writing prompts. Both prompts can be used to launch a discussion after a close reading. Examples include:

- To connect to the argumentative writing prompt (*Support, refute, or modify the statement: Laws are the most important factor in overcoming discrimination*):

  - What is the role of laws and government in reuniting a country that has experienced a civil war? How might Lincoln connect ideas about healing and justice to the work of overcoming discrimination?

- To connect to the informative writing prompt: *Historian Eric Foner calls Reconstruction "America's unfinished revolution." What debates and dilemmas from the Reconstruction era remain unresolved? After researching informational texts on Reconstruction, write an essay in which you explain one debate that was central to this period that remained unresolved. Explain why the debate was significant to the history of Reconstruction. In your conclusion, discuss the legacy of the debate not being resolved.*

  - Ask students to find connections between Lincoln's message about healing the country and contemporary issues surrounding the idea of unifying American society today. What aspects of Lincoln's approach remain "unfinished" in the twenty-first century?

- To connect to more general Facing History and Ourselves themes:

  - How does Lincoln try to reunite the country through his word choice and tone? What does this suggest about how he views the divisions in American society ("we" and "they")? What can you infer about how he views his role as president in a democracy?

  - What does Lincoln suggest about how it might be possible to create a just society?

  - What is the role of an individual in building a democracy? Is it possible and just for an individual, group, or nation to have "malice toward none" and "charity for all" after war?

- It's also possible to have students themselves create the questions for a discussion. To do this, you might guide students by asking them to find connections between the essential questions and the text or to write questions based on what resonates for them. They might choose to make connections to the author's purpose, the structure of the text, the tone of the text, or the main messages of the text. Alternatively, they may want to make connections to issues related to the individual and society, to examples of healing and justice, to the role of leaders in a democracy, and beyond.

CLOSE READING B Teacher Guide

Text of Lincoln's Second Inaugural Address

March 4, 1865

Fellow-Countrymen:

At this second appearing to take the oath of the Presidential office there is less occasion for an extended address than there was at the first. Then a statement somewhat in detail of a course to be pursued seemed fitting and proper. Now, at the expiration of four years, during which public declarations have been constantly called forth on every point and phase of the great contest which still absorbs the attention and engrosses the energies of the nation, little that is new could be presented. The progress of our arms, upon which all else chiefly depends, is as well known to the public as to myself, and it is, I trust, reasonably satisfactory and encouraging to all. With high hope for the future, no prediction in regard to it is ventured.

On the occasion corresponding to this four years ago all thoughts were anxiously directed to an impending civil war. All dreaded it, all sought to avert it. While the inaugural address was being delivered from this place, devoted altogether to saving the Union without war, insurgent agents were in the city seeking to destroy it without war—seeking to dissolve the Union and divide effects by negotiation. Both parties

74

Guided Close Reading
with Text-Dependent Questions

1. **In the first sentence, what do we learn is the reason for Lincoln's address?**

   A good close reading begins with some "easy wins" for students, and this question should clearly draw out the response that Lincoln gave this speech after taking the oath of office for the second time.

2. **According to what Lincoln says in the first paragraph, what are the differences between this speech and his previous inaugural address?**

   Lincoln states that four years prior, a detailed address that laid out the course for his first term as president was "fitting and proper." However, Lincoln points out that the four years after that first speech were full of other public addresses speaking to the progress of the war, making his current speech less of an "occasion" and leaving him with much less new information to present to the nation.

3. **Given what Lincoln says at the end of the first paragraph, what can you infer that he believes about the course of the war?**

   Based on Lincoln's mention of the "progress of our arms," which he calls "reasonably satisfactory and encouraging to all," one might infer that he is addressing a Northern audience and that the North is at present winning the war. Notably, however, despite the "high hope" that the North will emerge the victor, he is careful not to make any concrete claims about the outcome of the war.

4. **Paraphrase in your own words Lincoln's second paragraph describing the events surrounding his speech four years prior.**

   Students should note three things about the events during the period of his first inaugural address: (a) all parties were fearful of the impending conflict and looking for ways to avoid it, (b) Lincoln's address was directed at preserving the Union without provoking war, and (c) deprecated war, but one of them would make war rather than let the nation survive, and the other would accept war rather than let it perish, and the war came.

One-eighth of the whole population were colored slaves, not distributed generally over the Union, but localized in the southern part of it. These slaves constituted a peculiar and powerful interest. All knew that this interest was somehow the cause of the war. To strengthen, perpetuate, and extend this interest was the object for which the insurgents would rend the Union even by war, while the Government claimed no right to do more than to restrict the territorial enlargement of it. Neither party expected for the war the magnitude or the duration which it has already attained. Neither anticipated that the cause of the conflict might cease with or even before the conflict itself should cease. Each looked for an easier triumph, and a result less fundamental and astounding. Both read the same Bible and pray to the same God, and each invokes His aid against the other. It may seem strange that any men should dare to ask a just God's assistance in wringing their bread from the sweat of other men's faces, but let us judge not, that we be not judged. The prayers of both could not be answered. That of neither has been answered fully.

"insurgent agents" were simultaneously attempting to dissolve the Union through negotiation. The war resulted from the differences with regard to the Union's survival.

5. **Lincoln repeatedly uses the word *all* in the second paragraph (as well as *both*) to emphasize the commonalities between the two sides. How does Lincoln differentiate between the roles of the North and the South in the second paragraph?**

Lincoln is careful not to place blame on the South for the Civil War. In the opening lines of the paragraph, Lincoln recognizes that all Americans were fearful of any coming conflict and that they all looked for other solutions to the disagreements within the nation. While he does note that the South "[made] war rather than let the nation survive," he also notes that the North accepted this outcome because it did not want the dissolution of the Union.

6. **What does Lincoln claim is the cause of the Civil War?**

In the beginning of the third paragraph, Lincoln says that "all knew" that the issue of slavery was "somehow" the cause of the war. He goes on to elaborate by saying that despite the government's efforts to reassure the South that its only interest was in restricting the spread of slavery to the territories, the "southern part" of the country started the war to "strengthen, perpetuate, and extend" its hold on slaves.

7. **What additional similarities between Northerners and Southerners does Lincoln note in the third paragraph?**

Lincoln says that neither side expected the war to last as long as it had at that point, and both sides sought an easy victory with less "astounding" results. The result he references—and another commonality between both sides—is a shared surprise that the (legal) end of slavery had come before the end of the conflict itself ("Neither anticipated that the cause of the conflict might cease with or even before the conflict itself should cease"). In addition, Lincoln notes that "Both read the same

Text of Lincoln's Second Inaugural Address

The Almighty has His own purposes. "Woe unto the world because of offenses; for it must needs be that offenses come, but woe to that man by whom the offense cometh." If we shall suppose that American slavery is one of those offenses which, in the providence of God, must needs come, but which, having continued through His appointed time, He now wills to remove, and that He gives to both North and South this terrible war as the woe due to those by whom the offense came, shall we discern therein any departure from those divine attributes which the believers in a living God always ascribe to Him? Fondly do we hope, fervently do we pray, that this mighty scourge of war may speedily pass away. Yet, if God wills that it continue until all the wealth piled by the bondsman's two hundred and fifty years of unrequited toil shall be sunk, and until every drop of blood drawn with the lash shall be paid by another drawn with the sword, as was said three thousand years ago, so still it must be said "the judgments of the Lord are true and righteous altogether."

Bible and pray to the same God," emphasizing this common ground and understanding between the two sides even though they have been engaged in a long and difficult conflict.

8. **In the context of the third paragraph, what is the meaning of the word *wringing*? Explain what Lincoln is describing with the phrase "wringing their bread from the sweat of other men's faces."**

Students should understand that with this phrase, Lincoln is alluding to slavery, in that slave owners acquire their "bread," or earnings, via the sweat, or work, of their slaves rather than their own labor. The imagery of slavery should also suggest to students the violent nature of the word wringing, which can be contextually defined as "obtaining by force."

9. **According to Lincoln, who is responsible for the "offense" of slavery?**

In the beginning of the paragraph, Lincoln notes that slavery had been "localized in the southern part" of the United States, and he goes so far as to question the strangeness of Southerners praying to God for assistance in winning the war when they had long been "wringing their bread from the sweat of other men's faces"—but he is quick to follow with a reminder to his listeners to "let us judge not, that we be not judged." Lincoln recognizes that despite the different sides that the North and South take in the war, the entire country is responsible for the perpetuation of the "offense" of "American slavery," and therefore God "gives to both the North and South this terrible war."

10. **What role does Lincoln hypothetically ("If we shall suppose") imagine God playing in slavery and the Civil War? Does this conception of the deity run counter to the traditional understanding of God?**

In the second half of the speech, Lincoln entertains the notion that slavery and the ensuing fight over it were the will of God. As noted above, rather than blaming the South specifically for the history of slavery, Lincoln suggests that both sides are responsible and can be seen as "those by whom the offense came." As a result, God's response to the offense is a war that engages both sides of the nation. Because the war is

Text of Lincoln's Second Inaugural Address

With malice toward none, with charity for all, with firmness in the right as God gives us to see the right, let us strive on to finish the work we are in, to bind up the nation's wounds, to care for him who shall have borne the battle and for his widow and his orphan, to do all which may achieve and cherish a just and lasting peace among ourselves and with all nations.

Guided Close Reading with Text-Dependent Questions

God's punishment for the offense of slavery, both sides must understand that even though they hope and pray that the conflict will end quickly, the length and course of the war are determined by God.

11. **What is Lincoln referring to with the phrase "until every drop of blood drawn with the lash shall be paid by another drawn with the sword"?**

The "lash" references a common practice of punishing slaves, and the "sword" alludes to the war. Lincoln is speaking to the idea that the Civil War is God's punishment to the United States for the legacy of slavery. He is professing that if God wills that the same amount of blood must be spilled in the Civil War as the amount lost by those who suffered under slavery, the country must accept the length of the war as the proper sentence.

12. **What clues are in the fourth paragraph as to the meaning of the word malice? What is the significance of the phrase "with malice toward none" in Lincoln's speech?**

Lincoln uses this paragraph to describe how the nation's people need to come together and care for each other. From the context of the paragraph, and using clues from other phrases such as "charity for all," the reader should understand the word malice to be contextually defined as "hatred" or "ill will." The significance of this phrase is that Lincoln calls for Northerners to treat their Southern compatriots with compassion and kindness despite the bitterness of the war.

13. **At the conclusion of the speech, what does Lincoln call on the nation to do in order to "achieve and cherish a just and lasting peace among ourselves and with all nations"?**

Lincoln notes that in order to move on after finishing "the work we are in" (e.g., winning the war), the country must "bind up the nation's wounds" and "care for him who shall have borne the battle and for his widow and his orphan." He demonstrates that the next steps for the nation should be about unity and working together rather than placing blame on the South.

Guided Close Reading
with Text-Dependent Questions

14. **How does the message of the final paragraph connect to Lincoln's message in the third paragraph?**

In the third paragraph, Lincoln is careful to explain that the Civil War is the consequence for slavery for the entire nation. Rather than singling out the South or the states that seceded, he understands that the entire nation must carry the burden of the past and that therefore the South should not be treated with "malice" and everyone should be treated with "charity" as the country works to rebuild itself.

In the third paragraph, Lincoln also extensively contemplates the consequences of accepting that "the Almighty has His own purposes" that we may not fully understand—a fact that he reiterates in the final paragraph when tasking his listeners to carry on "with firmness in the right" while understanding that their knowledge is limited to what "God gives us to see the right."

Lastly, Lincoln ends the third paragraph by vividly comparing the bloodletting caused by slavery to the bloodletting caused by the war, and in the fourth paragraph he envisions that the end of both would lead to a binding up of "the nation's wounds" such that "a just and lasting peace" may emerge.

Text of Lincoln's Second Inaugural Address

March 4, 1865

Fellow-Countrymen:

At this second appearing to take the oath of the Presidential office there is less occasion for an extended address than there was at the first. Then a statement somewhat in detail of a course to be pursued seemed fitting and proper. Now, at the expiration of four years, during which public declarations have been constantly called forth on every point and phase of the great contest which still absorbs the attention and engrosses the energies of the nation, little that is new could be presented. The progress of our arms, upon which all else chiefly depends, is as well known to the public as to myself, and it is, I trust, reasonably satisfactory and encouraging to all. With high hope for the future, no prediction in regard to it is ventured.

On the occasion corresponding to this four years ago all thoughts were anxiously directed to an impending civil war. All dreaded it, all sought to avert it. While the inaugural address was being delivered from this place, devoted altogether to saving the Union without war, insurgent agents were in the city seeking to destroy it without war—seeking

Guided Close Reading
with Text-Dependent Questions

1. In the first sentence, what do we learn is the reason for Lincoln's address?

2. According to what Lincoln says in the first paragraph, what are the differences between this speech and his previous inaugural address?

3. Given what Lincoln says at the end of the first paragraph, what can you infer that he believes about the course of the war?

4. Paraphrase in your own words Lincoln's second paragraph describing the events surrounding his speech four years prior.

5. Lincoln repeatedly uses the word *all* in the second paragraph (as well as *both*) to emphasize the commonalities between the two sides. How does Lincoln differentiate between the roles of the North and the South in the second paragraph?

6. What does Lincoln claim is the cause of the Civil War?

7. What additional similarities between Northerners and Southerners does Lincoln note in the third paragraph?

Text of Lincoln's Second Inaugural Address

to dissolve the Union and divide effects by negotiation. Both parties deprecated war, but one of them would make war rather than let the nation survive, and the other would accept war rather than let it perish, and the war came.

One-eighth of the whole population were colored slaves, not distributed generally over the Union, but localized in the southern part of it. These slaves constituted a peculiar and powerful interest. All knew that this interest was somehow the cause of the war. To strengthen, perpetuate, and extend this interest was the object for which the insurgents would rend the Union even by war, while the Government claimed no right to do more than to restrict the territorial enlargement of it. Neither party expected for the war the magnitude or the duration which it has already attained. Neither anticipated that the cause of the conflict might cease with or even before the conflict itself should cease. Each looked for an easier triumph, and a result less fundamental and astounding. Both read the same Bible and pray to the same God, and each invokes His aid against the other. It may seem strange that any men should dare to ask a just God's assistance in wringing their bread from the sweat of other men's faces, but let us judge not, that we be not judged. The prayers of both could not be answered. That of neither has been answered fully. The Almighty has His own purposes. "Woe unto the world because of

Text of Lincoln's Second Inaugural Address

offenses; for it must needs be that offenses come, but woe to that man by whom the offense cometh." If we shall suppose that American slavery is one of those offenses which, in the providence of God, must needs come, but which, having continued through His appointed time, He now wills to remove, and that He gives to both North and South this terrible war as the woe due to those by whom the offense came, shall we discern therein any departure from those divine attributes which the believers in a living God always ascribe to Him? Fondly do we hope, fervently do we pray, that this mighty scourge of war may speedily pass away. Yet, if God wills that it continue until all the wealth piled by the bondsman's two hundred and fifty years of unrequited toil shall be sunk, and until every drop of blood drawn with the lash shall be paid by another drawn with the sword, as was said three thousand years ago, so still it must be said "the judgments of the Lord are true and righteous altogether."

Guided Close Reading
with Text-Dependent Questions

8. In the context of the third paragraph, what is the meaning of the word *wringing*? Explain what Lincoln is describing with the phrase *"wringing their bread from the sweat of other men's faces."*

9. According to Lincoln, who is responsible for the "offense" of slavery?

10. What role does Lincoln hypothetically ("If we shall suppose") imagine God playing in slavery and the Civil War? Does this conception of the deity run counter to the traditional understanding of God?

81

Guided Close Reading
with Text-Dependent Questions

11. What is Lincoln referring to with the phrase "until every drop of blood drawn with the lash shall be paid by another drawn with the sword"?

12. What clues are in the fourth paragraph as to the meaning of the word *malice*? What is the significance of the phrase "with malice toward none" in Lincoln's speech?

13. At the conclusion of the speech, what does Lincoln call on the nation to do in order to "achieve and cherish a just and lasting peace among ourselves and with all nations"?

Text of Lincoln's Second Inaugural Address

With malice toward none, with charity for all, with firmness in the right as God gives us to see the right, let us strive on to finish the work we are in, to bind up the nation's wounds, to care for him who shall have borne the battle and for his widow and his orphan, to do all which may achieve and cherish a just and lasting peace among ourselves and with all nations.

Guided Close Reading
with Text-Dependent Questions

14. How does the message of the final paragraph connect to Lincoln's message in the third paragraph?

LESSON 5 Healing and Justice

ESSENTIAL QUESTION

After a civil war, how can a nation simultaneously heal and provide justice to all of its inhabitants?

TRANSITION

Students learned about two unresolved challenges facing the United States immediately after the Civil War: how to define freedom and how to reunite two parts of the country torn apart by a miserable and bitter war. Students will look closely at the actions of President Andrew Johnson to resolve these dilemmas through his plan for Reconstruction. They will debate the fairness of this plan and, in the process, reflect on deeper issues of *healing* and *justice* in the aftermath of both a devastating war and a profound transformation of society.

RATIONALE

As the Civil War ended, the country and its lawmakers faced the daunting challenge of bringing the North and South back together and forming a unified nation. This task was all the more complicated given the fact of Emancipation, the aspirations of freedpeople across the South, and the tension between these factors and the belief in white supremacy held by many Americans. Historian David Blight describes the challenges of the era as a balancing act between two competing, and sometimes mutually exclusive, goals:

> The challenge of Reconstruction, and it's the challenge we've had ever since, is: How do you do two profound things at the same time? One was healing and the other was justice. How do you have them both? What truly constitutes healing of a people, of a nation, that's suffered this scale of violence and destruction, and how do you have justice? And justice for whom?[1]

Students will see that one of the primary political conflicts of the era stemmed from disagreement over exactly what the proper balance of these principles—healing and justice—should be. In the two years following the end of the Civil War and the Lincoln assassination, a political battle between President Andrew Johnson and a group of Republicans in Congress known as the Radicals ensued. In this lesson, students will look closely at Johnson's Presidential Reconstruction plan, and they will be exposed to the Radical Republican criticism of that plan. In the process, they will uncover disagreements between Americans over the rights of the victorious North to impose its will on the defeated South and over the rights and status that white and black Southerners each ought to be granted in the Southern states.

---

1 David Blight, "Andrew Johnson and the Radicals: A Contest over the Meaning of Reconstruction," lecture presented at Yale University (iTunes U audio file), https://itunes.apple.com/us/itunes-u/civil-war-reconstruction-era/id341650730 (accessed Apr. 25, 2013).

The Presidential Reconstruction Plan

Andrew Johnson assumed the presidency following Lincoln's assassination in April 1865, and within a month he began to implement his plans for Reconstruction, which became known as Presidential Reconstruction. Johnson was a Democrat from eastern Tennessee whose loyalties toward poor Southern whites led him to detest the slaveholder aristocracy and remain a staunch supporter of the Union during the Civil War. In fact, he was permitted to keep his seat in the United States Senate after the war began because he remained loyal to the Union, despite his state's secession. Later in the war, Lincoln appointed Johnson military governor of Tennessee, where he earned a reputation for taking strong action against Confederates in his state. Lincoln then brought Johnson onto the 1864 ticket because he had the backing of loyalist white Southerners to whom Republicans could appeal for support after the war. However, Johnson had little concern for the rights or needs of freedpeople beyond their emancipation. He believed in white supremacy, and, as his Reconstruction policies and public speeches reflected, his belief in white supremacy was stronger than his dislike for the wealthy Southern planter class.

Johnson argued that, since he believed secession was illegal, the rebellious states had never truly left the Union. Therefore, their relationship to the federal government ought to be restored as expediently as possible, and white supremacy, the political and social order that prevailed before the war, ought to continue, absent slavery. Announced in May 1865 while Congress was in recess (Congress would not reconvene until December), Johnson's plan granted amnesty, including the restoration of property, to the vast majority of Southern whites who supported the Confederacy as long as they were willing to take an oath of loyalty to the Union. (The text of the oath is included in this lesson's resources.) High-ranking Confederate military officers, political leaders, and planters with more than $20,000 in wealth were required to apply individually to Johnson for a pardon in order to regain their rights and property. Johnson ultimately granted requested pardons liberally, so by the fall of 1865, most ex-Rebels were considered citizens in good standing. Presidential Reconstruction also provided for the rapid readmission of Southern states to the Union. Johnson called for Southern states to hold constitutional conventions to amend their prewar constitutions to comply with federal law and accept the Thirteenth Amendment. Eligibility to vote for convention delegates was determined by each state's prewar constitution, thus excluding those who were enslaved before the war (as well as anyone not yet granted amnesty or pardon) from the process of revising the state constitutions. This guaranteed that white supremacy would continue to prevail in the postwar state governments even in the absence of slavery. David Blight summarizes Johnson's philosophy of Reconstruction with this phrase: "The Constitution as it is, and the Union as it was."

The Radical Republican Vision

Radical Republicans, a progressive minority of the Republican Party, believed that Johnson's approach was wholly unacceptable, and the Radicals' position gained support from moderate Republicans as conflict between the president and Congress erupted in 1865 and 1866. What was especially threatening to Republicans was that under Johnson's plan, Southern Democrats stood to gain a level of representation in Congress greater even than it was before the war. This was because the "three-fifths" clause was no longer operative in the Constitution after the abolition of slavery.

Each freedperson now counted as a full person when determining the number of representatives each state would send to Congress and the Electoral College. However, as former Confederates regained control of Southern governments under Presidential Reconstruction, it became clear that they would prohibit freedpeople from voting, enabling white Democrats to dominate the elections.

Radical Republicans maintained that the federal government, as the victor in war over the former Confederacy, had the right to impose significant political and social changes, chief among them voting rights for freedpeople. Countering Johnson's goal of *restoring* the states of the South, Representative Thaddeus Stevens argued that Congress must *remake* them: "The whole fabric of southern society *must* be changed, and never can it be done if this opportunity is lost. Without this, this Government can never be, as it never has been, a true republic."[2] If the Southern states would not be remade, Radical Republicans asked, then which side had really won the war?

While they had not formulated a specific plan for Reconstruction in 1865, Radical Republicans coalesced around the ideal of equal rights. In particular, their vision for remaking the South included voting rights for black males, the establishment of new state governments in the South recognizing these voting rights, and strong federal protection for the rights of former slaves. Moderate Republicans were more pragmatic than the Radicals, whom they outnumbered. Moderates initially hoped to work with President Johnson to restore the Union rather than wholly remake it As we will see in subsequent lessons, the realities of Presidential Reconstruction, as well as Andrew Johnson's combative response to Republican efforts to modify his policies, would prompt moderate Republicans to take positions closer to those of the Radicals.[3]

By examining the opposing philosophies for Reconstruction put forth by Andrew Johnson and Radical Republicans, students can begin to consider the difficulties of balancing healing and justice after a cataclysm such as the Civil War. They might consider the difficult choices and questions faced by political leaders at the time: Whose voices should be included in the process of "binding up the nation's wounds"? Who should be included and who should be excluded in the nation that would emerge from Reconstruction? Could the nation heal if former Confederates felt that they were being punished by a loss of power and status? Could democracy thrive if African Americans were not guaranteed equal rights in the new nation? How *could* the nation balance the goals of healing and justice?

LEARNING GOALS

Understanding: Students will understand that:

- Achieving the goals of *healing* and *justice* simultaneously after a civil war is a significant challenge for any country.

- In times of crisis, negotiating a society's universe of obligation can be a significant source of conflict and reveal the fragility of democracy.

---

2 From *The Selected Papers of Thaddeus Stevens, Vol. 2: April 1865–August 1868* (University of Pittsburgh Press, 1998), 23.
3 Eric Foner, *Forever Free: The Story of Emancipation and Reconstruction* (Vintage Books, 2006), 111–121.

Knowledge: *Students will know that:*

- Presidential Johnson enacted a plan for Reconstruction that prioritized healing and reconciliation between the North and South over justice for freedpeople.

- Radical Republicans, a minority in their party, criticized Johnson's Reconstruction plan. At the heart of the differences between President Johnson and the Radical Republicans was the debate over citizenship and who can be a full member of American society.

RESOURCE LIST

- "Healing and Justice" (anticipation guide)

- "Creating a Plan for Reconstruction" (activity)

- "Debating Reconstruction Policies" (document)

- "Presidential Reconstruction" (document)

- "PARDON: Shall I Trust These Men?" and "FRANCHISE: And Not This Man?" (images)

LESSON PLAN

ESTIMATED DURATION: 2 CLASS PERIODS

SKILLS ADDRESSED:

- **Literacy:** Citing specific textual evidence to support conclusions drawn from a text

- **Historical thinking:** Analyzing evidence, reasoning, contexts, and points of view to interpret the past

- **Social-emotional:** Relationship skills—negotiating consensus and shared understanding of important concepts

I. Exploring Healing and Justice

By reflecting on the meanings of *healing* and *justice*, and then creating concept maps for these terms, students will have the opportunity to engage with some of the dilemmas that Americans faced after the Civil War.

PROCEDURE

1. Distribute the Lesson 5 anticipation guide "Healing and Justice" (**Handout 5.1**). Ask students to complete the handout individually.

2. Divide the class into groups of three, four, or five. Prompt the members of each group to share and discuss their positions from the anticipation guide.

3. Explain that the statements on the anticipation guide relate to two important concepts: *healing* and *justice*. As a class, create a working definition for each word. Remind students that a working definition is one that they can expand, focus, or revise as they learn more about a concept. You might also allow students to

consult a dictionary or thesaurus to determine the meaning of each word best suited for describing the challenges a nation faces in the aftermath of war. Start two "durable" concept maps, which can be saved and posted in the classroom for later reference, for *healing* and *justice*. Write the class definitions for the terms on the maps, as well as related ideas and concepts that come up in the discussion.

4. Provide each group with two sets of self-stick notes, each set in a different color. Designate one color for *healing* and the other for *justice*. Working with information from the anticipation guide, ask each group to discuss what Americans could do to help bring about healing and justice after the Civil War. Groups should record as many specific ideas as they can agree on for each concept on appropriately colored self-stick notes. As students finish the task, a representative from each group can attach the notes to the concept maps in the room.

5. Give students the opportunity to read the concept maps after they are complete before beginning a whole-group wrap-up of this activity. End the activity by asking students to record and share their thoughts about the following questions:

   • What did you notice about the concept maps? Did you notice consensus among the groups as to what might bring about healing or justice? Did you notice any disagreement between the groups?

   • How did you experience the process of coming to agreement with your group members as to what would bring about healing and justice? What dilemmas did you wrestle with? What sticking points did you encounter?

II. Creating a Plan for Reconstruction

Students will now build on their exploration of the concepts of healing and justice by creating their own plans for Reconstruction that attempt to balance both of these goals. In the process, they will look more deeply at some of the dilemmas that Americans faced after the Civil War, and they will create a basis from which they can evaluate the actual plans President Johnson and, later, Congress enacted.

PROCEDURE

1. Students will work in pairs or triads. Provide each group with a piece of chart paper, markers, and a copy of **Handout 5.2** ("Creating a Plan for Reconstruction").

2. Explain to students that their task is to create a specific plan for Reconstruction that balances *healing* and *justice*. Their plan will have to address many of the dilemmas from the anticipation guide that they discussed earlier.

3. Give the groups 20 minutes to discuss the dilemmas presented on the handout "Creating a Plan for Reconstruction" and decide on a specific proposal that addresses each one. Students should record their proposals on the chart paper.

4. After they complete their plans for Reconstruction, each group should briefly evaluate its own plan by discussing the following questions (also provided at the end of the handout):

   • Who benefits from your plan and who is harmed?

- How will your plan help to reunite and heal the country?

- How will your plan bring about justice after the war? Does it deny justice to any group of Americans?

5. If time permits, you might give students time to circulate around the classroom to see the plans of other groups. They might revise their own group's plan based on ideas they learn from other groups.

III. Evaluating Presidential Reconstruction

Now that students have proposed their own plans for Reconstruction, they can turn their attention to the visions put forward in 1865 and 1866 by President Johnson and the Radical Republicans in Congress. In this activity, students will read an outline of Johnson's Presidential Reconstruction. They will consider the extent to which this vision for Reconstruction would lead to healing and justice.

PROCEDURE

1. Students will work in the same groups they formed to create their plans for Reconstruction. For each group, prepare a "Big Paper" teaching strategy setup (typically a sheet of poster paper) with **Handout 5.4** ("Presidential Reconstruction") from this lesson taped in the center. See facinghistory.org/reconstruction-era/strategies for more information about this strategy.

2. Make sure that all students have a pen or marker. Preferably, each student in the same group will have a different color.

3. Inform the class that this activity will be completed in silence. All communication is done in writing. Students should be told that they will have time to speak in pairs and in large groups later. Go over all of the instructions at the beginning so that students do not ask questions during the activity. Be sure to ask students if they have questions before the activity starts to minimize the chance that they will interrupt the silence once it has begun. You can also remind students of their task as they begin each new step.

4. Begin the activity by giving a "Big Paper" to each group. The groups will read the text in silence. After students have read, they will comment on the text and ask questions of each other in writing on the Big Paper. Tell students that their written conversations should focus on the same questions they used to evaluate their own plans:

- Who benefits from your plan and who is harmed?

- How will this plan help to reunite and heal the country?

- How will this plan bring about justice after the war? Does it deny justice to any group of Americans?

5. The written conversations should start by addressing the above question, but they can stray wherever students take them. If someone in the group writes a question, another member of the group should respond to the question by writing on the Big Paper. Students can draw lines connecting a comment to a particular question. Make sure students know that more than one of them can

write on the Big Paper at the same time. The length of this step is flexible, but it should last at least 10 minutes.

6. After this initial period of silent conversation, prompt students to read the other Big Papers in the room. They should start with a Big Paper that contains the plan they did not already discuss. Students should bring their markers or pens with them and can write comments or further questions for thought on other Big Papers. Determine the length of time to allot for this step based on the number of Big Papers and your knowledge of your students.

7. After reading and commenting on other Big Papers, silence is broken. Students should rejoin their original groups back at their own Big Paper and read the comments written by students from other groups. Now they can have a free, verbal conversation about the text, their own comments, what they read on other papers, and the comments their fellow students wrote back to them. They might also discuss how their group's own plan is similar to and different from President Johnson's plan. At this point, you might ask students to take out their journals and write down a question or comment from the activity that stands out to them.

8. Finally, debrief the process with the large group. Begin with the following questions:

   • What did you learn from doing this activity?

   • What conclusions can you draw about the possibilities of bringing about healing and justice in the United States after the Civil War?

   • What new questions do you have?

   You might also discuss the students' experience of the Big Paper process, touching on the importance and difficulty of staying silent and their level of comfort with this activity.

IV. Extensions: Introducing Critiques of Presidential Reconstruction

INTRODUCING THE RADICAL REPUBLICAN VISION

You might briefly introduce the core principles of a small but significant minority of Republicans in Congress in 1865, the Radicals. They coalesced around the belief that, as Representative Thaddeus Stevens stated, "the whole fabric of Southern society *must* be changed." Consider sharing this quotation with students along with the following core principles of Radical Republicans in 1865:

   • Voting rights should be extended to all black men.

   • New state governments should be formed in the South that guarantee these voting rights for black men.

   • The federal government should be willing to take strong action to protect the rights of former slaves when states do not.

In a brief class discussion, ask students to predict how Radical Republicans would respond to President Johnson's plan for Reconstruction.

INTERPRETING THE CRITIQUE IN A POLITICAL CARTOON

Alternatively, you might present to students the two-paneled image "PARDON: Shall I Trust These Men?" and "FRANCHISE: And Not This Man?" (**Handout 5.5**) by political cartoonist Thomas Nast. Using the "Visual Image Analysis" strategy, have students examine each panel of the image closely. Students can discuss which Reconstruction vision is represented by each panel of the image, and then they can interpret Nast's position on Reconstruction. What is he trying to say about Presidential Reconstruction? How would Nast answer the three questions students used to evaluate Presidential Reconstruction?

HEALING AND JUSTICE

Read the statement in the left column. Decide if you strongly agree (SA), agree (A), disagree (D), or strongly disagree (SD) with it. Circle your response and provide a one- to two-sentence explanation of your opinion (on separate paper if needed).

Statement	Your Opinion			
1. Those who win a war have the right to impose any punishment they wish on those who lost.	**SA** Explain:	**A**	**D**	**SD**
2. Allowing former Confederates to vote, hold office, and resume governing their states (but without slavery) is the quickest way to restore the Union and heal the hatreds that caused the Civil War.	**SA** Explain:	**A**	**D**	**SD**
3. During and after the Civil War, the federal government had the right to seize land owned by Southern planters and give it to freedpeople.	**SA** Explain:	**A**	**D**	**SD**
4. To ensure the strongest possible democracy after the Civil War, neither former slaves nor former Confederates should be excluded from voting and holding office.	**SA** Explain:	**A**	**D**	**SD**
5. Forcing ex-Confederates to take an oath in support of the United States and the Constitution is an effective way to ensure that they will accept the end of slavery and be loyal citizens.	**SA** Explain:	**A**	**D**	**SD**
6. Giving freedpeople citizenship, voting rights, and the ability to hold elected office would not be worth it if such steps make it difficult for healing to occur between the North and South.	**SA** Explain:	**A**	**D**	**SD**

CREATING A PLAN FOR RECONSTRUCTION

Create a proposal for a plan for Reconstruction after the Civil War. Your plan should seek to achieve two goals: (1) to reunite the nation, resolve the conflicts that led to the Civil War, and heal the wounds the war caused, and (2) to bring justice to the nation and its citizens.

Your plan should address each of the following dilemmas that the United States faced as the Civil War ended:

1. What will happen to each of the groups of ex-Confederates listed below? Will they be citizens? Will they be permitted to vote? Will they be permitted to hold office in the government?

    *   Confederate leaders (government officials/military officers)

    *   Wealthy, slave-owning planters

    *   Women who ran plantation households

    *   Low-ranking soldiers

    *   Working-class and poor whites

2. What will happen to freedpeople and other African Americans? Will they be citizens? Will they be permitted to vote and hold office? What other rights will they be provided?

3. What will happen to the land and other property confiscated by the Union army or abandoned during the war? Who has the right to use it? Who has the right to own it?

4. What is the best way to ensure that white Southerners will be loyal to the United States and accept the end of slavery?

After you have created a plan that addresses the dilemmas above, evaluate it by answering these questions:

*   Who are the winners and losers in your plan?

*   How will your plan help to reunite and heal the country?

*   How will your plan bring about justice after the war? Does it deny justice to any group of Americans?

DEBATING RECONSTRUCTION POLICIES

President Andrew Johnson argued for the nation as it was:

> On the 22d day of July, 1861, Congress declared by an almost unanimous vote of both Houses that the war should be conducted solely for the purpose of preserving the Union and maintaining the supremacy of the Federal Constitution and laws, without impairing the dignity, equality, and rights of the States or of individuals, and that when this was done the war should cease . . . [I]t was a solemn public, official pledge of the national honor, and I can not imagine upon what grounds the repudiation of it is to be justified.[1]

Republican Richard Dana presented his "grasp of war" theory:

> A war is over when its purpose is secured . . . When one nation has conquered another, in a war, the victorious nation does not retreat from the country and give up possession of it, because the fighting has ceased. No; it holds the conquered enemy in the grasp of war until it has secured whatever it has a right to require . . .
>
> We have a right to require, my friends, that the freedmen of the South shall have the right to hold land . . . We have the right to require that they shall be allowed to testify in state courts . . . We have a right to demand that they shall bear arms as soldiers in the militia . . . We have a right to demand that there shall be an impartial ballot . . .[2]

Representative Thaddeus Stevens argued for changing the fabric of Southern society:

> The whole fabric of southern society *must* be changed, and never can it be done if this opportunity is lost. Without this, this Government can never be, as it never has been, a true republic.[3]

---

1 Excerpted from Andrew Johnson's State of the Union Address on December 3, 1867, available at http://teachingamericanhistory.org/library/document/state-of-the-union-address-69/ (accessed Jan. 24, 2014).
2 From "Richard H. Dana, Jr., Presents His 'Grasp of War' Theory, June 1865," in Michael Perman and Amy M. Taylor, eds., *Major Problems in the Civil War and Reconstruction: Documents and Essays*, 3rd ed. (Boston: Wadsworth/Cengage Learning, 2011), 325.
3 From speech delivered by Thaddeus Stevens on Sept. 6, 1865, in *The Selected Papers of Thaddeus Stevens, Vol. 2: April 1865–August 1868* (University of Pittsburgh Press, 1998), 23. Text available at http://history.furman.edu/benson/hst41/red/stevens2.htm (accessed Jan. 24, 2014).

PRESIDENTIAL RECONSTRUCTION

The plan for Reconstruction created by President Andrew Johnson and his administration in May 1865 included the following provisions:

- Former Confederates who pledged loyalty to the Union received amnesty and pardon; all of their property was restored, except slaves but including any land that had been provided to freedpeople in the closing months of the war.

    Loyalty oath:

    I, _____ _____, do solemnly swear (or affirm), in presence of Almighty God, that I will henceforth faithfully support, protect, and defend the Constitution of the United States and the Union of the States thereunder, and that I will in like manner abide by and faithfully support all laws and proclamations which have been made during the existing rebellion with reference to the emancipation of slaves. So help me God.

- Some former Confederates, including the highest officials in the Confederacy and those who owned more than $20,000 of property, had to apply to Johnson in person for pardon. (Johnson granted pardons to nearly all who applied.)

- States could be restored fully into the Union after they wrote new constitutions that accepted the abolition of slavery, repudiated secession, and canceled the Confederate debt.

- State conventions charged with writing new constitutions were not required to allow African Americans to participate.[1]

---

1 Adapted from James D. Richardson, ed., *A Compilation of the Messages and Papers of the Presidents 1789–1897*, vol. 6 (1920), 310–312, excerpted at http://www.britannica.com/presidents/article-9116918 (accessed Jan. 24, 2014).

{IMAGES}

"PARDON: SHALL I TRUST THESE MEN?" "FRANCHISE: AND NOT THIS MAN?"

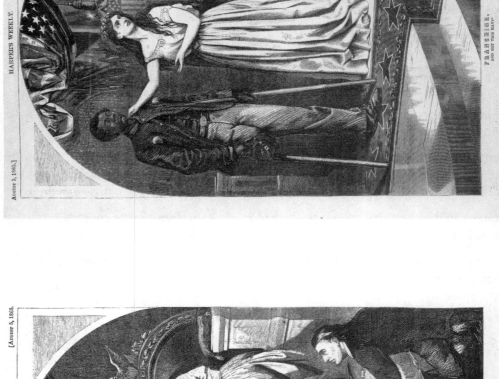

Wood engravings by Thomas Nast from Harper's Weekly (1865), Library of Congress

LESSON 6 The Union as It Was

ESSENTIAL QUESTIONS

What does it mean to be free? What rights and opportunities does one need in order to maintain and defend his or her freedom?

TRANSITION

In the last lesson, students learned about the opposing visions for Reconstruction offered by President Andrew Johnson and the Radical Republicans in Congress. In this lesson, students will examine documents that shed light on life in the South under the policies of Presidential Reconstruction in 1865 and 1866. In particular, they will see evidence of the reestablishment of the South "as it was," a society based on white supremacy, which led many of Presidential Reconstruction's opponents to wonder whether the Northern victory would bring about the changes in American society they desired.

RATIONALE

Andrew Johnson began to implement his plans for Reconstruction as soon as he became president of the United States following President Lincoln's assassination in April 1865. As students learned in the last lesson, Johnson's plan required states of the former Confederacy to ratify the Thirteenth Amendment, which abolished slavery. However, Presidential Reconstruction also permitted most former Confederates to resume political control in their respective states and, therefore, to determine what role freedpeople would play in state politics and economics. President Johnson was not interested in expanding or protecting the political, civil, or economic rights of African Americans, and neither were the white Southerners who governed their states under Presidential Reconstruction. While it was clear to Johnson's Radical Republican opponents in Congress that his plan would lead to the reestablishment of white supremacy, antebellum Southern aristocracy, and Democratic Party rule, they were temporarily powerless to stop the plan because Congress was in recess until December. Therefore, while Presidential Reconstruction policies were in effect, postwar Southern society began to resemble prewar Southern society in many ways.

Land Policy and Economic Justice

In 1865, nearly all elected officials but the radical minority in the Republican Party opposed granting political rights such as the vote to freedpeople, but in the war's closing months, a variety of policies providing some level of economic freedom and autonomy for former slaves had been implemented throughout the South. In large part, these policies were responses to two important questions students considered when they explored the aspirations of freedpeople in Lesson 3:

- What would freedpeople need in order to sustain their freedom?

- What, if anything, were freedpeople entitled to in compensation for their past labor as slaves?

One response to these questions was supplied by Union general William Tecumseh Sherman after his January 1865 meeting with freedpeople known as the Savannah Colloquy (see "Savannah Freedpeople Express Their Aspirations for Freedom," **Handout 3.2**). Sherman issued Special Field Order 15 on January 16, 1865, which ordered 400,000 acres of land along the coasts of South Carolina, Georgia, and Florida to be divided into 40-acre plots and provided to freedpeople and their families. Most of this land was vacated by its owners when the Union army invaded that area early in the Civil War. On smaller scales throughout other parts of the South, freedpeople had either claimed or been granted abandoned lands in territories controlled by the Union army. But by late spring of 1865, many Southern planters were returning to reclaim the land they had left behind.

Would it be just to return confiscated and abandoned land, such as that distributed to freedpeople by Sherman's field order, to the people who had owned it, in some cases, for generations before the war? Or would it be more just to give some or all of it to the former slaves whose families had labored on it for generations? The answers to these questions would have profound implications for how the competing demands of justice and healing would be addressed during Reconstruction. If confiscating land from Southern planters and giving it to freedpeople would be an act of justice, it would also most certainly set back the process of healing between white Americans who supported the Confederacy and those who supported the Union. How the nation resolved this dilemma would also provide evidence about how the postwar United States would define its universe of obligation.

Andrew Johnson's Presidential Reconstruction policies addressed this dilemma over land rights and economic justice by stipulating that all property (except, of course, for slaves) be returned to former Confederates who pledged loyalty to the Union. In this lesson, students will read some protests of freedpeople as the land they had been granted was taken from them, as well as arguments explaining why they believed they had a right to the land. Students will return to their exploration of the meaning of freedom, started earlier in the unit, and seek to explain why one group of South Carolina freedpeople, upon losing their land, argued that "this is not the condition of really free men."[1] Throughout the Reconstruction era, land would become a divisive issue that challenged even Republicans who advocated for full political rights for freedpeople.

"Black Codes" and Labor Contracts

Restoration of abandoned lands to their prewar owners was only one measure the federal and state governments took during Presidential Reconstruction to ensure that white supremacy would continue in postwar Southern society. By the fall of 1865, most Southern legislatures passed laws severely restricting the freedom of Southern blacks to negotiate the terms of their labor. Known as "Black Codes," these laws required all blacks, whether free or slave before the Civil War, to sign annual labor contracts with white employers. If they did not, or if they did not fulfill the terms of these contracts, they would be deemed vagrants and fined or imprisoned. When black Southerners could not pay fines that resulted from breaking these or any other laws, the Black Codes permitted local sheriffs to auction them off to white citizens willing to pay the fines

---

1 "Committee of Freedmen on Edisto Island, South Carolina, to the Freedmen's Bureau Commissioner," in Stephen Hahn et al., eds., *Land and Labor, 1865* (*Freedom: A Documentary History of Emancipation, 1861–1867*, Series 3, vol. 1) (University of North Carolina Press, 2008), available at http://www.history.umd.edu/Freedmen/Edisto%20petitions.htm.

on their behalf, creating a system of "slavery by another name." The excerpt from the Mississippi Black Codes included in this lesson reflects these requirements for labor contracts and the penalties for supposed vagrancy, and it also details other restrictions on the lives of African Americans (in marriage and gun ownership, among other areas).

Many Southern blacks, therefore, had no choice but to negotiate labor or sharecropping contracts with planters—sometimes the very planters who had enslaved them. Fairness in these negotiations was largely dependent on the goodwill of the landowner. The Freedmen's Bureau, charged with helping to facilitate fair labor contracts between planters and freedpeople, reported widespread acrimony over these agreements. Freedpeople protested that landowners were taking advantage of them and demanding that they work more than their contracts specified. Planters' complaints often invoked racist beliefs that blacks were lazy and disobedient. Sharecropping arrangements often left black farmers perpetually indebted to planters and therefore tied to the land in order to work off a debt they could never repay. In this lesson, students will examine a sharecropping contract from 1866 as well as a firsthand account from a black sharecropper of how the system worked to his disadvantage.

Progress in Education

Despite obstacles created by Presidential Reconstruction policies, black Southerners continued in crucial ways to display agency and make progress toward goals that were, perhaps, unthinkable only a few years prior to 1865. Education was one area in which freedpeople made notable progress during Presidential Reconstruction. Indeed, freedpeople followed through on the pledges made by the South Carolina Freedmen's Convention, which declared that "knowledge is power" in its November 1865 resolution (included in Lesson 3). In this lesson, students will read an excerpt from a January 1866 report by a Freedmen's Bureau inspector who estimates that freedpeople had created in the South 500 schools, supporting 125,000 students, without assistance from state or federal governments. The schools were in addition to the government-funded schools, numbering more than 1,000, established in the South by the Freedmen's Bureau in the late 1860s. The effects of the establishment of schools for freedpeople were significant. Historian Douglas Egerton writes: "Black literacy increased four hundred percent in the thirty-five years after Appomattox, a triumph not witnessed by any other nineteenth-century post-slavery society."[2] It is important for students to see that, even as political, civil, and economic rights were denied to freedpeople in states across the South in the first years after the Civil War, black Southerners continued to strive for better lives for their families, and in some ways they succeeded.

Andrew Johnson introduced his Reconstruction policies in May 1865, while Congress was in recess. By the time Congress returned to session in December 1865, Johnson declared that the task of Reconstruction was complete. But Republicans surveyed the status of freedpeople and former Confederates in the South and openly wondered who had really won the Civil War. Radicals, and eventually an increasing number of moderate Republicans, complained, as Egerton states, that Southern governments "clearly intended to devise a legal system in which blacks remained semi-enslaved, denied access to land, and relegated to a subordinate economic and social status."[3] Congressmen

---

2 Douglas R. Egerton, *The Wars of Reconstruction: The Brief, Violent History of America's Most Progressive Era* (New York: Bloomsbury Press, 2014), 167.

3 Ibid., 179.

elected by the former Confederate states traveled to Washington for the new session of Congress that December (including former Confederate vice president Alexander Stephens, who was elected to the Senate from Georgia), but Republicans refused to seat them. A bitter political conflict between the president and the Republican Congress would ensue as Republicans began to assert their own plan for Reconstruction.

LEARNING GOALS

Understanding: Students will understand that:

- Victory in a war does not necessarily mean that its underlying causes have been resolved.

- Different groups sometimes have competing claims on justice. During Reconstruction, white Southern planters equated justice with protection of property they legally obtained. Freedpeople equated justice with the right to possess land that they made valuable through their labor as slaves.

Knowledge: Students will know that:

- The reestablishment of a Southern society based on white supremacy under Presidential Reconstruction left many freedpeople in circumstances that in many ways resembled the conditions of slavery.

- Some argued that freedpeople had a right to land because their labor helped create the land's value. Students should know the basic tenets of the argument.

- Freedpeople established hundreds of schools for their children in the South, many without outside assistance or financial support.

RESOURCE LIST

- "Freedpeople Protest the Loss of Their Land" (document)
- "A Right to the Land" (document)
- "Sharecropping Contract" (document)
- "He Was Always Right and You Were Always Wrong" (document)
- "Mississippi Black Codes (1865)" (document)
- "Freedmen's Bureau Agent Reports on Progress in Education" (document)

ACTIVITY SUGGESTIONS

Consider using the following activity ideas and strategies when you implement this lesson in your classroom.

- Before exploring the documents in this lesson, first review the freedpeople's aspirations for freedom that students learned about in Lesson 3 ("Defining Freedom"). If the class created a concept map for *freedom* in that lesson, it would also be useful to review it at this time. These aspects of freedom—including civil rights, voting rights, land ownership, education, and social equality—can provide students with a standard for evaluating the extent to which freedpeople were truly free while the policies of Presidential Reconstruction were in place.

As you briefly review these ideas about the meaning of freedom, it might also be useful to discuss which of the aspirations could be achieved by freedpeople on their own and which might require cooperation from government and society.

- After reviewing the ideas about freedom that students discussed in the lesson "Defining Freedom," use the "Gallery Walk" strategy with the documents from this lesson. (For more information, see facinghistory.org/reconstruction-era/ strategies.) Students should consider what each document tells them about whether or not freedpeople were truly free under Presidential Reconstruction. They should record in their journals evidence that shows whether or not the experiences of freedpeople were meeting their aspirations for equal rights, land, and education. When students discover that freedpeople's experiences fell short of their aspirations, they should describe in their journals the obstacles that prevented the realization of those aspirations. When students discover that freedpeople were making progress toward their aspirations, they should describe in their journals the factors that helped them do so.

- Some of the documents in this lesson are challenging to understand because of their language and style. Consider using the "Chunking" strategy to help students break down these challenging texts. Chunking may be especially helpful with **Handouts 6.1**, **6.3**, and **6.5**: "Freedpeople Protest the Loss of Their Land," "Sharecropping Contract," and "Mississippi Black Codes (1865)." (See facinghistory. org/reconstruction-era/strategies to learn more about this strategy.)

The document "Mississippi Black Codes (1865)," is divided into many sections, each of which describes a single regulation. Therefore, it might be helpful to assign each section to a pair of students to summarize, and then have each partner group share its summaries with the class so that students get a sense of the breadth of the restrictions on freedom created by such laws.

- After an analysis of the documents in this lesson, the "Barometer" strategy can help students synthesize and share their thinking about what they have learned about the state of freedom experienced by freedpeople while Presidential Reconstruction policies were in place. This activity will force students to take and explain a position on the extent to which freedpeople were truly free. (See facinghistory.org/reconstruction-era/strategies to learn more about this strategy.)

Create a continuum in your classroom by posting signs that read "Strongly Agree" and "Strongly Disagree" at opposite ends of the room. Then read the following statement: *Under Presidential Reconstruction, freedpeople were not free.* Give students a few minutes to review the evidence from the documents that they recorded in their journals and decide on the extent to which they agree or disagree with the statement. Then have them stand along the continuum between the two signs to indicate their responses. Once students have taken their positions, call on several students to explain their position, using evidence from the documents. Allow students who are persuaded by the arguments of their classmates to change their positions throughout the activity.

FREEDPEOPLE PROTEST THE LOSS OF THEIR LAND

In January 1865, General Sherman acted on the testimony of the freedpeople of Savannah, Georgia (see the document "Savannah Freedpeople Express Their Aspirations for Freedom," **Handout 3.2**), *by issuing Special Field Order 15. The field order divided up land abandoned by Southern planters along the coasts of South Carolina, Georgia, and Florida and gave it to freedpeople in 40-acre plots. Under President Johnson's Reconstruction policies, most of that land was taken from the freedpeople and returned to its original owners later that year. The following is a letter from the Committee of Freedmen on Edisto Island, South Carolina, to Freedmen's Bureau Commissioner O. O. Howard responding to Johnson's land policy.*

[Edisto Island, S.C., October 20 or 21, 1865]

General   It Is with painfull Hearts that we the committe address you, we Have thorougholy considered the order which you wished us to Sighn, we wish we could do so but cannot feel our rights Safe If we do so,

General we want Homestead's; we were promised Homestead's by the government, If It does not carry out the promises Its agents made to us, If the government Haveing concluded to befriend Its late enemies and to neglect to observe the principles of common faith between Its self and us Its allies In the war you said was over, now takes away from them all right to the soil they stand upon save such as they can get by again working for *your* late and thier *all time ememies.*—If the government does so we are left In a more unpleasant condition than our former

we are at the mercy of those who are combined to prevent us from getting land enough to lay our Fathers bones upon. We Have property In Horses, cattle, carriages, & articles of furniture, but we are landless and Homeless, from the Homes we Have lived In In the past we can only do one of three things Step Into the public *road or the sea* or remain on them working as In former time and subject to thire will as then. We can not resist It In any way without being driven out Homeless upon the road.

You will see this Is not the condition of really freemen

You ask us to forgive the land owners of our Island, *You* only lost your right arm. In war and might forgive them. The man who tied me to a tree & gave me 39 lashes & who stripped and flogged my mother & my sister & who will not let me stay In His empty Hut except I will do His planting & be Satisfied with His price & who combines with others to keep away land from me well knowing I would not Have any thing to do with Him If I Had land of my own.—that man, I cannot well forgive. Does It look as If He Has forgiven me, seeing How He tries to keep me In a condition of Helplessness

General, we cannot remain Here In such condition and If the government permits them to come back we ask It to Help us to reach land where we shall not be slaves nor compelled to work for those who would treat us as such

we Have not been treacherous, we Have not for selfish motives allied to us those who suffered like us from a common enemy & then Haveing gained *our* purpose left our allies In thier Hands There Is no rights secured to us there Is no law likely to be made which our Hands can reach. The state will make laws that we shall not be able to Hold land even If we pay for It Landless, Homeless. Voteless. we can only pray to god & Hope for *His Help, your Infuence & assistance* With consideration of esteem your

Obt Servts
In behalf of the people

Henry Bram
Committe Ishmael Moultrie
yates Sampson[1]

---

1 Published in Stephen Hahn et al., eds., *Land and Labor, 1865 (Freedom: A Documentary History of Emancipation 1861–1867*, Series 3, vol. 1) (University of North Carolina Press, 2008), available at http://www.history.umd.edu/Freedmen/Edisto%20petitions.htm.

A RIGHT TO THE LAND

In 1866, after army officials forced freedman Bayley Wyatt to vacate the Virginia land he had occupied since the end of the war, he argued at a public meeting for freedpeople's right to the land as follows:

We now, as a people desires to be elevated, and we desires to do all we can to be educated, and we hope our friends will aid us all they can . . .

I may state to all our friends, and to all our enemies, that we has a right to the land where we are located. For why? I tell you. Our wives, our children, our husbands, has been sold over and over again to purchase the lands we now locate upon; for that reason we have a divine right to the land . . .

And then didn't we clear the land and raise the crops of corn, of cotton, of tobacco, of rice, of sugar, of everything? And then didn't them large cities in the North grow up on the cotton and the sugars and the rice that we made? Yes! I appeal to the South and the North if I hasn't spoken the words of truth. I say they have grown rich, and my people is poor.[1]

---

1 From Roy E. Finkenbine, *Sources of the African-American Past: Primary Sources in American History*, 2nd ed. (Pearson, 2003), 88.

SHARECROPPING CONTRACT

[December 23, 1865]

Thomas J. Ross agrees to employ the said Freedmen to plant and raise a crop on his Rosstown Plantation for the year 1866 in Shelby County, Tenn. On the following Rules, Regulations and Renumerations.

. . . Ross agrees to furnish the land to cultivate, and a sufficient number of mules & horses and feed them to make and house said crop and all necessary farming utensils to carry on the same and to give unto said Freedmen whose names appear below one half of all the cotton, corn and wheat that is raised there for the year 1866 after all the necessary expenses are deducted . . .

. . . And we the said Freedmen agrees to furnish ourselves & families in provisions, clothing, medicine and medical bills and all, and every kind of other expenses that we may incur on the plantation for the year 1866 free of charge to said Ross. Should the said Ross furnish us any of the above supplies or any other kind of expenses, during said year, we are to settle and pay him out of the nett proceeds of our part of the crop the retail price of the county at time of sale or any price we may agree upon—The said Ross shall keep a regular book account . . . to be adjusted and settled at the end of the year . . .

We furthermore bind ourselves to and with said Ross that we will do good work and labor ten hours a day on an average, winter and summer . . . The time we are going to and from work shall not be computed or counted in the time . . . We further agree that we will loose all lost time, or pay at the rate of one dollar per day, rainy days excepted . . .

We furthermore bind ourselves that we will obey the orders of Ross in all things in carrying out and managing the crop for the year and further bind ourselves that we said Freedmen will keep up the fences around the enclosures, and lots especially and if any rails be missing by burning or otherwise destroyed by said Freedmen, we will pay for them or otherwise reconstruct the fence anew at our expense . . .

All is responsible for all farming utensils that is on hand or may be placed in care of said Freedmen for the year 1866 to said Ross and are also responsible to said Ross if we carelessly, maliciously maltreat any of his stock for said year to said Ross for damages to be assessed out of our wages for said year, all of which is understood by us Freedmen in the foregoing contract, or agreement, Ross assigning his name and ours following. It is further agreed by us whose names appear below that we will keep a sufficiency of firewood hawled up at all times and make fires in the room of Ross, when desired, attend to all stock properly, under direction of said Ross . .[1]

---

1 Excerpted from records at *The Freedmen's Bureau Online*, http://freedmensbureau.com/tennessee/contracts/miscellaneouscontracts.htm.

HE WAS ALWAYS RIGHT AND YOU WERE ALWAYS WRONG

Henry Blake, a freedman from Arkansas, describes how sharecropping limited his freedom in these words:

When we worked on shares, we couldn't make nothing, just overalls and something to eat. Half went to the other man and you would destroy your half, if you weren't careful. A man that didn't know how to count would always lose. He might lose anyhow. They didn't give no itemized statement. No, you just had to take their word. They never give you no details. No matter how good account you kept, you had to go by their account, and now, Brother, I'm tellin' you the truth about this. It's been that way for a long time. You had to take the white man's work on note, and everything. Anything you wanted, you could git if you were a good hand. You could git anything you wanted as long as you worked. If you didn't make no money, that's all right; they would advance you more. But you better not leave him, you better not try to leave and get caught. They'd keep you in debt. They were sharp. Christmas come, you could take up twenty dollar, in somethin' to eat and as much as you wanted in whiskey. You could buy a gallon of whiskey. Anything that kept you a slave because he was always right and you were always wrong if there was a difference. If there was an argument, he would get mad and there would be a shooting take place.[1]

1 From *Henry Blake, Little Rock, Arkansas*, Federal Writer's Project, US Work Projects Administration (Manuscript Division), Library of Congress, available at the *History Matters* website, http://historymatters.gmu.edu/d/6377/.

MISSISSIPPI BLACK CODES (1865)

CIVIL RIGHTS OF FREEDMEN

Section 3: . . . [I]t shall not be lawful for any freedman, free negro or mulatto to intermarry with any white person; nor for any person to intermarry with any freedman, free negro or mulatto; and any person who shall so intermarry shall be deemed guilty of felony, and on conviction thereof shall be confined in the State penitentiary for life; and those shall be deemed freedmen, free negroes and mulattoes who are of pure negro blood, and those descended from a negro to the third generation, inclusive, though one ancestor in each generation may have been a white person.

Section 5: . . . Every freedman, free negro and mulatto shall, on the second Monday of January, one thousand eight hundred and sixty-six, and annually thereafter, have a lawful home or employment, and shall have written evidence thereof . . .

Section 6: . . . All contracts for labor made with freedmen, free negroes and mulattoes for a longer period than one month shall be in writing, and a duplicate, attested and read to said freedman, free negro or mulatto by a beat, city or county officer . . . and if the laborer shall quit the service of the employer before the expiration of his term of service, without good cause, he shall forfeit his wages for that year up to the time of quitting.

Section 7: . . . Every civil officer shall, and every person may, arrest and carry back to his or her legal employer any freedman, free negro, or mulatto who shall have quit the service of his or her employer before the expiration of his or her term of service without good cause . . .

VAGRANT LAW

Section 1: . . . That all rogues and vagabonds, idle and dissipated persons, beggars, jugglers, or persons practicing unlawful games or plays, runaways, common drunkards, common night-walkers, pilferers, lewd, wanton, or lascivious persons, in speech or behavior, common railers and brawlers, persons who neglect their calling or employment, misspend what they earn, or do not provide for the support of themselves or their families, or dependents, and all other idle and disorderly persons, including all who neglect all lawful business, habitually misspend their time by frequenting houses of ill-fame, gaming-houses, or tippling shops, shall be deemed and considered vagrants, under the provisions of this act, and upon conviction thereof shall be fined not exceeding one hundred dollars, with all accruing costs, and be imprisoned, at the discretion of the court, not exceeding ten days.

Section 2: . . . All freedmen, free negroes and mulattoes in this State, over the age of eighteen years, found on the second Monday in January, 1866, or thereafter, with no lawful employment or business, or found unlawful assembling themselves together, either in the day or night time, and all white persons assembling themselves with freedmen, Free negroes or mulattoes, or usually associating with freedmen, free negroes or mulattoes, on terms of equality, or living in adultery or fornication with a freed woman, freed negro or mulatto, shall be deemed vagrants, and on conviction thereof shall be fined in a sum not exceeding, in the case of a freedman, free negro or mulatto, fifty dollars, and a white man two hundred dollars, and imprisonment at the discretion of the court, the free negro not exceeding ten days, and the white man not exceeding six months . . .

Section 5: . . . All fines and forfeitures collected by the provisions of this act shall be paid into the county treasury of general county purposes, and in case of any freedman, free negro or mulatto shall fail for five days after the imposition of any or forfeiture upon him or her for violation of any of the provisions of this act to pay the same, that it shall be, and is hereby, made the duty of the sheriff of the proper county to hire out said freedman, free negro or mulatto, to any person who will, for the shortest period of service, pay said fine and forfeiture and all costs . . .

CERTAIN OFFENSES OF FREEDMEN

Section 1: . . . That no freedman, free negro or mulatto, not in the military service of the United States government, and not licensed so to do by the board of police of his or her county, shall keep or carry fire-arms of any kind, or any ammunition, dirk or bowie knife, and on conviction thereof in the county court shall be punished by fine . . .

Section 2: . . . Any freedman, free negro, or mulatto committing riots, routs, affrays, trespasses, malicious mischief, cruel treatment to animals, seditious speeches, insulting gestures, language, or acts, or assaults on any person, disturbance of the peace, exercising the function of a minister of the Gospel without a license from some regularly organized church, vending spirituous or intoxicating liquors, or committing any other misdemeanor, the punishment of which is not specifically provided for by law, shall, upon conviction thereof in the county court, be fined not less than ten dollars, and not more than one hundred dollars, and may be imprisoned at the discretion of the court, not exceeding thirty days.

Section 3: . . . If any white person shall sell, lend, or give to any freedman, free negro, or mulatto any fire-arms, dirk or bowie knife, or ammunition, or any spirituous or intoxicating liquors, such person or persons so offending, upon conviction thereof in the county court of his or her county, shall be fined not exceeding fifty dollars, and may be imprisoned, at the discretion of the court, not exceeding thirty days . . .[1]

---

1 Excerpted from William E. Gienapp, ed., *The Civil War and Reconstruction: A Documentary Collection* (New York: W. W. Norton, 2001), 325.

FREEDMEN'S BUREAU AGENT REPORTS ON PROGRESS IN EDUCATION

The following is an excerpt from a January 1866 Freedmen's Bureau report on education for freedpeople in the South, written by Freedmen's Bureau inspector John W. Alvord.

Not only are individuals seen at study, and under the most untoward circumstances, but in very many places I have found what I will call "native schools," often rude and very imperfect, but *there they are,* a group, perhaps, of all ages, *trying to learn.* Some young man, some woman, or old preacher, in cellar, or shed, or corner of a negro meeting-house, with the alphabet in hand, or a torn spelling-book, is their teacher. All are full of enthusiasm with the new knowledge The Book is imparting to them . . .

A still higher order of this native teaching is seen in the colored schools at Charleston, Savannah, and New Orleans. With many disadvantages they bear a very good examination. One I visited in the latter city, of 300 pupils, and wholly taught by educated colored men, would bear comparison with any ordinary school at the north. Not only good reading and spelling were heard, but lessons at the black-board in arithmetic, recitations in geography and English grammar. Very creditable specimens of writing were shown, and all the older classes could read or recite as fluently in French as in English. This was a free school, wholly supported by the colored people of the city . . . All the above cases illustrate the remark that this educational movement among the freedmen has in it a self-sustaining element. I took special pains to ascertain the facts on this particular point, and have to report that there are schools of this kind in some stage of advancement (taught and supported wholly by the people themselves) in all the large places I visited—often *numbers* of them, and they are also making their appearance through the *interior* of the entire country. The superintendent of South Carolina assured me that there was not a place of any size in the whole of that State where such a school was not attempted. I have much testimony, both oral and written, from others well informed, that the same is true of other States. There can scarcely be a doubt, and I venture the estimate, that at least 500 schools of this description are already in operation throughout the south. If, therefore, all these be added, and including soldiers and individuals at study, we shall have at least 125,000 as the *entire educational census of this lately emancipated people.*

This is a wonderful state of things. We have just emerged from a terrific war; peace is not yet declared. There is scarcely the beginning of reorganized society at the south; and yet here is a people long imbruted by slavery, and the most despised of any on earth, whose chains are no sooner broken than they spring to their feet and start up an exceeding great army, clothing themselves with intelligence. What other people on earth have ever shown, while in their ignorance, such a passion for education?[1]

---

1 United States Bureau of Refugees, Freedmen, and Abandoned Lands and John W. Alvord, *Freedmen's Schools and Textbooks,* vol. 1, *Semi-annual report on schools for freedmen: numbers 1–10, January 1866–July 1870* (AMS Press, 1868), 1–10.

Connecting to the Writing Prompt

This is an appropriate time to return to the writing prompt for this unit. Encourage students to review the documents they encountered in Lessons 4, 5, and 6. Which events, arguments, and other information in the documents connect to the writing prompt? Provide students with the opportunity to continue the evidence logs they began previously in the unit.

Consider using the "Annotating and Paraphrasing" strategy in the "Teaching Strategies" section, available on our website at facinghistory.org/reconstruction-era/strategies, to help students record information in their evidence logs in a manner that will be more helpful as they advance through the writing process later in this unit.

Finally, ask students to reflect on the new evidence they have recorded. Does it confirm or conflict with their thinking about the question posed in the prompt? Has their thinking about the prompt changed based on what they have learned about the aftermath of the Civil War and the debates over justice and healing? Have students record their thoughts in their journals.

SECTION 4
RADICAL RECONSTRUCTION AND INTERRACIAL DEMOCRACY

This section contains the following lessons:

LESSON 7 Radical Reconstruction and the Birth of Civil Rights

ESSENTIAL QUESTION

What can a nation's laws reveal about that nation's universe of obligation?

TRANSITION

In the previous two lessons, students analyzed the Reconstruction policies of President Andrew Johnson and learned about the conditions for freedpeople that emerged in Southern states under Presidential Reconstruction. In this lesson, they will learn about the responses to Johnson's policies by Republicans in Congress. In particular, they will look closely at the laws passed by Republicans that modified, and then overturned, Presidential Reconstruction. These include landmark legislation such as the Civil Rights Act of 1866 and the Fourteenth Amendment that introduced the concepts of *national citizenship*, *civil rights*, and *equality* into federal law and the US Constitution.

RATIONALE

As students learned in the previous lesson, President Johnson's Reconstruction policies largely restored the pre-Civil War political, economic, and social hierarchy in the South. Freedpeople were denied participation in the political process as well as land or any other compensation for their prior labor as slaves, and Black Codes in every Southern state severely restricted their basic civil rights. As a result, many were trapped in a state of dependence on white landowners enforced in many of the same ways as before the Civil War. This was not the postwar Southern society that African Americans and Radical Republicans in Congress imagined.

The Radical Republicans, however, never constituted a majority in their party; they required support from the more numerous moderate Republicans in Congress to enact the changes they sought. Moderates did not initially share the belief in universal black male suffrage central to the Radical Republican vision of the reconstructed nation. It would take a political battle with President Johnson in 1866 to unite both moderates and Radicals behind a single Republican plan.

At first, moderate Republicans sought cooperation rather than conflict with President Johnson. Once Congress returned to session in December 1865, a Joint Committee on Reconstruction was created to study postwar conditions in the South under Presidential Reconstruction. Troubled by the Black Codes passed in every Southern state, moderates embraced the principle of equality before the law—the idea that governments should not be permitted to pass laws that designate certain actions as crimes for some groups but not for others.

In early 1866, Republicans passed two bills that sought to bolster protection for freedpeople under Presidential Reconstruction: the Civil Rights Act of 1866 and an extension of the Freedmen's Bureau. The Civil Rights Act was a landmark law for the following reasons:

- For the first time, it legislated a national definition of citizenship. Previously, citizenship was defined by individual states.

- It declared all persons born in the United States to be national citizens (except American Indians, because tribes were considered "sovereign dependent nations" with their own governments).

- It declared all citizens equal before the law. Historian Eric Foner writes: "No longer could states enact laws such as the Black Codes declaring certain actions crimes for black persons but not white."[1]

- It declared for all citizens the rights of free labor, including the rights to make contracts, bring lawsuits, and have protection of their persons and property.

However, President Johnson shocked Republicans in Congress by vetoing both laws. It became clear to moderate Republicans that President Johnson would rebuff their efforts to cooperate. In response, moderate and Radical Republicans united to override the president's veto of the Civil Rights Act with two-thirds majorities in both houses of Congress, marking the first time in American history that a presidential veto of a piece of major legislation was overridden.[2]

As a bitter conflict between President Johnson and the Republicans in Congress erupted in 1866, Republicans sought to pass a new amendment to the Constitution in order to protect their vision of the post-Civil War nation from the ever-changing political landscape. The result was the Fourteenth Amendment, a product of intense debate between conservative, moderate, and Radical Republicans. While the amendment is often associated with the Radicals, historians assert that it was an inherently moderate one. Many Radicals, such as Thaddeus Stevens, ultimately supported the amendment while believing it did not go far enough to guarantee universal male suffrage. Explaining why he supported "so imperfect a proposition" as the Fourteenth Amendment, Stevens said, "Because I live among men and not among angels; among men as intelligent, as determined, and as independent as myself, who, not agreeing with me, do not choose to yield their opinions to mine."

Passed by Congress in June of 1866 (and eventually adopted by the states in 1868), the Fourteenth Amendment has been hailed by historians as the "Second Constitution" because of the manner in which it redefined the United States as a modern nation. The amendment's important provisions include the following:

- It enshrined birthright citizenship in the Constitution, making the definition of citizenship permanently a national responsibility (rather than a state matter).

- It nationalized the protection of rights guaranteed by the Bill of Rights. States were now forbidden from violating those rights, when previously the rights were only protected from violation by the federal government.

- It provided for "equal protection of the law" for all American citizens (although the meaning of this clause would be contested over the course of the following century).

- It penalized states for denying to any male citizen the right to vote by reducing the state's representation in Congress. By imposing a penalty only when male citizens

---

1 Eric Foner, *Forever Free: The Story of Emancipation and Reconstruction* (Vintage Books, 2006), 115.
2 Eric Foner, *Reconstruction: America's Unfinished Revolution, 1863–1877*, Perennial Classics ed. (HarperCollins, 2002), 239–251.

were denied the right to vote, the amendment made the first reference to gender in the Constitution.

- It banned former Rebels who held prewar political office from holding office again.

- It prohibited payments to former slaveholders in compensation for the loss of their slaves after Emancipation.

- It prohibited the payment of any debts amassed by the Confederacy to fight the war, but it guaranteed the payment of all such debts incurred by the Union.

The importance of the Fourteenth Amendment is underscored by the fact that, nearly from the moment of its adoption to the present day, its history has been one of constant interpretation and reinterpretation.

Violence in Memphis and New Orleans

With the political battle lines drawn, voters would have their say in the battle between the president and congressional Republicans in the 1866 congressional elections. The Fourteenth Amendment was one of the primary issues of the campaign, but two other events—riots in Memphis and New Orleans—further united Republicans against Presidential Reconstruction and galvanized public opinion in their favor. In Memphis, three days of violence in May followed a confrontation between former black Union soldiers and Irish-immigrant police. The violence resulted in the deaths of 48 people (46 of whom were black), the rape of five black women, and the widespread destruction of black homes and property.[3] In New Orleans in July, local whites attacked about 200 African Americans who were marching in support of black voting rights. Thirty-four blacks and three white supporters were killed, more than 100 were injured, and the violence ended only when federal troops intervened.[4]

Radical Republicans Implement Their Plan

The violence of 1866 was a sign to many Americans that perhaps the Union had been *restored* but not adequately *reconstructed*; that the way freedom had been defined for black Americans was not adequate; and that Presidential Reconstruction had led to neither healing nor justice. As a result, Republicans swept the elections and gained more than two-thirds of the seats in both chambers of Congress, a majority that could override any presidential veto. Republicans needed such a majority to pass their Reconstruction plans over Johnson's constant opposition.

Despite the Republicans' overwhelming success in the 1866 congressional elections, they still needed cooperation from the Southern states in order to add the Fourteenth Amendment to the Constitution. Except for Tennessee, all of the states of the former Confederacy refused. Therefore, it became clear to moderate Republicans that a new plan for Reconstruction was needed—something closer to the Radical Reconstruction vision of *remaking* the Southern states. Republicans united again to pass the Reconstruction Acts of 1867, which ended the era of Presidential Reconstruction and enacted the plan often referred to as Radical Reconstruction. The Reconstruction Acts included the following measures:

---

3 Foner, *Reconstruction: America's Unfinished Revolution*, 262.
4 Ibid., 263.

- The South was divided into five military districts and governed by military governors until acceptable state constitutions could be written and approved by Congress.

- All males, regardless of race, but excluding former Confederate leaders, were permitted to participate in the constitutional conventions that formed the new governments in each state.

- New state constitutions were required to provide for *universal manhood suffrage* (voting rights for all men) without regard to race.

- States were required to ratify the Fourteenth Amendment in order to be readmitted to the Union.

Although tensions between Congress and President Johnson continued to rise after the 1866 elections (ultimately leading to Johnson's 1868 impeachment and decision not to seek a second term), Johnson was not able to prevent the era of Radical Reconstruction from beginning. The Fifteenth Amendment, prohibiting the denial of voting rights "on account of race, color, or previous condition of servitude," passed Congress during Johnson's final weeks in office in February 1869 (and was adopted by the states in 1870). With African Americans now voting in every state, an "unprecedented experiment in interracial democracy,"[5] the subject of the next lesson, had begun.

While the Fourteenth and Fifteenth Amendments significantly expanded the scope of American citizenship and extended political rights to millions of Americans, they are also notable because they continued to exclude large numbers of Americans. In particular, the protection of voting rights in both amendments was not extended to women. The Fifteenth Amendment, furthermore, did not prevent the implementation of literacy tests, poll taxes, and other methods of indirectly disenfranchising freedpeople and other minority groups. As a result of these limitations, the laws and amendments brought about by the Republican Congress of the late 1860s left many inhabitants of the United States wondering to what extent they belonged.

LEARNING GOALS

Understanding: Students will understand that:

- One way a nation can define, both explicitly and implicitly, its universe of obligation is through its constitution and laws.

- A nation's requirements for citizenship are one way that it uses laws to define who belongs, but nations do not always treat citizens as equals.

- By striving for the goal of equality of opportunity, democracy can be strengthened.

Knowledge: Students will know that:

- The Civil Rights Act of 1866 and the Fourteenth Amendment expanded the universe of obligation of the United States by making freedpeople citizens and promising equal protection of the law to all people.

---

5 Foner, *Forever Free*, 108.

- The Civil Rights Act of 1866 and the Fourteenth Amendment were the first attempts to define specifically through law what freedom meant for all Americans, including freedpeople.

- While the Fourteenth and Fifteenth Amendments led to significant expansions of rights and equality, they also did not prevent many Americans from being excluded from political participation and civil rights protection.

RESOURCE LIST

- "The Civil Rights Act of 1866" (document)

- "The Fourteenth Amendment" (document)

- "Congress Debates the Fourteenth Amendment" (document)

- "The Reconstruction Acts of 1867" (document)

ACTIVITY SUGGESTIONS

Consider using the following activity ideas and strategies when you implement this lesson in your classroom.

- Historians point to three different groups within the Republican Party in the late 1860s: Radical Republicans, moderates, and conservatives. Therefore, the terms *radical, moderate*, and *conservative* are three words whose meanings are worth exploring before looking at the documents and history presented in this lesson. It may also be worth pointing out, for clarity, that the way these words are used to label political constituencies has changed over time, like the orientations of the parties themselves. Consider using concept maps to explore the meaning of each word with the class. You might ask students to find definitions in the dictionary to get the discussion started.

  Once you have established working definitions for each term, write them along a continuum on the chalkboard or a piece of chart paper. Students can then analyze the laws and amendments included in this lesson's documents and place them along the continuum. Have students add the outline of Presidential Reconstruction from Lesson 5 to the continuum, as well. Ask them to explain the reasoning behind their conclusions about how conservative, moderate, or radical each law or policy is. What can they conclude from this activity about the differences between President Johnson and the Republicans in Congress? What can they conclude about the differences within the Republican Party? What do they notice about the way the nation's Reconstruction policies changed between 1865 and 1867?

- The Fourteenth Amendment is a complex text, but the quotations from the 1866 congressional debate over the amendment provided in **Handout 7.3** ("Congress Debates the Fourteenth Amendment") can help clarify for students both what the amendment says and its significance. The following activity can be used on its own or as preparation for use of the "Socratic Seminar" strategy (described below).

  Consider using the quotations from **Handout 7.3** to create a "Thought Museum." Choose one or two quotations pertaining to each section of the Fourteenth Amendment. Focus especially on the first through third sections. Post the quotations around the room; each quotation will make up one "exhibit."

Before students leave their seats, take a few minutes to read the Fourteenth Amendment together. Explain to students that reading quotations from the 1866 congressional debate over the amendment can illuminate the document's language. Then give students several self-stick notes each and provide sufficient time for them to visit and respond to as many exhibits as possible. They should bring their copy of the Fourteenth Amendment with them for reference as they move around the room. After reading the quotation(s) at each exhibit, students can add a note to the exhibit with a comment or question that it raises for them. They might also post a connection between a quotation and another historical event, current event, or personal experience.

Once students have spent sufficient time exploring the exhibits, assign one student to "curate" each exhibit. This will entail going to the assigned exhibit and choosing two to three notes that seem particularly important or clarifying. While the curators are working, everyone else should return to their seats. These students can talk in pairs and discuss the following questions:

- What story do these quotations tell?

- Is the Fourteenth Amendment a conservative, moderate, or radical document?

When the curators are finished, they should each report to the class by first reading the clause of the amendment to which their exhibit pertains and then sharing the notes they chose and explaining their reasoning. After each curator finishes his or her report, allow time for questions and comments. You may need to provide additional clarification about the Fourteenth Amendment and its meaning throughout the activity.

After students have had an opportunity to explore the text of the Fourteenth Amendment and some of the ideas at the heart of the congressional debate, they will be prepared to apply the "Socratic Seminar" strategy using the amendment text. (For more information about this strategy, visit facinghistory.org/reconstruction-era/strategies.) The goal of this activity is for students to help one another understand the ideas, issues, and values reflected in a specific text. Students are responsible for facilitating a discussion centered around ideas in the text rather than asserting opinions. Through a process of listening, making meaning, and finding common ground, students will work toward a shared understanding instead of trying to prove a particular argument. Use the following questions to help students focus the seminar:

- What does the Fourteenth Amendment say about the universe of obligation of the United States over time?

- Through what other words, actions, or events might American citizens and their government contribute to a definition of who belongs in the United States?

- As an extension activity for this lesson, you might give students the opportunity to compare President Johnson's Presidential Reconstruction plan, enacted in 1865, with the Reconstruction Acts, enacted by Congress in 1867. In Lesson 5, students reflected on how well Presidential Reconstruction struck a balance between providing healing and justice for the nation after the war. You might ask students to review their silent "Big Paper" conversations from that lesson. You might also ask students to repeat the activity, using this lesson's "The Reconstruction Acts of 1867" (**Handout 7.4**) document as the basis for the silent written discussion. Use the same questions to focus this version of the activity:

- Who benefits from your plan and who is harmed?

- How will this plan help to reunite and heal the country?

- How will this plan bring about justice after the war? Does it deny justice to any group of Americans?

See facinghistory.org/reconstruction-era/strategies for more information on the "Big Paper" teaching strategy.

THE CIVIL RIGHTS ACT OF 1866

April 9, 1866

An Act to protect all Persons in the United States in their Civil Rights, and furnish the Means of their Vindication.

Be it enacted by the Senate and House of Representatives of the United States of America in Congress assembled, That all persons born in the United States and not subject to any foreign power, excluding Indians not taxed*, are hereby declared to be citizens of the United States; and such citizens, of every race and color, without regard to any previous condition of slavery or involuntary servitude, except as a punishment for crime whereof the party shall have been duly convicted, shall have the same right, in every State and Territory in the United States, to make and enforce contracts, to sue, be parties, and give evidence, to inherit, purchase, lease, sell, hold, and convey real and personal property, and to full and equal benefit of all laws and proceedings for the security of person and property, as is enjoyed by white citizens, and shall be subject to like punishment, pains, and penalties, and to none other, any law, statute, ordinance, regulation, or custom, to the contrary notwithstanding . . .[1]

---

* The phrase "Indians not taxed" appears in several laws and articles of the Constitution. American Indian tribes were considered "sovereign dependent nations" with their own governments. As a result, those who lived on Indian reservations or in unsettled US territories were not subject to state or federal taxes and did not count toward population totals used to determine representation in Congress. Until 1924, Native Americans born on reservations were not automatically citizens.

---

1 Civil Rights Act, 14 Stat. 27–30, April 9, 1866, text available at http://www.pbs.org/wgbh/amex/reconstruction/activism/ps_1866.html.

THE FOURTEENTH AMENDMENT

The following Constitutional amendment was approved by Congress on June 13, 1866, and ratified on July 9, 1868.

Section 1. All persons born or naturalized in the United States, and subject to the jurisdiction thereof, are citizens of the United States and of the State wherein they reside. No State shall make or enforce any law which shall abridge the privileges or immunities of citizens of the United States; nor shall any State deprive any person of life, liberty, or property, without due process of law; nor deny to any person within its jurisdiction the equal protection of the laws.

Section 2. Representatives shall be apportioned among the several States according to their respective numbers, counting the whole number of persons in each State, excluding Indians not taxed.* But when the right to vote at any election for the choice of electors for President and Vice-President of the United States, representatives in Congress, the executive and judicial officers of a State, or the members of the legislature thereof, is denied to any of the male inhabitants of such State, being twenty-one years of age, and citizens of the United States, or in any way abridged, except for participation in rebellion, or other crime, the basis of representation therein shall be reduced in the proportion which the number of such male citizens shall bear to the whole number of male citizens twenty-one years of age in such State.

Section 3. No person shall be a senator, or representative in Congress, or elector of President and Vice-President, or hold any office, civil or military, under the United States, or under any State, who having previously taken an oath, as a member of Congress, or as an officer of the United States, or as a member of any State legislature, or as an executive or judicial officer of any State, to support the Constitution of the United States, shall have engaged in insurrection or rebellion against the same, or given aid or comfort to the enemies thereof. But Congress may by a vote of two-thirds of each House remove such disability.

Section 4. The validity of the public debt of the United States, authorized by law, including debts incurred for payment of pensions and bounties for services in suppressing insurrection or rebellion, shall not be questioned. But neither the United States nor any State shall assume or pay any debt or obligation incurred in aid of insurrection or rebellion against the United States, or any claim for the loss or emancipation of any slave; but all such debts, obligations, and claims shall be held illegal and void.

Section 5. The Congress shall have the power to enforce, by appropriate legislation, the provisions of this article.[1]

---

* *The phrase "Indians not taxed" appears in several laws and articles of the Constitution. American Indian tribes were considered "sovereign dependent nations" with their own governments. As a result, those who lived on Indian reservations or in unsettled US territories were not subject to state or federal taxes and did not count toward population totals used to determine representation in Congress. Until 1924, Native Americans born on reservations were not automatically citizens.*

1 Constitution of the United States, Amendment XIV, Sections 1–5. Text available at http://memory.loc.gov/cgi-bin/ampage?collId=llsl&fileName=014/llsl014.db&recNum=389.

CONGRESS DEBATES THE FOURTEENTH AMENDMENT[1]

GENERAL STATEMENTS:

Rep. Eben Ingersoll (Republican from Illinois) comments on the potential of the amendment to change the nation:

"Carry out the policy of Andrew Johnson, and you will restore the old order of things, if the Government is not entirely destroyed: you will have the same old slave power, the enemy of liberty and justice, ruling this nation again, which ruled it for so many years."

Scholar Garrett Epps describes the Democratic Party's argument against the amendment:

"They dismissed the amendment as a useless contraption designed only for temporary partisan advantage; at the same time, they warned that the measure would transform the nation into a centralized despotism."

Senator Luke Poland (Republican from Vermont) comments on the difference he expects the amendment will make:

"[The South] will be opened and expanded by the influence of free labor and free institutions . . . All causes of discord between North and South being over, we shall become a homogenous nation of freemen, dwelling together in peace and unity."

Senator Edgar Cowan (Democrat from Pennsylvania) comments on how the amendment will expand federal power:

"What conceivable difference could it make to a citizen of Pennsylvania as to how Ohio distributes her political power? . . . To touch, to venture upon that ground is to revolutionize the whole frame and texture of the system of our government."

Rep. Thaddeus Stevens (Republican from Pennsylvania) comments on the compromises in the amendment:

"Do you inquire why, holding these views and possessing some will of my own, I accept so imperfect a proposition? I answer, because I live among men and not among angels; among men as intelligent, as determined, and as independent as myself, who, not agreeing with me, do not choose to yield their opinions to mine. Mutual concession, therefore is our only resort, or mutual hostilities."

SECTION 1:

Rep. Thaddeus Stevens (Republican from Pennsylvania) comments on Section 1:

"[Section 1] allows Congress to correct the unjust legislation of the states, so far that the law which operates upon one man shall operate equally upon all. Whatever law punishes a white man for a crime shall punish the black man precisely in the same way and to the same degree. Whatever law protects the white man shall afford 'equal protection' to the black man."

Scholar Garrett Epps describes Democratic opposition to Section 1:

"Andrew Rogers of New Jersey gave the fullest explanation of the opposition when he warned that the first section would take away the government's traditional power to choose groups among

---

1 Except where noted, all quotations excerpted from Garrett Epps, *Democracy Reborn: The Fourteenth Amendment and the Fight for Equal Rights in Post-Civil War America* (Henry Holt, 2006), 224–239.

citizens who are worthy of 'privileges and immunities,' and would instead confer these treasured prerogatives as rights on the unworthy. 'The right to vote is a privilege,' he said. 'The right to marry is a privilege. The right to contract is a privilege. The right to be a juror is a privilege. The right to be a judge or President of United States is a privilege. I hold if [Section 1] ever becomes a part of the fundamental law of the land it will prevent any state from refusing to allow anything to anybody embraced under this term of privileges and immunities,' he said. 'That, sir, will be an introduction to the time when despotism and tyranny will march forth undisturbed and unbroken, in silence and in darkness, in this land which was once the land of freedom . . .'"

Senator Jacob Howard (Republican from Michigan) comments on Section 1:

"[Section 1] will, if adopted by the states, forever disable every one of them from passing laws trenching upon those fundamental rights and privileges which pertain to citizens of the United States, and to all persons who may happen to be within their jurisdiction. It establishes equality before the law, and it gives to the humblest, the poorest, the most despised of the race the same rights and the same protection before the law as it gives to the most powerful, the most wealthy, or the most haughty. That, sir, is republican government, as I understand it, and the only one which can claim the praise of a just Government."

Scholar Garrett Epps describes the impact of the amendment's definition of citizenship:

"Nearly a century and a half later, the citizenship language seems almost obvious. But in 1866, the idea of a preeminent national citizenship was a radical repudiation of the 'state sovereignty' theory, which held that each state had a right to define its own qualifications for citizenship, and that Americans were state citizens first and only secondarily citizens of the Union. Edgar Cowan of Pennsylvania spoke for the Democrats in repudiating the radical implications of the new language, which would make both the nation and each state within it into multiracial republics, in which equality was a birthright and not a gift of the majority. The language, he said in horror, would make citizens of even the most undesirable nomads."

Senator Edgar Cowan (Democrat from Pennsylvania) warns about the ramifications of the amendment's definition of citizenship:

"There is a race in contact with this country which, in all characteristic except that of simply making fierce war, is not only our equal but perhaps our superior. I mean the yellow race; the Mongol race. They outnumber us largely. Of their industry, their skill, and their pertinacity in all worldly affairs, nobody can doubt . . . They may pour in their millions upon our Pacific Coast in a very short time. Are the states to lose control over this immigration? Is the United States to determine that they are to be citizens?"

SECTION 2:

Scholar Garrett Epps describes Thaddeus Stevens's support for Section 2:

"To Stevens . . . the second section was 'the most important in the article,' because it would 'either compel the states to grant universal suffrage or so . . . shear them of their power as to keep them forever in a hopeless minority in the national Government.'"

Scholar Garrett Epps describes Senator Jacob Howard's (Republican from Michigan) support for Section 2:

"'[I favor black suffrage] to some extent at least, for I am opposed to the exclusion and proscription of an entire race.' But the committee did not believe a suffrage amendment could be ratified. So the second section 'is so drawn as to make it the political interest of the once slaveholding States to admit their colored population to the right of suffrage.' It would operate whether the Southern states drew a racial line to exclude freed slaves from voting or used a formally nonracial category like a literacy test, he said."

Rep. James Brooks (Democrat from New York) responds to the exclusion of women from Section 2:

"I raise my voice here on behalf of 15 million of our countrywomen, the fairest, brightest portion of creation, and I ask why they are not permitted to be represented under this resolution . . . Why, in organizing a system of liberality and justice, not recognize in the case of free women as well as free negroes the right of representation?"[2]

SECTION 3:

Scholar Garrett Epps describes revisions made to Section 3 during the debate in the Senate, changing the penalties for former Confederates:

"The Senate unanimously struck out Section 3, which would have disenfranchised former Confederates from voting until 1870 . . . [Senator] Howard brought forward a new disenfranchisement section, far more lenient than the [previous] House version; it did not limit ex-Confederates' right to vote, but only excluded a small group from holding office: those who had 'previously taken an oath' to support the U.S. Constitution and then had afterward participated in the Confederate cause."

Historian Eric Foner describes the level of support for disenfranchising former Confederates:

"[A] majority of Republicans considered disenfranchisement [of former Confederates until 1870] vindictive, undemocratic, and likely to arouse opposition in the North."[3]

SECTION 5:

Senator Jacob Howard (Republican from Michigan) comments on Section 5:

"[Section 5] casts upon Congress the responsibility of seeing to it, for the future, that all the sections of the amendment are carried out in good faith, and that no State infringes the rights of persons or property . . . It enables Congress, in case the States shall enact laws in conflict with the principles of the amendment, to correct that legislation by a formal congressional enactment."

Sen. Thomas Hendricks (Democrat from Indiana) comments on Section 5:

"When these words were used in the amendment abolishing slavery they were thought to be harmless; but during the session there has been claimed for them such force and scope of meaning as that Congress might invade the jurisdiction of the States, rob them of their reserved rights, and crown the Federal Government with absolute and despotic power."

---

2 Epps, *Democracy Reborn*, 111.
3 Eric Foner, *Reconstruction: America's Unfinished Revolution, 1863–1877*, Perennial Classics ed. (HarperCollins, 2002), 254.

THE RECONSTRUCTION ACTS OF 1867

The Reconstruction Acts of 1867 began the period of time known as Radical Reconstruction. These laws included the following measures:

- The South was divided into five military districts and governed by military governors until acceptable state constitutions could be written and approved by Congress.

- All males, regardless of race, but excluding former Confederate leaders, were permitted to participate in the constitutional conventions that formed the new governments in each state.

- New state constitutions were required to provide for *universal manhood suffrage* (voting rights for all men) without regard to race.

- States were required to ratify the Fourteenth Amendment in order to be readmitted to the Union.

LESSON 8 Interracial Democracy

ESSENTIAL QUESTION

What are the consequences of how a nation defines its universe of obligation?

TRANSITION

In the previous lesson, students examined the laws and amendments that were signal achievements of the Reconstruction era. While doing so, they reflected on the ways that nations determine who belongs and express who is included in their universes of obligation. In this lesson, students will explore the consequences of the laws passed as part of Radical Reconstruction, and they will reflect on how the revolutionary changes that occurred because of these laws in the late 1860s and early 1870s affected the strength of American democracy.

RATIONALE

The "unprecedented experiment in interracial democracy"[1] that resulted from the policies of Radical Reconstruction is a story largely unknown to many Americans. The laws passed by the Republican Congress in the late 1860s constituted a momentous expansion of civil and political rights in the United States, and they were followed by an equally unparalleled increase in civic participation and social transformation. Millions of freedpeople, as well as thousands of black Americans in the North, were no longer prohibited from voting in the United States, and they were eager for their voices to be heard. Historian Eric Foner writes:

> Never before in history had so large a group of emancipated slaves suddenly achieved political and civil rights. And the coming of black suffrage in the South in 1867 inspired a sense of millennial possibility second only to emancipation itself. Former slaves now stood on equal footing with whites, declared a speaker at a mass meeting in Savannah; before them lay "a field, too vast for contemplation."[2]

It is important for students to understand the unparalleled nature of the expansion of political and civil rights in the United States under Radical Reconstruction and the impact this expansion had on life in the South, where the majority of African Americans lived at the time. Although it didn't last, for reasons that future lessons will explore, this period of interracial democracy is considered by historians to be one of the successes of the Reconstruction era.

A Revolution in African American Political Participation

Once Radical Reconstruction policies were enacted in 1866 and 1867, Southern blacks joined civic organizations, such as Union Leagues, en masse. Meeting in schools

---

1 Eric Foner, *Forever Free: The Story of Emancipation and Reconstruction* (Vintage Books, 2006), 108.
2 Ibid., 129.

and churches, Union Leagues educated freedpeople on the workings of politics and government. They instructed them on the responsibilities of jury duty and offered advice on entering into contracts. The leagues also organized rallies and parades in support of local, state, and national political issues.[3]

These civic groups provided a foundation from which African American political leaders at all levels of government would emerge. Historians believe that the number of black officeholders in federal, state, and local governments during Reconstruction peaked at about 2,000. This was a dramatic change in the life and government of the South, only a decade removed from the Supreme Court's *Dred Scott* decision, and this number of black officeholders was unmatched until after the Voting Rights Act of 1965. According to Eric Foner, "It is safe to say that nowhere do black officials as a group exercise the political power they enjoyed in at least some Southern states during Reconstruction."[4] Sixteen African Americans were elected to Congress in Washington, and several dozen more were appointed to federal government posts. More than 600 were elected to Southern legislatures, and hundreds more served in local government positions such as justice of the peace, registrar, city councillor, and county commissioner.

A Coalition of Outsiders

Despite the unprecedented influence of black voters and elected officials during Reconstruction, it is also important to note that African Americans never constituted a majority in the Republican Party, only one African American held the governorship of a state, and in only one state (South Carolina between 1872 and 1876) did African Americans hold a majority in either house of state legislature.[5] Nevertheless, the Republican Party supported the rights of African Americans by controlling state and local governments across the South under Radical Reconstruction. Black votes, while essential, were not solely responsible for the Republican Party's ascendance; the party needed support from white Republicans to cement an effective political coalition. Historian Steven Hahn describes the coalition that transformed Southern politics:

> [D]uring Radical Reconstruction there was a *shift away* from the former slave-holding elite toward a collection of groups who had been outsiders to the formal arenas of southern politics. They included white northerners who had served in the U.S. Army and Freedmen's Bureau, had taken up planting or merchandising, or had been engaged in teaching and missionary work; white southerners who had been Unionists or unenthusiastic Confederates, had been nonslaveholders and small slaveholders, or had lived beyond the immediate orbit of the planter class; black northerners, some having escaped from slavery, who had acquired education and skills, had joined the Union military effort, or had served as ministers and missionaries . . . ; and black southerners who either had been free before the Civil War or had gained their freedom as a result of it. Together, they were substantially less wealthy, less experienced politically, and less committed to perpetuating the old plantation order. And together, they usually owed their positions to black slaves.[6]

---

3 Foner, *Forever Free*, 130–131.
4 Eric Foner, *Freedom's Lawmakers: A Directory of Black Officeholders during Reconstruction*, revised ed. (Baton Rouge, LA: Louisiana State University Press, 1996), xxxi.
5 Ibid.
6 Steven Hahn, "A Society Turned Bottomside Up," in Michael Perman and Amy M. Taylor, eds., *Major Problems in the Civil War and Reconstruction: Documents and Essays*, 3rd ed. (Boston: Wadsworth/Cengage Learning, 2011), 405–406.

Thus the policies of Radical Reconstruction led to Southern state governments in which white and black men alike voted and held elective office. This transformation, spurred on by the codification of the idea of *equality* in both law and the Constitution, prompted Americans of every gender, race, ethnicity, and class to begin to assert themselves as equal members of American society.

LEARNING GOALS

Understanding: Students will understand that:

- The success of a democracy is dependent upon its definition of citizenship, how opportunities to participate in civic life are granted and protected, and how citizens choose to participate in its civic life.

- Democracy can be understood as an aspiration that nations strive toward. At the same time, nations can successfully become more democratic without fully achieving the goals of equality and justice.

- Oppressed groups often need support from people outside of their groups in order to create a more equal society.

Knowledge: Students will know that:

- Radical Reconstruction brought about revolutionary changes to the nature of democracy and the structure of American society, especially in the South.

- African Americans had more political representation in the years of Radical Reconstruction than at any other time in American history, perhaps including the present day.

- Southern Republican governments, sustained by black votes, rebuilt Southern political institutions and introduced public education to the South.

RESOURCE LIST

- "Black Officeholders in the South" (document)
- "The First South Carolina Legislature After the 1867 Reconstruction Acts" (image)
- "The Honoured Representative of Four Millions of Colored People" (document)
- "The Role of 'Carpetbaggers'" (document)
- "Reconstructing Mississippi" (document)
- "Improving Education in South Carolina" (document)

LESSON PLAN

ESTIMATED DURATION: 1 CLASS PERIOD

SKILLS ADDRESSED:

- **Literacy:** Conducting short research projects based on focused questions; demonstrating understanding of the subject under investigation

- **Historical thinking:** Extracting useful information and drawing appropriate conclusions from historical evidence

- **Social-emotional:** Self-management—respectful communication and deliberation while engaging with others over complex issues that elicit different perspectives and opinions

I. Opener: Predicting the Effects of Radical Reconstruction

In this lesson, students will deepen their understanding of historical causation by examining evidence pertaining to the impact of Radical Reconstruction laws and amendments on both Southern states and American democracy as a whole. Before analyzing the statistics and documents in this lesson, it will be helpful for students to reflect on the laws and amendments they learned about in the last lesson and make predictions about the impact they had. Ask students to reflect for a few minutes in their journals on the following prompt: *In the last lesson, you learned about several laws and amendments passed by Republicans in Congress during Reconstruction, including the Civil Rights Act of 1866, the Fourteenth Amendment, and the Reconstruction Acts of 1867. What impact do you think these laws had?*

After students have had a few minutes to reflect and record their thoughts in their journals, you might briefly discuss their predictions using the "Think, Pair, Share" strategy. (See facinghistory.org/reconstruction-era/strategies for more information about this teaching strategy.)

II. Evaluating the Effects of Radical Reconstruction

Now that students have made predictions about the impact of the Reconstruction laws and amendments passed by Republicans in 1866 and 1867, they will examine evidence and draw conclusions about the actual impact of these measures.

PROCEDURE

1. Explain to students that they will be looking at documents, statistics, and an image that provide evidence related to the impact of the Reconstruction laws and amendments they learned about in the previous lesson.

2. Have students examine the documents and statistics provided in this lesson and record evidence and conclusions they can draw from them that help to characterize the impact of the Reconstruction laws and amendments. This can be accomplished in a variety of ways:

    - You might arrange the documents in stations, so that students travel around the room in small groups to read and discuss each document one at a time, recording evidence in their journals.

    - Instead, you might combine the documents into packets and provide a copy to each student. Students can then read the documents individually and underline or highlight relevant evidence.

3. After students have read and analyzed the documents, give them a few minutes to reflect on the evidence they have gathered.

4. Give each student a notecard. Then have them each write a newspaper headline at the top of the card that captures how the Radical Reconstruction laws and amendments changed the country. Explain that a good headline usually summarizes an idea or event in 12 words or less. Alternatively, you might have students compose a Tweet (which is 140 characters or less).

5. Below their headlines, have students list three pieces of evidence they recorded from the documents and statistics that support or explain their headline. Optionally, you might have students write complete newspaper articles to support and explain their headlines.

6. Finally, consider asking students to rethink their headlines with the following conditions:

- Imagine you are writing this headline for a newspaper with a Radical Republican bias. How might your headline be different?

- Imagine you are writing this headline for a newspaper with a Southern Democrat bias. How might your headline be different?

III. Wrap Up: Evaluating the Strength of Democracy

In the lessons that follow, students will learn about the variety of ways that Americans—Northern and Southern, black and white—reacted to the interracial democracy that arose in the South during Reconstruction. However, the end of this lesson is an opportune time, before an exploration of such responses begins, to have students reflect on how the unprecedented changes brought on by Radical Reconstruction affected the health of democracy in the United States. Ask students to reflect on the following prompt in their journals, and then conclude the lesson with another brief "Think, Pair, Share" activity:

Based on what you have learned, how did the expansion of citizenship and voting rights during Reconstruction affect the health of democracy in the United States?

Later lessons will likely complicate students' thinking about the state of democracy in the United States. Therefore, it might be useful to ask students to revisit their responses to this prompt at intervals as the class proceeds through this unit.

BLACK OFFICEHOLDERS IN THE SOUTH

The following seven tables provide information about the numbers of African American officeholders in the South during Reconstruction and the backgrounds of those officeholders.[1]

TABLE 1 Black Officeholders during Reconstruction by State

Alabama	173
Arkansas	46
District of Columbia	11
Florida	58
Georgia	135
Louisiana	210
Mississippi	226
Missouri	1
North Carolina	187
South Carolina	316
Tennessee	20
Texas	49
Virginia	85
Total	**1,510***

* Historians estimate the total number of black officeholders is closer to 2,000, but these numbers reflect only those for whom definite records exist.

TABLE 2 Black Officeholders during Reconstruction: Federal

Ambassador	2
Census Marshal	6
Census Taker	14
Clerk	12
Congressman: Senate	2
Congressman: House of Representatives	14
Customs Appointment	40
Deputy US Marshal	11
Engineer	1
Mail Agent	14
Pension Agent	1
Postmaster / Post Office Official	43
Register of Bankruptcy	1
Timber Agent	1
US Assessor	10
US Grand jury	3
US Land Office	5
US Treasury Agent	3
Unidentified Patronage Appointment	2

TABLE 3 Black Members of Congress during Reconstruction

Alabama	**Louisiana**	**South Carolina**
Jeremiah Haralson	Charles E. Nash	Richard H. Cain
James T. Rapier		Robert C. DeLarge
Benjamin S. Turner	**Mississippi**	Robert B. Elliott
	Blanche K. Bruce*	Joseph H. Rainey
Florida	John R. Lynch	Alonzo J. Ransier
Josiah T. Walls	Hiram Revels*	Robert Smalls
Georgia	**North Carolina**	
Jefferson Long	John A. Hyman	

* = Served in US Senate

---

1 All data adopted from Eric Foner, *Freedom's Lawmakers: A Directory of Black Officeholders during Reconstruction*, revised ed. (Baton Rouge, LA: Louisiana State University Press, 1996), xi–xxxii.

TABLE 4 Black Officeholders during Reconstruction: State

Assistant Commissioner of Agriculture	1
Assistant Secretary of State	3
Assistant Superintendent of Education	2
Board of Education	1
Constitutional Convention 1867–69: Delegate	267
Constitutional Convention 1875: Delegate (North Carolina)	7
Deaf and Dumb Asylum, Superintendent	1
Governor	1
Justice of Supreme Court	1
Land Commission, including County Agents (South Carolina)	10
Legislative Clerk	7
Legislator: House of Representatives	683
Legislator: Senate	112
Lieutenant Governor	6
Lunatic Asylum, Assistant Physician	1
Lunatic Asylum, Board of Regents	7
Militia Officer	60
Orphan Asylum, Board of Trustees	6
Secretary of State	9
Speaker of House	4
State Commissioner	5
Superintendent of Education	4
Treasurer	2

TABLE 5 Major Black State Officials during Reconstruction

Governor
Louisiana
  P. B. S. Pinchback

Lieutenant Governor
Louisiana
  Caesar C. Antoine
  Oscar J. Dunn
  P. B. S. Pinchback
Mississippi
  Alexander K. Davis
South Carolina
  Richard H. Cleaves
  Alonzo J. Ransier

Treasurer
Louisiana
  Antoine Dubuclet
South Carolina
  Francis L. Cardozo

Superintendent of Education
Arkansas
  Joseph C. Corbin
Florida
  Jonathan C. Gibbs
Louisiana
  William G. Brown
Mississippi
  Thomas C. Cardozo

Speaker of the House
Mississippi
  John R. Lynch
  Isaac D. Shadd
South Carolina
  Robert B. Elliott
  Samuel J. Lee

Secretary of State
Florida
  Jonathan C. Gibbs
Louisiana
  Pierre G. Deslonde
Mississippi
  Hannibal C. Carter
  James Hill
  James Lynch
  M. M. McLeod
  Hiram Revels
South Carolina
  Francis L. Cardozo
  Henry E. Hayne

Supreme Court
South Carolina
  Jonathan J. Wright

State Commissioner
Arkansas
  William H. Grey, Commr. of Immigration and State Lands
  James T. White, Commr. of Public Works
Mississippi
  Richard Griggs, Commr. of Immigration and Agriculture
South Carolina
  Robert G. DeLarge, Land Commr.
  Henry E. Hayne, Land Commr.

TABLE 6 Black Officeholders during Reconstruction: County or Local

Assessor	32	Harbor Master	3
Auditor	7	Health Officer	1
Board of Education	79	Inspector	10
Board of Health	1	Jailor	9
Chancery Clerk	1	Judge	11
Charitable Institutions, Supervisor of	1	Jury Commissioner	1
City Attorney	1	Justice of the Peace or Magistrate	232
City Clerk	1	Lumber Measurer	1
City Council	146	Mayor	5
City Marshal	7	Notary Public	5
City Office (unidentified)	3	Ordinary	3
City Public Works Commissioner	2	Overseer of Poor	7
Claims Commissioner	1	Overseer of Roads	1
Clerk	12	Park Commission	1
Clerk of Court	24	Police Officer	71
Clerk of Market	2	Recorder	9
Constable	41	Register of Bankruptcy	1
Coroner	33	Register of Deeds	2
County Attorney	1	Register of Mesne Conveyances	1
County Clerk	2	Registrar	116
County Commissioner*	113	Sheriff	41
County Superintendent of Schools	14	Solicitor	1
County Treasurer	17	Street Commissioner	5
Deputy Sheriff	25	Streetcar Commissioner	1
Detective	2	Tax Collector	35
District Attorney	1	Trustee	2
District Clerk	1	Warden	4
Election Official	52	Weigher	4

TABLE 7 Antebellum Status of Black Officeholders during Reconstruction

State	Slave	Free	Both	Unknown
Alabama	42	9	8	114
Arkansas	12	5	3	26
Florida	15	8	2	32
District of Columbia	0	6	2	3
Georgia	20	15	5	95
Louisiana	33	81	2	93
Mississippi	59	28	6	131
Missouri	0	0	1	0
North Carolina	22	34	3	126
South Carolina	131	88	5	91
Tennessee	4	7	2	7
Texas	28	6	4	11
Virginia	21	40	12	12
Total	**387**	**327**	**54**	**741**

THE FIRST SOUTH CAROLINA LEGISLATURE AFTER THE 1867 RECONSTRUCTION ACTS

In 1868, South Carolina had the first state legislature with a black majority. This image includes 63 of the legislature's members, and it was distributed throughout South Carolina by opponents of Radical Reconstruction.[1]

Photo montage (1876), Library of Congress

---

1 Julie L. Mellby, "Radical Members of the South Carolina Legislature," *Graphic Arts* (blog), entry posted May 19, 2011, http://blogs.princeton.edu/graphicarts/2011/05/radical_members_of_the_south_c.html (accessed Oct. 9, 2014).

"THE HONOURED REPRESENTATIVE OF FOUR MILLIONS OF COLORED PEOPLE"

We have chosen to include certain racial epithets in this handout in order to honestly communicate the bigoted language of the time. We recommend that teachers review the section "Addressing Dehumanizing Language from History" on page xiv before using this material.

Historian Douglas R. Egerton describes the life and political career of Mississippi politician Blanche K. Bruce, the first African American to serve a full six-year term in the United States Senate.

Portrait of Blanche K. Bruce, via Wikimedia Commons

Just ten years after President Abraham Lincoln, in his final public address, advocated voting rights for the "very intelligent [blacks], and on those who serve in our cause as soldiers," Blanche Kelso Bruce, a former slave, raised his right hand to take the oath of office as a U.S. senator from Mississippi. Garbed in a black suit and starched white cotton shirt, his black waistcoat adorned with a fourteen-karat-gold pocket watch, the stout, slightly balding statesman looked older than his thirty-four years. His dark "wavy" hair and newly trimmed van dyke revealed his mother's heritage, while his light skin was the legacy of his father and former master. Preceded in the Senate by Hiram Revels, who had served a partial term from 1870 to 1871, Bruce took his oath less than two decades after Chief Justice Roger B. Taney announced that blacks were not citizens in the country of their birth. "Unpretending and unostentatious," the *Memphis Planet* [newspaper] conceded, "he moves quietly on, the honoured representative of four millions of colored people."

Born in 1841 in Farmville, Virginia, the child then known as Branch and his five siblings were slaves because their mother, Polly Bruce, was a slave. Blanche later insisted that his father, Pettis Perkinson, had treated him as "tenderly" as he had treated his white children, and the young slave—who changed his name to Blanche while still in his teens—was employed as a domestic to his half brother and taught to read. But in an act that demonstrated that the war truly could be a conflict of brothers, in 1861 Blanche's white half brother William left to join the Confederate cause. Blanche decided "to emancipate [him]self" and decamped for the abolitionist stronghold of Lawrence, Kansas, where he found employment as a teacher. The decision nearly proved a fatal one when in August 1863 the town was sacked by Confederate guerrillas led by William Clarke Quantrill. The raiders murdered 183 men and boys, slaughtering anybody above the age of fourteen, but Bruce was able to hide in bushes behind his house. "Quantrill's band certainly would not have spared a colored man," Bruce later wrote.

After the war, Bruce briefly attended Oberlin College, the rural Ohio school widely known for its abolitionist origins and progressive attitudes on educational integration. His meager financial resources soon forced him to withdraw, but while working on a Mississippi River steamboat, Bruce heard about opportunities for ambitious black men in the lower South. Arriving in Mississippi in February 1869, at a time when the state had not yet been readmitted to Congress, Bruce settled in Bolivar County, a devoutly Republican region with a four-to-one advantage in black voters. . . . He quickly won elections for sheriff, then tax collector and superintendent of education, all while editing a local newspaper. Senators were then chosen by state assemblies, and on February 3, 1874, Bruce was chosen by the Mississippi legislature to serve in the national Senate. He journeyed north toward Washington to begin what would become the first full term served by an African American senator. There he joined black Congressmen John Adams Hyman of North Carolina and Robert Smalls, who succeeded Richard "Daddy" Cain in South Carolina's fifth district. Congressman John Roy Lynch, one of the youngest members of the House, continued to represent Mississippi's sixth district. "A turn in fortune's wheel" was one white editor's characterization of just how dramatically the political world had been turned upside down.

As the only man of color in the [Senate] chamber, Bruce sought to position himself as the servant of his state's entire population and dispel any notions that he was a single-issue politician. That meant seeking to appease his state's other senator, James L. Alcorn. Just one month into his term, Bruce stepped across the aisle to converse with Alcorn, a conservative Republican and former Confederate officer who routinely caucused with the chamber's Democrats. Alcorn had not seen fit to honor the tradition of escorting his junior colleague to his swearing-in ceremony, but Bruce was not a man to carry a grudge. The two were engaged in "harmonious conservation" when above them in the gallery, two white observers began to loudly discuss the novelty of "a nigger coming over to sit with Democrats in the United States Senate." The second man, a Marylander, admitted that Bruce "looks clean, and maybe he will keep his place and be respectful." But most senators, well aware of just how far their country had progressed since 1861, accepted his presence, if perhaps grudgingly. "He has made a most favorable impression upon the members of the Senate and those with whom he came into contact," observed one black editor. In politics, power and influence could trump race. If Mississippi Unionists preferred their senator to be white, the reality was that Bruce held the seat, and he shared their vision of regional prosperity, even if they did not share his of an interracial democracy. One Pennsylvania Republican visited Bruce's office and was surprised to find a "small army of white Mississippians" in his waiting room, all of them "ready to swear by you." The northern man thought that curious. He had never before met white southerners, and he "had a lurking idea that these people were all down on a negro on general principles." But Reconstruction was an era of new opportunities, and southern whites, whether they dreaded it or accepted it, had seen this day coming for nearly a decade.[1]

1 Douglas R. Egerton, *The Wars of Reconstruction: The Brief, Violent History of America's Most Progressive Era* (New York: Bloomsbury Press, 2014), 245–247.

THE ROLE OF "CARPETBAGGERS"

Alexander White, a white congressman from Alabama, described the role that "carpetbaggers" and "scalawags" played in Reconstruction politics as follows:

These white republicans are known by the contemptuous appellation of carpet-bagger and scalawag . . . [T]hey are a northern growth, and unless going South expatriates them, they are still northern men . . . But who are they? . . . Most of them have titles, not empty titles complaisantly bestowed in the piping times of peace, but titles worthily won by faithful and efficient service in the Federal armies, or plucked with strong right arm from war's rugged front upon the field of battle . . . These men either went South with the Union armies and at the close of the war remained there; or went there soon after, in the latter part of 1865 or early in 1866, to make cotton. The high price of cotton in 1865 and 1866, and the facility with which cheap labor could be obtained, induced many enterprising northern men, especially the officers in the Federal armies in the South who had seen and become familiar with the country, to go or remain there to make cotton. Many purchased large plantations and paid large sums of money for them; others rented plantations, in some instances two or three, and embarked with characteristic energy in planting. This, it should be remembered, was before the civil-rights bill or the reconstruction acts, before the colored people had any part in political matters, and two years before they ever proposed to vote or claimed to have the right to vote at any election in the Southern States.

When the political contests of 1868 came on in which the colored people first took part in politics, as near all the native population in the large cotton-growing sections were opposed to negro suffrage and opposed to the republican party, they very naturally turned to these northern men for counsel and assistance in the performance of the new duties and exercise of their newly acquired political rights, and they as naturally gave them such counsel and became their leaders, and were intrusted with official power by them.

This brief summary will give you a correct idea of the manner in which, as I believe, nine-tenths of those who are called carpet-baggers became involved in political affairs [in the] South . . .

Without their co-operation and assistance the colored republicans could neither organize nor operate successfully in political contests, and without them the [Republican] party would soon be extinguished in the Southern States . . .[1]

---

1 Excerpted from William E. Gienapp, ed., *The Civil War and Reconstruction: A Documentary Collection* (New York: W. W. Norton, 2001), 374–375.

RECONSTRUCTING MISSISSIPPI

Freedman John Roy Lynch was elected to the Mississippi House of Representatives in the elections of 1868, the first elections in which African Americans voted. In his autobiography, he described the accomplishments of the first interracial legislature in Mississippi.

The [1868] campaign was aggressive from beginning to end . . . [T]he election resulted in a sweeping Republican victory. That party not only elected the state ticket by a majority of about thirty thousand, but also had a large majority in both branches of the state legislature.

The new administration had an important and difficult task before it. A state government had to be organized from top to bottom. A new judiciary had to be inaugurated, consisting of three justices of the state supreme court, fifteen judges of the circuit court, and twenty chancery court judges, all of whom had to be appointed by the governor, by and with the advice and consent of the [state] senate. In addition to this, a new public school system had to be organized and established. There was not a public school building anywhere in the state except in a few of the larger towns, and they, with possibly a few exceptions, were greatly in need of repair. To erect the necessary schoolhouses and to reconstruct and repair those already in existence so as to afford educational facilities for both races was by no means an easy task. It necessitated a very large outlay of cash in the beginning which resulted in a material increase in the rate of taxation for the time being, but the constitution called for the establishment of the system and, of course, the work had to be done. It was not only done, but it was done creditably and as economically as circumstances and conditions at that time made possible. That system, though slightly changed, still stands as a creditable monument to the work of the first Republican state administration that was organized in the state of Mississippi under the Reconstruction Acts of Congress.

It was also necessary to reorganize, reconstruct, and in many instances, rebuild some of the penal, charitable, and other public institutions of the state. A new code of laws also had to be adopted to take the place of the old one, and thus wipe out the black laws that had been passed by what was known as the Johnson legislature. Also it was necessary to change the statutes of the state to harmonize with the new order of things. This was no easy task, especially in view of the fact that a heavy increase in the rate of taxation was thus made necessary. That this great and important work was splendidly, creditably, and economically done, no fair-minded person who is familiar with the facts will question or dispute.[1]

---

1 From John Hope Franklin, ed., *Reminiscences of an Active Life: The Autobiography of John Roy Lynch* (University Press of Mississippi, 2008), 69–71.

IMPROVING EDUCATION IN SOUTH CAROLINA

Freedman Samuel J. Lee was elected to the South Carolina House of Representatives in the elections of 1868, the first elections in which African Americans voted. He became Speaker of the House in 1872. In 1874, he reported on the improvements to the state education system made by the Republican legislature during Reconstruction.

Permit me, now to refer to our increased educational advantages. It is very pleasing, gentlemen, to witness how rapidly the schools are springing up in every portion of our State, and how the number of competent, well trained teachers are increasing. . . .

Our State University has been renovated and made progressive. New Professors, men of unquestionable ability and erudition, now fill the chairs once filled by men who were too aristocratic to instruct colored youths. A system of scholarships has been established that will, as soon as it is practically in operation, bring into the University a very large number of students. . . . The State Normal School is also situated here, and will have a fair attendance of scholars. We have, also, Claflin University, at Orangeburg, which is well attended, and progressing very favorably; and in the different cities and large towns of the State, school houses have been built, and the school master can be found there busily instructing "the young idea how to shoot" [a quotation from poet James Thomson, who uses *shoot* to mean "grow" or "advance"]. The effects of education can also be perceived; the people are becoming daily more enlightened; their minds are expanding, and they have awakened, in a great degree, from the mental darkness that hitherto surrounded them. . . .[1]

---

1 Excerpt from Final Report to the South Carolina House, 1874, *Journal of the House of Representatives of the State of South Carolina, for the Regular Session of 1874–1874* (Columbia, 1874), 549–553. Reprinted in William Loren Katz, *Eyewitness* (New York: Simon & Schuster, 1995). Available at http://www.pbs.org/wgbh/amex/reconstruction/schools/ps_report.html.

LESSON 9 Equality for All?

ESSENTIAL QUESTIONS

What does it mean to be equal? Is equality essential for democracy?

TRANSITION

In the previous two lessons, students examined the landmark legislation and amendments of the Radical Reconstruction era, and they learned about the unprecedented period of interracial democracy that resulted. In this lesson, students will learn about some of the limits to the transformation of American democracy at this time and about several groups of Americans who demanded that the promise of equality be made a reality for them.

RATIONALE

While the rights of African Americans were greatly expanded under Radical Reconstruction, many forms of discrimination remained unregulated by law. Additionally, the limited rights of many Americans—including women, immigrants, workers, and Native Americans—remained untouched by Radical Reconstruction in the 1860s and 1870s. Yet the spirit of equality, newly enshrined in the Constitution by the Fourteenth Amendment, prompted many of these Americans to demand new rights.

This lesson provides students with a survey of American voices demanding to be included, each in his or her own way, in the universe of obligation of the nation that emerged from the Civil War. Some of these voices envision an equal society, while others express a belief that some Americans deserve more rights than others. Some of these voices envision an integrated society, while others express a desire to live apart. By learning about these demands, students might consider the challenges of democracy. How can a democracy balance the competing demands of its inhabitants for rights and power? How can it achieve equality when not all of its inhabitants believe in equality? How can it achieve a harmonious society when not all of its inhabitants wish to live together? While the histories of each of the groups represented in this lesson deserve extended study in a course on American history, the goal of this lesson is to show how the revolutionary changes that Radical Reconstruction brought to Southern society invigorated the desires of Americans everywhere to have their voices heard and their rights respected.

The following paragraphs provide context for the groups that are represented in this lesson.

African Americans: While Radical Reconstruction legislation and amendments dramatically changed the lives of African Americans, many forms of discrimination based on race were not explicitly forbidden by law. In 1874, Congress debated a new civil rights bill, written by Republican senator Charles Sumner from Massachusetts, which banned racial discrimination in public accommodation and transportation. Alabama congressman James Rapier argues for the bill's passage in **Handout 9.3** ("Arguing for

Civil Rights") by describing the discrimination he faced when traveling south from Washington. The bill became law in 1875, and it was the last piece of Reconstruction legislation passed by Congress. It was declared unconstitutional by the Supreme Court in the Civil Rights Cases of 1883.

Women: Women's rights advocates had a long history as part of the coalition demanding the abolition of slavery, but after the Thirteenth Amendment was ratified, some women and African Americans diverged in their efforts for equality. As compromises in the Fourteenth and Fifteenth Amendments left women's suffrage off the agenda, some women's rights advocates, such as Frances Gage and Lucy Stone, continued to support the amendments, while others, notably Susan B. Anthony and Elizabeth Cady Stanton, strongly opposed them. Gage and Stone argued that any expansion of rights, even if inadequate in scope, ought to be supported because it would make society more democratic. Anthony and Stanton argued that women deserved the franchise before African Americans and other groups. This perspective is represented in **Handout 9.1** ,"The Fifteenth Amendment (Illustrated)" (though the image itself is the work of an Austrian immigrant who was not affiliated the women's suffrage movement). Although women had not been extended the franchise, Anthony voted in the 1872 election anyway, and she was arrested for committing a crime. She was convicted and fined $100 for "the crime of having voted," a common topic in her speeches thereafter.

Workers: The 1870s are known as the beginning of the Gilded Age (a term coined in 1873 by Mark Twain and fellow writer Charles Dudley Warner), a time of expanding industrialism, economic inequality, graft, and corruption. At the same time that the federal government continued to deny the provision of land to freedpeople in the South, it was granting free land to railroad corporations in the West. This policy facilitated the rapid expansion of railroads and the economic development of the West, but it also encouraged land speculation as corporations sold for enormous profit the land they were given for free. Workers across the country decried such policies that favored the wealthy and resulted in enormous economic inequality. The title of one pamphlet from the decade sums up this sentiment: "The Rich Are Growing Richer, While the Poor Are Growing Poorer." American laborers began to organize into unions to demand higher wages, better working conditions, and government policies more favorable to workers. The ideas of socialism and communism also arrived in the United States from Europe in the 1870s, fueling the demands of some workers for economic equality. Labor groups such as the Workingmen's Party of California not only demanded economic equality but also sought to exclude immigrants from employment, viewing them as competitors for jobs.

Immigrants: After the Civil War, Congress passed laws to encourage immigration from Europe. According to Census Bureau statistics, between 1860 and 1880, the number of foreign-born Americans from Europe grew by two million, a 50% increase. During the same two decades, the number of foreign-born residents of the United States from China tripled, from roughly 35,000 in 1860 to nearly 105,000 in 1880. Chinese workers were crucial to the completion of the transcontinental railroad, and many others worked in manufacturing jobs. While Chinese immigrants represented less than 2% of the total immigrant population in the United States, some Americans, including members of the Workingmen's Party of California, perceived them as a threat to jobs and economic security. By 1875, there was enough anti-Chinese sentiment to prompt Congress to pass the Page Act, the first law to limit immigration of groups considered "undesirable." In 1882, the Chinese Exclusion Act further restricted Chinese immigration. It is in this context that a group of Chinese immigrants wrote to President Ulysses S. Grant in 1877 defending their value to American society and asking for protection from discrimination.

Native Americans: The circumstances of Native Americans during Reconstruction were complex and frequently dire. The American government's policies toward Native Americans at this time were the culmination of several centuries of oppression and what some scholars have labeled genocide. Westward expansion, including the extension of railroads, was the goal of national economic policy during the 1860s and 1870s. As a result, the United States confiscated the western lands of a variety of Indian nations. The army was sent to battle the nations that resisted. Under President Grant's Indian policies, many Native Americans were encouraged (and often forced) to attend schools that would teach them how to assimilate into the culture of white America, while others were confined to reservations. In **Handout 9.7** ("Creating a New Policy for Native Americans"), Grant's advisors present assimilation and reservations as preferable alternatives to "extermination." Sioux leader Sitting Bull responds to this policy by maintaining that all creatures have an equal right to inhabit the land. He pledges to fight if the Americans claim the land "for their own, and fence their neighbors away."

LEARNING GOALS

Understanding: Students will understand that:

- Democracy can be understood as an aspiration that nations strive toward. Nations can successfully become more democratic without fully achieving the goals of equality and justice.

- Progress in making a society more democratic is often slow and uneven. Rights provided to some groups often continue to be denied to others.

- When some members of society attain new rights, others are often inspired in their efforts to achieve justice.

Knowledge: Students will know that:

- While African Americans continued to push for additional civil rights protection, women, immigrants, workers, and Native Americans sought equal rights in the United States.

- Some of these groups viewed themselves as in competition with each other for membership in the United States.

RESOURCE LIST

- "The Fifteenth Amendment (Illustrated)" (image)

- "The Fifteenth Amendment" (document)

- "Arguing for Civil Rights" (document)

- "Speech by Susan B. Anthony: Is It a Crime for Women to Vote?" (document)

- "Platform of the Workingmen's Party of California (1877)" (document)

- "Chinese Immigrants Write to President Grant" (document)

- "Creating a New Policy for Native Americans" (document)

- "They Fence Their Neighbors Away" (document)

ACTIVITY SUGGESTIONS

Note that a detailed Common Core–aligned close reading protocol for an extended version of the speech in the document "Speech by Susan B. Anthony: Is It a Crime for Women to Vote?" (**Handout 9.4**) *follows this lesson. The Common Core standards recommend that students begin a close reading activity with little, if any, prior knowledge of the text at the heart of the activity. Therefore, if you plan to include a close reading of this document in your unit, we recommend that you complete the activity prior to using any of the suggested activities below.*

Consider using the following activity ideas and strategies when you implement this lesson in your classroom.

- Begin the lesson by asking students to reflect in their journals on what they think it means to be an equal member of a nation. Consider using the following journal prompt: *What is equality? How do you know if you are an equal member of a group or nation?*

  Start a concept map for the term *equality*. Have students suggest attributes for the map based on their journal reflections. Add new attributes to the map as they come up throughout the lesson. Save the concept map for reference later in the unit.

- Briefly read the Fifteenth Amendment together (**Handout 9.2**) to establish that it prohibits states from denying voting rights to citizens on the basis of race, color, or the fact that an individual used to be a slave. Then have students analyze the image in **Handout 9.1**, "The Fifteenth Amendment (Illustrated)," using the "Analyzing Visual Images" strategy. (More information about this strategy can be found at facinghistory.org/reconstruction-era/strategies.) This strategy will help students look closely at this image and reflect deeply on the perspective on equality it represents, and it will also help students sharpen their media literacy, critical thinking, observation, and interpretive skills. As you complete this five-step analysis, ask students to discuss the following questions:

  - What does equality look like?

  - Is the artist who created this image seeking equality in American society?

- Explain to students that in this lesson they will examine the state of equality in the United States during the time period that the ideal was established in the Constitution through the Fourteenth Amendment. They will look beyond the issue of equality between black and white Americans and consider that status of a variety of other groups, including women, workers, immigrants, and Native Americans.

  To help students acquire some knowledge about the status of all of these groups, use the "Jigsaw" strategy with the documents in this lesson. This strategy asks a group of students to become "experts" on a specific document and then share their knowledge with another group of students. Each "expert" group should discuss its assigned documents and record the following pieces of information and analysis to share once the groups have been shuffled into "teacher" groups:

- The name of the group of Americans represented in the document

- The extent to which that group was included in the universe of obligation of the United States

- The rights or opportunities that, if enjoyed by the members of that group, would show that they are equal members of society

- After analyzing the documents in this lesson, have students reflect in their journals, or participate in a "Barometer" activity, about the following question:

  - Can democracy exist without equality? Why or why not?

- Finally, ask students to revisit their journal reflection from the previous lesson evaluating the strength of democracy in the United States during Reconstruction. The question was the following: *Based on what you have learned so far, how did the expansion of citizenship and voting rights during Reconstruction affect the health of democracy in the United States?* Give students a few moments to expand or revise their thinking on this question.

"THE FIFTEENTH AMENDMENT (ILLUSTRATED)"

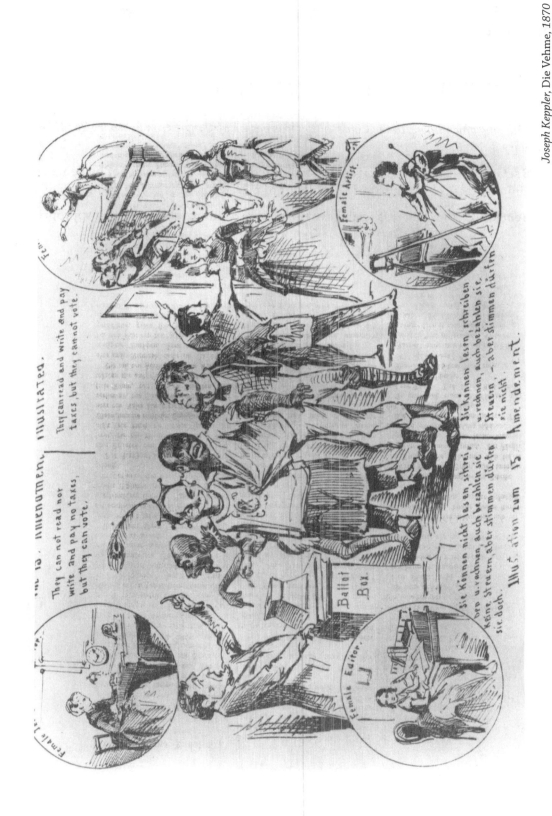

Joseph Keppler, Die Vehme, 1870

THE FIFTEENTH AMENDMENT

The following amendment to the Constitution was passed by Congress on February 26, 1869, and ratified on February 3, 1870.

Section 1. The right of citizens of the United States to vote shall not be denied or abridged by the United States or by any State on account of race, color, or previous condition of servitude.

Section 2. The Congress shall have the power to enforce this article by appropriate legislation.[1]

---

1 Constitution of the United States, Amendment XV, Sections 1–2. Text available at http://memory.loc.gov/cgi-bin/ampage?collId=llsl&fileName=015/llsl015.db&recNum=379.

ARGUING FOR CIVIL RIGHTS

The following is an excerpt from a speech by James T. Rapier, a black congressman from Alabama, arguing for passage of the Civil Rights Bill in 1874.

[A]ny white ex-convict (I care not what may have been his crime . . .) may start with me today to Montgomery, that all the way down he will be treated as a gentleman, while I will be treated as the convict. He will be allowed a berth in a sleeping car with all its comforts, while I will be forced into a dirty, rough box with the drunkards, apple sellers, railroad hands, and next to any dead that be in transit, regardless of how far decomposition may have progressed. Sentinels are placed at the doors of the better coaches, with positive instructions to keep persons of color out . . .

[T]here is not an inn between Washington and Montgomery, a distance of more than a thousand miles, that will accommodate me to bed or meal. Now, then, is there a man upon this floor who is so heartless, whose breast is so void of the better feelings, as to say that this brutal custom needs no regulation? I hold that it does and that Congress is the body to regulate it . . . Every day my life and property are exposed, are left to the mercy of others, and will be so as long as every hotelkeeper, railroad conductor, and steamboat captain can refuse me with impunity the accommodations common to other travelers . . .

[T]here is a cowardly propensity in the human heart that delights in oppressing somebody else, and in the gratification of this base desire we always select a victim that can be outraged with safety . . . [H]ere the Negro is the most available for this purpose; for this reason in part he was seized upon, and not because he is naturally inferior to anyone else. Instead of his enemies believing him to be incapable of a high order of mental culture, they have shown that they believe the reverse to be true, by taking the most elaborate pains to prevent his development . . .

By their acts, not by their words, the civilized world can and will judge how honest my opponents are in their declarations that I am naturally inferior to them. No one is surprised that this class opposes the passage of the civil rights bill, for if the Negro were allowed the same opportunities, the same rights of locomotion, the same rights to comfort in travel, how could they prove themselves better than the Negro?[1]

---

1 Excerpted from William E. Gienapp, ed., *The Civil War and Reconstruction: A Documentary Collection* (New York: W. W. Norton, 2001), 362–364.

SPEECH BY SUSAN B. ANTHONY: IS IT A CRIME FOR WOMEN TO VOTE?

Susan B. Anthony voted in the 1872 presidential election. Because women did not have the right to vote, she was arrested, put on trial, convicted, and fined $100. The following is an excerpt from a speech she delivered in 1873, prior to her trial.

Friends and Fellow-citizens: I stand before you to-night under indictment for the alleged crime of having voted at the last Presidential election, without having a lawful right to vote. It shall be my work this evening to prove to you that in thus voting, I not only committed no crime, but, instead, simply exercised my *citizen's right*, guaranteed to me and all United States citizens by the National Constitution, beyond the power of any State to deny . . .

The preamble of the federal constitution says: "We, the people of the United States, in order to form a more perfect union, establish justice, insure *domestic* tranquility, provide for the common defense, promote the general welfare and secure the blessings of liberty to ourselves and our posterity, do ordain and establish this constitution for the United States of America."

It was we, the people; not we, the white male citizens; nor yet we, the male citizens; but we, the whole people, who formed this Union. And we formed it, not to give the blessings of liberty, but to secure them; not to the half of ourselves and the half of our posterity, but to the whole people— women as well as men. And it is downright mockery to talk to women of their enjoyment of the blessings of liberty while they are denied the use of the only means of securing them provided by this democratic-republican government—the ballot . . .

To [women], this government has no just powers derived from the consent of the governed. To them this government is not a democracy. It is not a republic. It is an odious aristocracy; a hateful oligarchy of sex. The most hateful aristocracy ever established on the face of the globe. An oligarchy of wealth, where the rich govern the poor; an oligarchy of learning, where the educated govern the ignorant; or even an oligarchy of race, where the Saxon rules the African, might be endured; but this oligarchy of sex, which makes father, brothers, husband, sons, the oligarchs over the mother and sisters, the wife and daughters of every household; which ordains all men sovereigns, all women subjects, carries dissension, discord, and rebellion into every home of the nation . . .

The only question left to be settled, now, is: Are women persons? And I hardly believe any of our opponents will have the hardihood to say they are not. Being persons, then, women are citizens, and no state has a right to make any law, or to enforce any old law, that shall abridge their privileges or immunities. Hence, every discrimination against women in the constitutions and laws of the several states, is to-day null and void, precisely as is every one against negroes . . .[1]

1 Excerpts from "Is It a Crime for a Citizen of the United States to Vote?" (speech), delivered April 3, 1873, transcribed in Susan Brownell Anthony, *An Account of the Proceedings on the Trial of Susan B. Anthony, on the Charge of Illegal Voting* (Daily Democrat and Chronicle Book Print, 1874), 151–178. Full text available at http://law2.umkc.edu/faculty/projects/ftrials/anthony/anthonyaddress.html.

PLATFORM OF THE WORKINGMEN'S PARTY OF CALIFORNIA (1877)

We have chosen to include certain racial epithets in this handout in order to honestly communicate the bigoted language of the time. We recommend that teachers review the section "Addressing Dehumanizing Language from History" on page xiv before using this material.

The object of this Association is to unite all poor and working men and their friends into one political party, for the purpose of defending themselves against the dangerous encroachments of capital on the happiness of our people and the liberties of our country.

- We propose to wrest the government from the hands of the rich and place it in those of the people, where it properly belongs.

- We propose to rid the country of cheap Chinese labor as soon as possible, and by all the means in our power, because it tends still more to degrade labor and aggrandize capital.

- We propose to destroy land monopoly in our state by such laws as will make it impossible.

- We propose to destroy the great money power of the rich by a system of taxation that will make great wealth impossible in the future.

- We propose to provide decently for the poor and unfortunate, the weak, the helpless, and especially the young, because the country is rich enough to do so, and religion, humanity, and patriotism demand that we should do so.

- We propose to elect none but competent workingmen and their friends to any office whatever. The rich have ruled us until they have ruined us. We will now take our own affairs in our own hands. The republic must and shall be preserved, and only workingmen will do it. Our shoddy aristocrats want an emperor and a standing army to shoot down the people.

- For these purposes, we propose to organize ourselves into the Workingmen's Party of California, and to pledge and enroll therein all who are willing to join us in accomplishing these ends.

- When we have 10,000 members, we shall have the sympathy and support of 20,000 other workingmen.

- The party will then wait upon all who employ Chinese and ask for their discharge, and it will mark as public enemies those who refuse to comply with their request.

- This party will exhaust all peaceable means of attaining its ends, but it will not be denied justice when it has the power to enforce it. It will encourage no riot or outrage, but it will not volunteer to repress, or put down, or arrest, or prosecute the hungry and impatient who manifest their hatred of the Chinamen by a crusade against "John" or those who employ him. Let those who raise the storm by their selfishness, suppress it themselves. If they dare raise the devil, let them meet him face to face. We will not help them . . .[1]

---

1 Quoted in Ira Brown Cross, *A History of the Labor Movement in California*, vol. 14 (University of California Press, 1935), 96–97. Text available at http://instruct.westvalley.edu/kelly/History20_on_campus/Online%20Readings/Cross_Kearney.htm.

CHINESE IMMIGRANTS WRITE TO PRESIDENT GRANT

We have chosen to include certain racial epithets in this handout in order to honestly communicate the bigoted language of the time. We recommend that teachers review the section "Addressing Dehumanizing Language from History" on page xiv before using this material.

A MEMORIAL FROM REPRESENTATIVE CHINAMEN IN AMERICA To His Excellency U. S. GRANT, President of the United States of America.

Sir: — In the absence of any consular representative, we, the undersigned, in the name and in behalf of the Chinese people now in America, would most respectfully present for your consideration the following statements regarding the subject of Chinese immigration to this country:

First — We understand that it has always been the settled policy of your honorable government to welcome immigration to your shores, from all countries, without let or hinderance. The Chinese are not the only people who have crossed the ocean to seek a residence in this land.

Second — The treaty of amity and peace between the United States and China makes special mention of the rights and privileges of Americans in China, and also of the rights and privileges of Chinese in America.

Third — American steamers, subsidized by your honorable government, have visited the ports of China, and invited our people to come to this country to find employment and improve their condition.

Fourth — Our people in this country, for the most part, have been peaceable, law-abiding and industrious. They performed the largest part of the unskilled labor in the construction of the Central Pacific Railroad, and also of other railroads on this coast. They have found useful employment in all the manufacturing establishments of this coast, in agricultural pursuits, and in family service. While benefiting themselves with the honest reward of their daily toil, they have given satisfaction to their employers, and have left all the results of their industry to enrich the State. They have not displaced white laborers from these positions, but have simply multiplied industries.

Fifth — The Chinese have neither attempted nor desired to interfere with the established order of things in this country, either of politics or religion. They have opened no whiskey saloons for the purpose of dealing out poison, and degrading their fellow men. They have promptly paid their duties, their taxes, their rents and their debts.

Sixth — It has often occurred, about the time of the State and general elections, that political agitators have stirred up the mind of the people in hostility to the Chinese; but formerly the hostility has subsided after the elections were over.

Seventh — At the present time an intense excitement and bitter hostility against the Chinese in this land, and against further Chinese immigration, has been created in the minds of the people, led on by his Honor the Mayor of San Francisco and his associates in office, and approved by his Excellency the Governor of the State and other great men of the State. These great men gathered some twenty thousand of the people of this city together on the evening of April 5, and adopted an address and resolutions against Chinese immigration . . .

Eighth — In this address, numerous charges are made against our people, some of which are highly colored and sensational, and others, having no foundation in fact, are only calculated to mislead honest minds, and create an unjust prejudice against us. We wish most respectfully to call your attention, and through you the attention of Congress, to some of the statements of that remarkable paper, and ask a careful comparison of the statements there made with the facts in the case . . .

> With sentiments of profound respect, LEE MING How, President, Sam Yeep Company. LEE CHEE KWAN, President, Yung Wo Company. LAW YEE CHUNG, President, Kong Chow Company. CHAN LEUNG Kox, President, Wing Lung Company. LEE CHEONG CHIP, President, Hop Wu Company. CHANG KONG CHEW, President, Yan Wo Company. LEE TONG HAY, President, Chinese Y. M. C. A.[1]

---

1 Excerpted from the "California As I Saw It: First-Person Narratives of California's Early Years, 1849–1900" collection, Library of Congress website. Text available at http://www.loc.gov/teachers/classroommaterials/presentationsandactivities/presentations/timeline/riseind/chinimms/briggs.html (accessed March 22, 2013).

CREATING A NEW POLICY FOR NATIVE AMERICANS

The following is excerpted from the Indian Peace Commission report delivered to President Johnson in 1868. President Grant later made the report the basis for his "Indian Peace Policy."

To the President of the United States:

The undersigned, commissioners appointed under the act of Congress approved July 20, 1867, "to establish peace with certain hostile Indian tribes," were authorized by said act to call together the chiefs and headmen of such bands of Indians as were then waging war, for the purpose of ascertaining their reasons for hostility, and, if thought advisable, to make treaties with them, having in view the following objects, viz:

1st. To remove, if possible, the causes of war.

2d. To secure, as far as practicable, our frontier settlements and the safe building of our railroads looking to the Pacific; and

3d. To suggest or inaugurate some plan for the civilization of the Indians.

. . . If it be said that the savages are unreasonable, we answer, that if civilized they might be reasonable. At least they would not be dependent on the buffalo and the elk, they would no longer want a country exclusively for game, and the presence of the white man would become desirable. If it be said that because they are savages they should be exterminated, we answer that, aside from the humanity of the suggestion, it will prove exceedingly difficult, and if money considerations are permitted to weigh, it costs less to civilize than to kill. . . .

The white and Indian must mingle together and jointly occupy the country, or one of them must abandon it. . . . What prevented their living together? First. The antipathy of race. Second. The difference of customs and manners arising from their tribal or clannish organizations. Third. The difference in language, which in a great measure barred intercourse and a proper understanding each of the other's motives and intentions. . . .

But one thing then remains to be done with honor to the nation, and that is to select a district or districts of country, as indicated by Congress, on which all the tribes east of the Rocky mountains may be gathered. . . .[1]

---

1 Excerpted from "Report to the President by the Indian Peace Commission, January 7, 1868," transcribed by Carolyn Sims, Furman University Department of History, from the Annual Report of the Commissioner of Indian Affairs for the Year 1868 (Washington, D.C.: Government Printing Office, 1868), 26–50. Text available at http://eweb.furman.edu/~benson/docs/peace.htm (accessed Jan. 24, 2014).

THEY FENCE THEIR NEIGHBORS AWAY

The following is an excerpt from Sioux chief Sitting Bull's speech at the Powder River Council in 1877.

Behold, my brothers, the spring has come; the earth has received the embraces of the sun and we shall soon see the results of that love! Every seed has awakened and so has all animal life. It is through this mysterious power that we too have our being and we therefore yield to our neighbors, even our animal neighbors, the same right as ourselves, to inhabit this land. Yet hear me, my people, we have now to deal with another race—small and feeble when our fathers first met them, but now great and overbearing. Strangely enough they have a mind to till the soil and the love of possessions is a disease with them . . . They claim this mother of ours, the earth, for their own, and fence their neighbors away; they deface her with their buildings and their refuse. They threaten to take [the land] away from us. My brothers, shall we submit, or shall we say to them: "First kill me before you take possession of my Fatherland."[1]

---

1 Text available from the Gilder Lehrman Institute of American History, http://www.gilderlehrman.org/sites/default/files/inline-pdfs/Speech%20 Excerpts.pdf.

Speech by Susan B. Anthony: Is It a Crime for Women to Vote?

*Close reading is carefully and purposefully **rereading** a text. It's an encounter with the text in which we closely focus on what the author has to say, what the author's purpose is, what the words mean, and what the structure of the text tells us. Close reading ensures that we truly understand what we've read. At Facing History and Ourselves, we use this careful investigation of text to make connections to essential questions about history, human behavior, and ourselves. This protocol can be used to implement a close reading for select documents during the Reconstruction unit. Adapt this procedure to meet your goals and the needs of your students.*

FIRST READ: Read aloud. Either the teacher or an extremely fluent student can read the text aloud. Ask students to circle unfamiliar words as they listen. After the read-aloud, as students share these words with the class, decide which words to define immediately to limit confusion and which definitions you want students to uncover through careful reading.

SECOND READ: Individual read. Ask students to read silently to get a feel for the text. They can note specific words or phrases that jump out at them for any number of reasons: because they are interesting, familiar, strange, confusing, funny, troubling, difficult, etc. Share some of these as a class. Particular questions to ask students at this stage of the reading are:

- What can you already infer about the author of this text?

- How is the text structured?

- Does this structure make it easy or difficult to make meaning?

- Does this structure tell us anything about the author's style or purpose?

THIRD READ: Text-dependent questions. In small groups, have students read the text in chunks and answer a set of text-dependent questions. These questions are included with each close reading exemplar. Sample answers are provided to help guide the teacher. See the "Close Reading C: Student Handout" form for a student version of the document. See "Close Reading C: Teacher Notes" for the teacher's version.

FOURTH READ: Visual image. In small groups, have students create a visual image on paper that captures the essence of the text. You may also ask them to include three words or a sentence summary of each section of text. Groups can be assigned either the entire text or sections of text for this portion of the close reading.

FIFTH READ: Gallery read. Ask students to do a "gallery read" of the images that have been created.

TRANSITION TO DISCUSSION

At this point, we recommend organizing a class discussion so that students can make connections beyond the text. This discussion can be informal or can use the format of the "Socratic Seminar" or "Save the Last Word for Me" strategy (see the "Teaching Strategies" section on our website at facinghistory.org/reconstruction-era/strategies for details).

DISCUSSION SUGGESTIONS

As mentioned earlier, this unit includes two writing prompts. Both prompts can be used to launch a discussion after a close reading. Examples include:

- To connect to the argumentative writing prompt (*Support, refute, or modify the statement: Laws are the most important factor in overcoming discrimination*):

  - What is the role of laws in creating a just democracy? How do you think Susan B. Anthony would answer that question? How do you answer that question? What else might we need to create a just democracy?

- To connect to the informative writing prompt: *Historian Eric Foner calls Reconstruction "America's unfinished revolution." What debates and dilemmas from the Reconstruction era remain unresolved? After researching informational texts on Reconstruction, write an essay in which you explain one debate that was central to this period that remained unresolved. Explain why the debate was significant to the history of Reconstruction. In your conclusion, discuss the legacy of the debate not being resolved.*

  - Ask students to find connections between Anthony's debate on women's rights and contemporary issues about membership in American society today. What aspects or elements of Anthony's argument remain "unfinished" in the twenty-first century?

- To connect to more general Facing History and Ourselves themes:

  - How does Anthony's speech connect to issues of 'we" and "they"? What does her speech teach us about the different divisions in American society during Reconstruction? How does the speech connect to issues about belonging and exclusion in communities today?

  - What does it mean to be a citizen? What does it mean to be equal? How might Anthony answer these questions? How do you answer these questions?

- It's also possible to have students themselves create the questions for a discussion. To do this, you might guide students by asking them to find connections between the essential questions and the text or to write questions based on what resonates for them. They might choose to make connections to the author's purpose, the structure of the text, the tone of the text, or the main messages of the text. Alternatively, they may want to make connections to issues related to the individual and society, to examples of discrimination, to the role of voting in a democracy, and beyond.

CLOSE READING C Teacher Guide

Text of Susan B. Anthony's Speech

Friends and Fellow-citizens: I stand before you to-night, under indictment for the alleged crime of having voted at the last Presidential election, without having a lawful right to vote. It shall be my work this evening to prove to you that in thus voting, I not only committed no crime, but, instead, simply exercised my *citizen's right*, guaranteed to me and all United States citizens by the National Constitution, beyond the power of any State to deny.

Our democratic-republican government is based on the idea of the natural right of every individual member thereof to a voice and a vote in making and executing the laws. We assert the province of government to be to secure the people in the enjoyment of their unalienable rights. We throw to the winds the old dogma that governments can give rights. Before governments were organized, no one denies that each individual possessed the right to protect his own life, liberty and property. And when 100 or 1,000,000 people enter into a free government, they do not barter away their natural rights; they simply pledge themselves to protect each other in the enjoyment of them, through prescribed judicial and legislative tribunals. They agree to abandon the methods of brute force in the adjustment of their differences, and adopt those of civilization.

Guided Close Reading with Text-Dependent Questions

1. **While reading the first paragraph, what two things do you learn about Susan B. Anthony?**
   A good close reading starts with some "easy wins" for students, and this question should definitely elicit the response that Anthony is accused of illegally voting in the last presidential election. Students should further note that she believes she did not commit a crime but rather simply exercised her right as a citizen.

2. **What document does Anthony claim gives her the right to vote?**
   Anthony claims that the Constitution of the United States gives her (and every citizen) the right to vote and that it is a right that cannot be denied by any state.

3. **Why was it a crime for Anthony to vote in the last presidential election?**
   Based on the title, students should recognize that Anthony did not have the lawful right to vote at the time because she was a woman. It can also be inferred that state laws made it illegal for her to vote.

4. **In the context of the second paragraph, what is the meaning of inalienable? How does it inform Anthony's definition of a natural right?**
   Based on the paragraph, the meaning of inalienable is connected to the idea that this can be neither conferred nor taken away by a government. Anthony believes that natural rights are inalienable—that people possess the rights to life, liberty, and property independent of the existence of a government.

5. **Given what Anthony says in the second paragraph, what can you infer about what she thinks the role of government is?**
   Anthony claims that the role of government is therefore to "secure" and protect the natural rights of citizens and ensure that all individuals can enjoy their "unalienable rights." It is important to note that in creating a democratic-republican government centered on recognizing rights, the people agree to defer to its "judicial and legislative tribunals" rather than resolve their differences through "brute force."

Guided Close Reading with Text-Dependent Questions

6. How does Anthony connect her refutation of the "old dogma" in paragraph 2 to the documents written by the "fathers" mentioned in paragraph 3?

She asserts that rather than following the "old dogma" that holds that governments create or confer rights, the foundational documents of this country—the Declaration of Independence, the constitutions of both the individual states and the United States, and even the laws of the territories—maintain that rights are bestowed by God.

7. What can you infer about the purpose and source of the lengthy quotation offered by Anthony that begins "All men are created equal . . .":

It is logical to infer that the quotation is intended to prove the point she has made in the previous paragraph, and that it therefore stems from one of the "grand documents" written by the Founding Fathers (in the next paragraph, Anthony indicates that it stems from "the declaration").

8. How does Anthony's explanation of the quotation support her overarching claim?

She begins by noting that the quotation does not give the government any power to create rights or exclude individuals from their enjoyment. She goes on to assert that inherent in the idea of "all men" is the notion that all women, as well, possess the aforementioned rights. And she rounds out her analysis of the passage by pointing out that it ends by implying that the right to vote is a "natural" right of everyone in its championing of the notion of "the consent of the governed."

9. Paraphrase the quotation that starts with "That whenever any form of government . . ." in your own words.

Answers should capture two key ideas in the passage: (1) that the purpose of government is to protect the rights mentioned earlier—life, liberty, the pursuit of happiness, and also the implied right to vote—and (2) that the people have the right to change the government, or even to eliminate it and set up a new government, should it fail to support those rights.

Text of Susan B. Anthony's Speech

Nor can you find a word in any of the grand documents left us by the fathers that assumes for government the power to create or to confer rights. The Declaration of Independence, the United States Constitution, the constitutions of the several states and the organic laws of the territories, all alike propose to protect the people in the exercise of their God-given rights. Not one of them pretends to bestow rights.

"All men are created equal, and endowed by their Creator with certain unalienable rights. Among these are life, liberty and the pursuit of happiness. That to secure these, governments are instituted among men, deriving their just powers from the consent of the governed."

Here is no shadow of government authority over rights, nor exclusion of any from their full and equal enjoyment. Here is pronounced the right of all men, and "consequently," as the Quaker preacher said, "of all women," to a voice in the government. And here, in this very first paragraph of the declaration, is the assertion of the natural right of all to the ballot; for, how can "the consent of the governed" be given, if the right to vote be denied. Again:

"That whenever any form of government becomes destructive of these ends, it is the right of the people to alter or abolish it, and to institute a new government, laying its foundations on such principles, and organizing its powers in such forms as to them shall seem most likely to effect their safety and happiness."

10. What is the significance of the quote for Anthony's argument?

To Anthony, the quote explains that citizens have the right to change a destructive government and that without the ability to vote, that right could only be achieved through brute force—a method that earlier was identified as what the institution of government was designed to avoid. Hence the right of all people to vote so as to alter a government that is not adequately representing them is "clearly implied."

11. What does Anthony claim is "in direct violation of the spirit and letter of the declarations of the framers of this government"?

Anthony argues that because women do not have the right to vote, they are being ruled by men, putting one half of the country at the mercy of the other half. According to Anthony, when women do not have the right to vote, the government is compelling them to obey laws to which they have not consented.

12. What clues are in this passage as to the meaning of the word serf? Does serf have a negative or positive connotation in this context?

Anthony uses this passage to contrast "kings, priests, popes" and "aristocrats" with the "lowliest born subject." She claims that the early declarations by the Founding Fathers abolished "all class and caste distinction." Serf is therefore contextually defined as a member of the lowest class. From the perspective of the upper class, the word would have a negative association, but from Anthony's vantage point, the egalitarian notion of reducing everyone—serfs, women, and aristocrats alike—to the same "level" effectively raises the status of women and therefore confers a positive association.

13. What importance does the first line of the preamble to the federal Constitution have for Anthony's argument?

Anthony notes that the very first line of the preamble is "We, the people" and not "We, the white male citizens" or even "We, the male citizens." The fact that the preamble begins by calling together all of the people in the Union and not just the men suggests to her the significance of women

---

Text of Susan B. Anthony's Speech

Surely, the right of the whole people to vote is here clearly implied. For however destructive in their happiness this government might become, a disfranchised class could neither alter nor abolish it, nor institute a new one, except by the old brute force method of insurrection and rebellion. One-half of the people of this nation to-day are utterly power- less to blot from the statute books an unjust law, or to write there a new and a just one. The women, dissatisfied as they are with this form of government, that enforces taxation without representation,— that compels them to obey laws to which they have never given their consent,— that imprisons and hangs them without a trial by a jury of their peers, that robs them, in marriage, of the custody of their own persons, wages and children,—are this half of the people left wholly at the mercy of the other half, in direct violation of the spirit and letter of the declarations of the framers of this government, every one of which was based on the immutable principle of equal rights to all. By those declarations, kings, priests, popes, aristocrats, were all alike dethroned, and placed on a common level politically, with the lowliest born subject or serf. By them, too, men, as such, were deprived of their divine right to rule, and placed on a political level with women. By the practice of those declarations all class and caste distinction will be abolished; and slave, serf, plebeian, wife, woman, all alike, bound from their subject position to the proud platform of equality.

The preamble of the federal constitution says:

"We, the people of the United States, in order to form a more perfect union, establish justice, insure domestic tranquility, provide for the common defense, promote the general welfare and secure the blessings of liberty to ourselves and our posterity, do ordain and establish this constitution for the United States of America."

Guided Close Reading
with Text-Dependent Questions

within the Constitution: that the Constitution formed a government that did not confer the "blessings of liberty" but was intended to "secure" them for both men and women. Women, then, must be granted the right to vote in order not to make a "mockery" of the way in which citizens protect and defend the "blessings of liberty" within a democratic-republican government.

14. How does Anthony define the difference between a monarchy and a republic? What is the importance of this distinction for Anthony's argument?

Anthony claims that in a monarchy, certain people are "helpless, powerless, bound to obey laws made by superiors." On the other hand, in a republic, all people have "equal power, to make and unmake both their laws and lawmakers." By making this distinction, Anthony implicitly shows that the way women are currently treated by the government is not representative of a republic, but rather is more in line with the monarchical rule that the United States was founded in opposition to.

15. What is the meaning of Anthony's reference to a 15-million-headed monster?

Her point is that from the perspective of a powerless serf (i.e., from the vantage point of a woman), there is no essential difference between a monarch in the form of a single czar and the tyrannical rule of 15 million men: both effectively reduce women to the position of slaves.

16. Explain how, following Anthony's logic, the "only question left to be settled" is "Are women persons?"

Throughout her speech, Anthony argues that the founding documents of the United States give all citizens certain rights, and that in a republic, the rights of citizens cannot be taken away by the government. As the right to vote is not merely one among many God-given rights but the most important liberty a citizen can exercise, a government cannot

---

Text of Susan B. Anthony's Speech

It was we, the people, not we, the white male citizens, nor yet we, the male citizens; but we, the whole people, who formed this Union. And we formed it, not to give the blessings of liberty, but to secure them; not to the half of ourselves and the half of our posterity, but to the whole people—women as well as men. And it is downright mockery to talk to women of their enjoyment of the blessings of liberty while they are denied the use of the only means of securing them provided by this democratic-republican government—the ballot. . . .

What, I ask you, is the distinctive difference between the inhabitants of a monarchical and those of a republican form of government, save that in the monarchical the people are subjects, helpless, powerless, bound to obey laws made by superiors—while in the republican, the people are citizens, individual sovereigns, all clothed with equal power, to make and unmake both their laws and law makers, and the moment you deprive a person of his right to a voice in the government, you degrade him from the status of a citizen of the republic, to that of a subject, and it matters very little to him whether his monarch be an individual tyrant, as is the Czar of Russia, or a 15,000,000 headed monster, as here in the United States; he is a powerless subject, serf or slave; not a free and independent citizen in any sense . . .

The only question left to be settled, now, is: Are women persons? And I hardly believe any of our opponents will have the hardihood to say they are not. Being persons, then, women are citizens, and no state has a right to make any new law, or to enforce any old law, that shall abridge their privileges or immunities. Hence, every discrimination against women in the constitutions and laws of the several states, is to-day null and void, precisely as is every one against negroes.

Text of Susan B. Anthony's Speech

Is the right to vote one of the privileges or immunities of citizens? [It is] the one without which all the others are nothing . . .

Guided Close Reading
with Text-Dependent Questions

eliminate or curtail that right and remain republican in character. Since she believes [but does not argue] that all persons are citizens, the only question left in determining whether women should be allowed to exercise their natural right to vote in a republic is whether or not women are persons—a proposition so obvious that she claims, "I hardly believe any of our opponents will have the hardihood to say they are not."

160

CLOSE READING C   Student Handout

Text of Susan B. Anthony's Speech

Friends and Fellow-citizens: I stand before you to-night, under indictment for the alleged crime of having voted at the last Presidential election, without having a lawful right to vote. It shall be my work this evening to prove to you that in thus voting, I not only committed no crime, but, instead, simply exercised my *citizen's right*, guaranteed to me and all United States citizens by the National Constitution, beyond the power of any State to deny.

Our democratic-republican government is based on the idea of the natural right of every individual member thereof to a voice and a vote in making and executing the laws. We assert the province of government to be to secure the people in the enjoyment of their unalienable rights. We throw to the winds the old dogma that governments can give rights. Before governments were organized, no one denies that each individual possessed the right to protect his own life, liberty and property. And when 100 or 1,000,000 people enter into a free government, they do not barter away their natural rights; they simply pledge themselves to protect each other in the enjoyment of them, through prescribed judicial and legislative tribunals. They agree to abandon the methods of brute force in the adjustment of their differences, and adopt those of civilization.

Guided Close Reading with Text-Dependent Questions

1. While reading the first paragraph, what two things do you learn about Susan B. Anthony?

2. What document does Anthony claim gives her the right to vote?

3. Why was it a crime for Anthony to vote in the last presidential election?

4. In the context of the second paragraph, what is the meaning of *inalienable?* How does it inform Anthony's definition of a natural right?

5. Given what Anthony says in the second paragraph, what can you infer about what she thinks the role of government is?

Text of Susan B. Anthony's Speech

6. **How does Anthony connect her refutation of the "old dogma" in paragraph 2 to the documents written by the "fathers" mentioned in paragraph 3?**

Nor can you find a word in any of the grand documents left us by the fathers that assumes for government the power to create or to confer rights. The Declaration of Independence, the United States Constitution, the constitutions of the several states and the organic laws of the territories, all alike propose to protect the people in the exercise of their God-given rights. Not one of them pretends to bestow rights.

7. **What can you infer about the purpose and source of the lengthy quotation offered by Anthony that begins "All men are created equal . . ."?**

"All men are created equal, and endowed by their Creator with certain unalienable rights. Among these are life, liberty and the pursuit of happiness. That to secure these, governments are instituted among men, deriving their just powers from the consent of the governed."

8. **How does Anthony's explanation of the quotation support her overarching claim?**

Here is no shadow of government authority over rights, nor exclusion of any from their full and equal enjoyment. Here is pronounced the right of all men, and "consequently," as the Quaker preacher said, "of all women," to a voice in the government. And here, in this very first paragraph of the declaration, is the assertion of the natural right of all to the ballot; for, how can "the consent of the governed" be given, if the right to vote be denied. Again:

9. **Paraphrase the quotation that starts with "That whenever any form of government . . ." in your own words.**

"That whenever any form of government becomes destructive of these ends, it is the right of the people to alter or abolish it, and to institute a new government, laying its foundations on such principles, and organizing its powers in such forms as to them shall seem most likely to effect their safety and happiness."

Guided Close Reading
with Text-Dependent Questions

10. **What is the significance of the quote for Anthony's argument?**

11. **What does Anthony claim is "in direct violation of the spirit and letter of the declarations of the framers of this government"?**

12. **What clues are in this passage as to the meaning of the word** *serf*? **Does** *serf* **have a negative or positive connotation in this context?**

13. **What importance does the first line of the preamble to the federal Constitution have for Anthony's argument?**

Text of Susan B. Anthony's Speech

Surely, the right of the whole people to vote is here clearly implied. For however destructive in their happiness this government might become, a disfranchised class could neither alter nor abolish it, nor institute a new one, except by the old brute force method of insurrection and rebellion. One-half of the people of this nation to-day are utterly power- less to blot from the statute books an unjust law, or to write there a new and a just one. The women, dissatisfied as they are with this form of government, that enforces taxation without representation,— that compels them to obey laws to which they have never given their consent,— that imprisons and hangs them without a trial by a jury of their peers, that robs them, in marriage, of the custody of their own persons, wages and children,—are this half of the people left wholly at the mercy of the other half, in direct violation of the spirit and letter of the declarations of the framers of this government, every one of which was based on the immutable principle of equal rights to all. By those declarations, kings, priests, popes, aristocrats, were all alike dethroned, and placed on a common level politically, with the lowliest born subject or serf. By them, too, men, as such, were deprived of their divine right to rule, and placed on a political level with women. By the practice of those declarations all class and caste distinction will be abolished, and slave, serf, plebeian, wife, woman, all alike, bound from their subject position to the proud platform of equality.

The preamble of the federal constitution says:

"We, the people of the United States, in order to form a more perfect union, establish justice, insure domestic tranquility, provide for the common defense, promote the general welfare and secure the blessings of liberty to ourselves and our posterity, do ordain and establish this constitution for the United States of America."

Text of Susan B. Anthony's Speech

It was we, the people, not we, the white male citizens, nor yet we, the male citizens; but we, the whole people, who formed this Union. And we formed it, not to give the blessings of liberty, but to secure them; not to the half of ourselves and the half of our posterity, but to the whole people—women as well as men. And it is downright mockery to talk to women of their enjoyment of the blessings of liberty while they are denied the use of the only means of securing them provided by this democratic-republican government—the ballot. . . .

What, I ask you, is the distinctive difference between the inhabitants of a monarchical and those of a republican form of government, save that in the monarchical the people are subjects, helpless, powerless, bound to obey laws made by superiors—while in the republican, the people are citizens, individual sovereigns, all clothed with equal power, to make and unmake both their laws and law makers, and the moment you deprive a person of his right to a voice in the government, you degrade him from the status of a citizen of the republic, to that of a subject, and it matters very little to him whether his monarch be an individual tyrant, as is the Czar of Russia, or a 15,000,000 headed monster, as here in the United States; he is a powerless subject, serf or slave; not a free and independent citizen in any sense . . . .

The only question left to be settled, now, is: Are women persons? And I hardly believe any of our opponents will have the hardihood to say they are not. Being persons, then, women are citizens, and no state has a right to make any new law, or to enforce any old law, that shall abridge their privileges or immunities. Hence, every discrimination against women in the constitutions and laws of the several states, is to-day null and void, precisely as is every one against negroes.

14. **How does Anthony define the difference between a monarchy and a republic? What is the importance of this distinction for Anthony's argument?**

15. **What is the meaning of Anthony's reference to a 15-million-headed monster?**

16. **Explain how, following Anthony's logic, the "only question left to be settled" is "Are women persons?"**

Guided Close Reading
with Text-Dependent Questions

Text of Susan B. Anthony's Speech

Is the right to vote one of the privileges or immunities of citizens? [It is] the one without which all the others are nothing . . . .

Connecting to the Writing Prompt

This is an appropriate time to return to the writing prompt for this unit. Encourage students to review the documents they encountered in Lessons 7, 8, and 9. Which documents are relevant to the prompt? What helpful information do they provide? Give students the opportunity to continue their evidence logs.

Consider using the "Two-Minute Interview" activity, described in the "Teaching Strategies" section of our website at facinghistory.org/reconstruction-era/strategies, to give students the opportunity to share the evidence they have collected and identify questions they have about what they are learning.

After the activity, have students reflect in their journals on the following questions:

- How has what you have learned about the significant changes to the United States's universe of obligation during Reconstruction and the forms of inequality that persisted during the era changed your thinking about the prompt?

- What did you learn from the activity today? How does this information relate to the essay prompt?

- What else do you want to know?

SECTION 5
BACKLASH AND THE FRAGILITY OF DEMOCRACY

This section contains the following lessons:

LESSON 10 Backlash and the Ku Klux Klan

ESSENTIAL QUESTIONS

How should a democratic society respond to violence and terror? What power do bystanders and upstanders have in the response?

TRANSITION

In the previous two lessons, students learned about the transformation of American democracy that occurred as a result of Radical Reconstruction, and they explored some of its limitations. In this lesson, students will learn about the violent response these changes provoked from Americans who were opposed to Radical Reconstruction and shocked by the attempt to overthrow white supremacy in Southern society. By learning about the violence and intimidation perpetrated by the Ku Klux Klan in the 1860s and early 1870s, students will reflect on the effects that violence and terror can have on the choices made by individuals in a democracy.

RATIONALE

Lecturing on Reconstruction, historian David Blight argued: "Every revolution we have causes a counter-revolution." Indeed, the unprecedented period of interracial democracy that occurred after the passage of Radical Reconstruction policies also touched off a determined, violent backlash in the South.

By exploring the first stages of this backlash against interracial democracy, largely carried out by the secretive organization known as the Ku Klux Klan, this lesson probes the nature of violence, the effects of violence and intimidation on democracy, and what it takes to prevent or overcome such a backlash. The history of the Klan in the 1860s and early 1870s and the federal response to its actions together raise important questions about democracy, change, and violence:

- Is backlash inevitable in a time of great change?

- What motivates people to commit acts of violence? What are the roles of hatred, fear, and the loss of power in inspiring violent acts?

- How do the effects of violence and intimidation highlight the fragility of democracy?

- How can a democratic society respond to violence and overcome the effects of terror? What power do bystanders and upstanders have in the response?

The Formation of the Ku Klux Klan

The Ku Klux Klan was a collection of local extremist groups loosely affiliated (rather than centrally planned) around a unity of purpose: white supremacy. According to historian Eric Foner, "The Klan during Reconstruction offers the most extensive example of homegrown terrorism in American history."[1] First appearing in Tennessee in 1865, the Klan rose to prominence during the 1868 presidential election. Klansmen killed thousands of freedpeople and Republican supporters across the South, and they injured and threatened scores more. They often visited their victims at night, wearing hoods and robes to preserve anonymity and provoke fear.

In this lesson, students will explore what fueled the spread of the Klan and its acts of violence and intimidation. In one document in the lesson, W. E. B. Du Bois offers some provocative insights into the motivation for violence (from his 1935 book on Reconstruction). For Du Bois, hatred and human depravity are not sufficient explanations; he sees in every Klan group a "nucleus of ordinary men" driven by fear— of being "declassed, degraded, or actually disgraced"—and emboldened by the promise of anonymity. Records, such as those kept by the US Army major Lewis Merrill in South Carolina, show that, indeed, many business leaders, doctors, lawyers, and other prominent community members participated in the Klan. That Merrill was able to keep such documentation suggests that their hoods did not provide Klansmen with quite the level of anonymity they desired.

The Effects of Klan Violence

Regardless of the factors that fueled Klan violence, such attacks countered the spread of democracy during Radical Reconstruction. In the 1868 presidential election, few if any votes were cast for the Republican candidate, Ulysses S. Grant, in many heavily Republican Southern counties where Klan violence took place. Grant won the election anyway, and those who did vote Republican, as Abram Colby testifies in a document in this lesson, often later became Ku Klux Klan victims. The direct effects of violence on the ballot box are clear, but widespread brutality also chipped away at many citizens' confidence in the legitimacy of Republican-led government. As one victim of the Ku Klux Klan declared, "I consider a government that does not protect its citizens a failure."[2] As students will explore in lessons to come, unfounded doubts about the legitimacy and competence of government run by Republicans helped to undermine support for Reconstruction as the 1870s progressed.

Responding to Violence

Few good options existed for Southern states to respond effectively to Klan violence. Many Southern governors were hamstrung in fighting back against Klan violence because their state militias were largely comprised of African Americans. According to historian Michael Perman, these governors were faced with an impossible dilemma: using their militias against the Klan would exacerbate the perception of "Negro rule" fueling much of the violence, but not responding to the violence at all would signal weakness and fuel the belief that their governments were incompetent and illegitimate.[3]

The story of Yorkville, South Carolina, raises important questions about the role of bystanders and upstanders in responding to the Klan. As reports of widespread Klan violence around Yorkville reached Washington, Major Lewis Merrill was assigned to

---

1 Eric Foner, *Forever Free: The Story of Emancipation and Reconstruction* (Vintage Books, 2006), 171.

2 Quoted in "Illegitimacy and Insurgency in the Reconstructed South," in Michael Perman and Amy M. Taylor, eds., *Major Problems in the Civil War and Reconstruction: Documents and Essays*, 3rd ed. (Boston: Wadsworth/Cengage Learning, 2011), 456.

3 Ibid.

the area to monitor conditions there. Skeptical of the dramatic reports of violence he received before arriving, Merrill was shocked by the frequency and ferocity of the Klan brutality he witnessed. Without authority to make arrests or use force to stop the violence, Merrill compiled meticulous documentation of Klan activity and was able to identify many of the leaders and perpetrators in his records. He also tried to marshal public opinion against the violence. As an article in this lesson from the local Yorkville newspaper describes, he succeeded in persuading community leaders to publish a plea for an end to the violence. But many of those who signed the article were Klan members themselves, and the violence did not stop. Merrill continued to gather evidence that would eventually prove critical after the federal government decided to intervene. First, Congress would have to act.[4]

In 1870 and 1871, Congress passed a series of laws known as the Enforcement Acts. The third of these laws is known as the Ku Klux Klan Act, and it, especially, provided the federal government with the power to respond to Klan violence and intimidation. With the passage of this law, according to Eric Foner, "conspiracies to deprive citizens of the right to vote, hold office, serve on juries, and enjoy the equal protection of the laws could now, if states failed to act effectively against them, be prosecuted by federal district attorneys, and even lead to military intervention and the suspension of the writ of habeas corpus."[5] This was the first law that enabled the federal government to put individual citizens on trial for a federal crime. Using the powers provided by the Ku Klux Klan Act, President Grant sent federal troops to South Carolina to arrest more than 500 Klansmen in York County alone, based on Merrill's evidence. Thousands of Klansmen were prosecuted nationwide. While only a small percentage of prosecutions led to convictions and prison sentences, Klan violence dramatically subsided by 1872. Thousands of Klansmen fled their home states and ceased Klan activities to avoid prosecution.

The federal response to the Klan in South Carolina made many Americans uneasy; they worried that the federal government had gone too far in interfering in the affairs of a state. The Ku Klux Klan trials prompted Frederick Douglass to declare, "The law on the side of freedom is of great advantage only when there is power to make that law respected." In 1872, it remained an open question whether or not the federal government would be willing to exercise such power again.[6] Because so many Klan members avoided prosecution and prison, conditions were ripe for a second wave of violence and backlash later in the 1870s.

LEARNING GOALS

Understanding: Students will understand that:

- Significant political and social change often provokes a backlash when large portions of the population do not support the change.

- Backlash is often rooted in people's fear of losing power and status, or in their belief that others have received undeserved power.

- When backlash includes violence and intimidation, it is corrosive to democracy.

---

4 Stephen Budiansky, *The Bloody Shirt: Terror After the Civil War* (Penguin, 2008), 107–146.
5 Eric Foner, *Reconstruction: America's Unfinished Revolution, 1863–1877*, Perennial Classics ed. (HarperCollins, 2002), 454–455.
6 Foner, *Reconstruction*, 457–458.

- The law and its enforcement by the government can play a powerful role in protecting the rights and freedom of individuals.

Knowledge: *Students will know that:*

- The Ku Klux Klan carried out the first significant violent backlash against Radical Reconstruction in the South by using terror, brutality, and secrecy to influence elections.

- Congress passed important laws in 1870 and 1871 to enforce the provisions of Radical Reconstruction. One of these laws, the Ku Klux Klan Act, empowered the federal government to arrest and put on trial individuals who participated in Klan activities. As a result, by 1872, Klan activity in the South was drastically reduced.

- Belief in white supremacy persisted throughout the country, providing fertile ground for continued backlash after 1872.

RESOURCE LIST

- "Klansmen Broke My Door Open" (document)
- "Essential Quote Worksheet" (activity)
- "A Nucleus of Ordinary Men" (document)
- "Collaborators and Bystanders" (document)
- "Protecting Democracy" (document)
- "Responding to Violence: Public Opinion and the Law" (document)
- "The Range of Human Behavior" (document)
- "Analyzing the Causes of Ku Klux Klan Violence" (activity)

LESSON PLAN

ESTIMATED DURATION: 2 CLASS PERIODS

SKILLS ADDRESSED:

- **Literacy:** Determining central ideas or themes of a text and analyzing their development
- **Historical thinking:** Causation—identifying, analyzing, and evaluating multiple cause-and-effect relationships in a historical context
- **Social-emotional:** Responsible decision making—reflecting on decisions made by people in history and the factors that influenced their decisions

DAY ONE

I. Introduce the Concept of Backlash

This lesson offers students their first opportunity to confront the significant violence that occurred during Reconstruction. To provide a framework for understanding some of the violence that occurred during this time, it is helpful to start this lesson by introducing the concepts of *backlash* and *counter-revolution*. Students can then begin to think about possible factors that motivate individuals or groups to commit acts of violence toward others.

PROCEDURE

1. Write the following sentences on the board:

    - "Every revolution we have causes a *counter-revolution*."—Historian David Blight

    - Radical Reconstruction was followed by a violent *backlash* in the former Confederate states.

2. Prompt students to use those sentences to write working definitions for the terms *counter-revolution* and *backlash* in their journals. Remind them that a working definition is one that they can expand, focus, or revise as they learn more about a concept.

3. Ask for volunteers to share their working definitions. Copy the key ideas that they share about these concepts on the board for other students to use to sharpen their definitions. For your reference, here are the *Oxford New American Dictionary*'s definitions for these terms:

    - *Backlash*: a strong and adverse reaction by a large number of people, especially to a social or political development

    - *Counter-revolution*: a revolution opposing a former one or reversing its results

4. Now explain to students that Radical Reconstruction and the interracial democracy that resulted from it provoked a backlash. Ask students to identify what changes brought about by Radical Reconstruction might have prompted some Americans to have a strong adverse reaction.

II. Read and Respond to "The Klansmen Broke My Door Open"

Handout 10.1 ("The Klansmen Broke My Door Open") provides firsthand testimony about the violence and terror inflicted on black Southerners by the Ku Klux Klan in the late 1860s and early 1870s. It is important to give students time, space, and structure to process this story both individually and together.

PROCEDURE

1. Ask students to reflect in their journals on the following question: *Why might someone join a group that advocates racial violence?* Have them discuss thoughts together in pairs or as a group.

2. Many students will have heard of the Ku Klux Klan, but their knowledge about its activity during Reconstruction may be inaccurate or incomplete. Transition to the reading by using information from this lesson's rationale to provide brief background information about the formation of the Ku Klux Klan in the late 1860s.

3. Distribute **Handout 10.1** and read it aloud once as a whole group. Then give students time to reread the document. As they do so, have them record the following in their journals:

- One sentence from the document that they find surprising, interesting, or troubling

- One word that describes their experience reading this testimony

Process the document as a whole group using the "Wraparound" strategy, which can be found at facinghistory.org/reconstruction-era/strategies. Start with the sentences students recorded. One at a time, have students share their sentences. It often works best to have students simply respond in the order in which they are sitting. This way, you do not have to call on students to respond; once their neighbor has had a turn, students know it is their turn to present. Be sure to tell students not to say anything except the sentence they identified, because otherwise the activity will lose the desired effect. *It is okay if the same sentence is read more than one time.*

4. After everyone has shared, you can ask students to report back on common themes that have emerged or on something that surprised them.

5. Repeat the activity a second time, asking students to read the word they wrote down to describe their experience reading the testimony.

III. Complete Exit Cards

Before ending the first day of this lesson, consider applying the "Exit Card" strategy by having students complete cards for you to review. Exit cards require students to answer particular questions on a piece of paper that is turned in before they leave class. These cards provide teachers with immediate information that can be used to assess students' understanding, monitor students' questions, or gather feedback on teaching. Visit facinghistory.org/reconstruction-era/strategies for more information on the "Exit Card" strategy.

Provide each student with an index card or half-sheet of paper, and then ask them to write a question, comment, or concern about today's class.

DAY TWO

IV. Acknowledge Exit Cards

Begin the second day of this lesson by acknowledging the exit cards that students completed at the end of the first day. Point out any patterns that you noticed in the students' comments and address any questions you received that might pertain to the experiences of the class as a whole. Unless you have permission from students, it is usually best to keep anonymous the authors of any specific exit card comments you discuss.

V. Analyze Documents and Reflect on Human Behavior

It is important that students not only learn about the violent backlash perpetrated by white supremacist groups such as the Ku Klux Klan but also reflect on the variety of factors that made such violence possible and acceptable to so many in American society during the Reconstruction era. The purpose of exploring the roots of this violence is not to justify it or to build empathy for its perpetrators but to better understand the factors that encourage and normalize such actions so that we may be vigilant in guarding against them in our own society. Students will read a variety of documents that provide more detail about the aspects of human behavior that seemed to drive the violence of the Klan, as well as some of the factors that helped to combat Klan activity by 1872. Students will reflect on the factors that made violence possible by selecting quotations from the documents, sharing the quotations with classmates, and finding common themes between them.

PROCEDURE

1. Distribute the "Essential Quote Worksheet" activity (**Handout 10.2**) to the class. Also give each student one of the following: "A Nucleus of Ordinary Men," "Collaborators and Bystanders," "Protecting Democracy," or "Responding to Violence: Public Opinion and the Law" (**Handouts 10.3, 10.4, 10.5,** and **10.6**).

2. Explain to students that the handouts provide evidence to help answer the following question: *What factors made Ku Klux Klan violence possible and acceptable to so many Americans as a reaction to Reconstruction and interracial democracy?*

3. Prompt students to read their assigned documents. You might choose to have students read together with others who have the same handout. After reading, each student will independently choose one "essential quote" from his or her document that helps to answer the question above.

4. After choosing quotations, students can complete boxes 1–3 on the worksheet.

5. Next, students will find a partner who has a different handout, share their quotations, and discuss how their quotations are related to each other. Do their ideas corroborate, complement, or contradict each other? After their partner discussions, students can complete boxes 4–6 on their worksheets.

6. Students will then find a new partner who has yet a different handout from those already represented on their worksheets. They will share and discuss their quotations, completing box 7 in the process.

7. Students will use the "final link" box (box 8) on their worksheets to link their quotation to one of the quotations on **Handout 10.7**, "The Range of Human Behavior." Before asking students to make this final link, distribute the handout and read it together.

8. Complete this activity by returning to the focusing question in Step 2. Ask students to review the notes they have taken on their worksheets and then write a short reflection in response to the question in their journals.

VI. Diagram the Causes of Klan Violence

In order to help students consolidate what they have learned and sharpen their reflections on the causes and nature of Ku Klux Klan violence as backlash to Reconstruction, consider using the "Iceberg Diagram" strategy. You can use this graphic organizer as the basis for a class discussion, or you can assign students the task of completing it independently as an assessment. (Visit facinghistory.org/reconstruction-era/strategies for more on iceberg diagrams.)

PROCEDURE

1. **Introduce the metaphor:** Ask students what they know about icebergs, or show them a picture of an iceberg, focusing on the idea that what you see

above the water is only the tip of the iceberg. The larger foundation rests below the surface. Pass out **Handout 10.8**, "Analyzing the Causes of Ku Klux Klan Violence," which includes a diagram of an iceberg. Alternatively you can have students draw their own diagrams in their journals.

2. **The tip of the iceberg:** In or around the tip of the iceberg, ask students to list all the facts they know about Ku Klux Klan violence in the late 1860s and early 1870s. Questions they should answer include: *What happened? What choices were made in this situation? By whom? Who was affected? When did it happen? Where did it happen?*

3. **Beneath the surface:** Ask students to think about what factors caused or enabled Klan violence. Answers to the question *What factors made Ku Klux Klan violence possible and acceptable to so many Americans as a reaction to Reconstruction and interracial democracy?* should be written in the bottom part of the iceberg (under the water line). If you are using this activity as an assessment, students should complete this part independently. If not, consider letting students work in small groups. Remind students to use the terms *perpetrator, collaborator, bystander, resister,* and *upstander* when appropriate in their analysis.

4. **Debrief:** Prompts you might use to guide journal writing and/or class discussion include:

   - Of the causes listed in the bottom part of the iceberg, which were corroborated by more than one document? Were any mentioned in one document and then contradicted in another?

   - Of the causes listed in the bottom part of the iceberg, which one or two do you think were most significant? Why?

   - What more would you need to know in order to better understand the factors that made Klan violence possible?

   - What could have happened, if anything, to prevent the rise of Ku Klux Klan violence?

KLANSMEN BROKE MY DOOR OPEN

The following is excerpted from the 1872 testimony of Abram Colby, an African American legislator from Georgia, given before a congressional committee formed to investigate violence against freedpeople in the South.

Colby: On the 29th of October 1869, [the Klansmen] broke my door open, took me out of bed, took me to the woods and whipped me three hours or more and left me for dead. They said to me, "Do you think you will ever vote another damned Radical ticket?" I said, "If there was an election tomorrow, I would vote the Radical ticket." They set in and whipped me a thousand licks more, with sticks and straps that had buckles on the ends of them.

Question: What is the character of those men who were engaged in whipping you?

Colby: Some are first-class men in our town. One is a lawyer, one a doctor, and some are farmers. They had their pistols and they took me in my night-clothes and carried me from home. They hit me five thousand blows. I told President Grant the same that I tell you now. They told me to take off my shirt. I said, "I never do that for any man." My drawers fell down about my feet and they took hold of them and tripped me up. Then they pulled my shirt up over my head. They said I had voted for Grant and had carried the Negroes against them. About two days before they whipped me they offered me $5,000 to go with them and said they would pay me $2,500 in cash if I would let another man go to the legislature in my place. I told them that I would not do it if they would give me all the county was worth.

The worst thing was my mother, wife and daughter were in the room when they came. My little daughter begged them not to carry me away. They drew up a gun and actually frightened her to death. She never got over it until she died. That was the part that grieves me the most.

Question: How long before you recovered from the effects of this treatment?

Colby: I have never got over it yet. They broke something inside of me. I cannot do any work now, though I always made my living before in the barber-shop, hauling wood, etc.

Question: You spoke about being elected to the next legislature?

Colby: Yes, sir, but they run me off during the election. They swore they would kill me if I stayed. The Saturday night before the election I went to church. When I got home they just peppered the house with shot and bullets.[1]

---

1 In Dorothy Sterling, ed., *The Trouble They Seen: The Story of Reconstruction in the Words of African Americans* (Da Capo Press, 1994), 374–375.

ESSENTIAL QUOTE WORKSHEET

1) Your **essential quote:**	2) Why did you pick this quote?

3) What does this quotation reveal about the factors that make violence possible and acceptable in a society?	4) Your partner's **essential quote** (describe what is it about):

5) Link your essential quote to your partner's essential quote. (Does it corroborate, complement, or contradict?)	6) What does this quotation reveal about the factors that make violence possible and acceptable in a society?

7) Link your essential quote to someone else's in class. (Does it corroborate, complement, or contradict?)	8) **Final link:** Link your essential quote to one from the handout "The Range of Human Behavior." (Does it corroborate, complement, or contradict?)

A NUCLEUS OF ORDINARY MEN

In his 1935 book Black Reconstruction in America, *W. E. B. Du Bois analyzes the sources of the power of the Ku Klux Klan this way:*

The method of force which hides itself in secrecy is a method as old as humanity. The kind of thing that men are afraid or ashamed to do openly, and by day, they accomplish secretly, masked, and at night. The method has certain advantages. It uses Fear to cast out Fear; it dares things at which open method hesitates; it may with a certain impunity attack the high and the low; it need hesitate at no outrage of maiming or murder; it shields itself in the mob mind and then throws over all a veil of darkness which becomes glamor. It attracts people who otherwise could not be reached. It harnesses the mob.

. . . Total depravity, human hate . . . do not explain fully the mob spirit in America. Before the wide eyes of the mob is ever the Shape of Fear. Back of the writhing, yelling, cruel-eyed demons who break, destroy, maim and lynch and burn at the stake, is a knot, large or small, of normal human beings, and these human beings at heart are desperately afraid of something. Of what? Of many things, but usually of losing their jobs, being declassed, degraded, or actually disgraced; of losing their hopes, their savings, their plans for their children; of the actual pangs of hunger, of dirt, of crime. And of all this, most ubiquitous in modern industrial society is that fear of unemployment.

It is its nucleus of ordinary men that continually gives the mob its initial and awful impetus. Around this nucleus, to be sure, gather snowball-wise all manner of flotsam, filth and human garbage, and every lewdness of alcohol and current fashion. But all this is the horrible covering of this inner nucleus of Fear.[1]

---

1 W. E. B. Du Bois, *Black Reconstruction in America, 1860–1880* (Free Press, 1999), 677.

COLLABORATORS AND BYSTANDERS

Historian Eric Foner writes that the Ku Klux Klan drew support from many more people than those who directly committed violent or threatening acts against freedpeople and white Republicans. He explains:

> Of course most white southerners did not commit criminal acts, and some spoke out against the Klan. But the large majority of southern whites remained silent. Indeed, the Democratic Party's constant vilification of carpetbaggers and scalawags as corrupt incompetents, their insistence that blacks were unfit for equal citizenship, and their public laments about the intractability of black labor created an atmosphere that made violence seem a legitimate response in the eyes of many white southerners. Community support for the Klan extended to lawyers who represented the criminals in court, editors who established funds for their defense, and the innumerable women who sewed costumes and disguises for them. While most white southerners were law-abiding citizens, they seemed willing to forgive the Klan's excesses because they shared the organization's ultimate goal—the overthrow of Reconstruction and the restoration of white supremacy.[1]

---

1 Eric Foner, *Forever Free: The Story of Emancipation and Reconstruction* (Vintage Books, 2006), 174.

PROTECTING DEMOCRACY

During the 1871 congressional debate over the Ku Klux Klan Act, Rep. Robert Elliott of South Carolina argued as follows in favor of passing the bill that would allow the federal government to prosecute individuals for acts of political violence and intimidation:

"The United States shall guaranty to every State in this Union a republican form of government" [a quotation from the Constitution].

To make this clear, let us consider what is "a republican form of government" within the meaning of the Constitution? . . . It is a government having a written constitution, or organic law, which provides that its executive and legislative functions shall be exercised by persons elected by the majority of its citizens. In other words, it is a government for the people and by the people.

Assuming this definition to be correct in substance, I ask, how can a republican government be maintained in a State if the majority of electors are prevented from exercising the elective franchise by force of arms, or if members of the majority, having thus exercised it according to their consciences, are, for that cause, put in terror and subjected to murder, exile, and the lash, through "domestic violence," organized and operated by the minority for the sole purpose of acquiring a political domination in the State? . . .

. . . If you cannot now protect the loyal men of the South, then have the loyal people of this great Republic done and suffered much in vain, and your free Constitution is a mockery and a snare.[1]

---

1 *Congressional Globe*, House, 42nd Cong., 1st sess. (April 1, 1871), 389–392.

RESPONDING TO VIOLENCE: PUBLIC OPINION AND THE LAW

On May 18, 1871, the Yorkville Enquirer *of South Carolina published the following editorial describing a meeting between Major Lewis Merrill of the US Army and community leaders. Lewis was stationed near Yorkville to monitor Klan violence and gather evidence for possible prosecutions once the Ku Klux Klan Act was passed. After the meeting, the community leaders, many of them members of the Klan themselves, published a call in the* Enquirer *for an end to the violence, but it did not stop. The federal government responded by prosecuting Klan leaders, using Merrill's stockpile of evidence. These prosecutions led to an end of Klan activity for several decades and decreased violence toward supporters of Radical Reconstruction for a few years.*

A number of our citizens, by invitation, visited Major Merrill, post commandant at this place, on Saturday last, to confer upon the subject of the disorderly and turbulent spirit which has prevailed in this section of the State.

Major Merrill expressed his regrets that bands of disguised men had recently been whipping and otherwise maltreating white and colored citizens of this section. He mentioned incidents connected with each of the most recent acts of violence, which impressed those present with the idea that he is kept informed as to the operations of disguised persons in this county. He stated that he had in his possession the names of a number of the parties who had engaged in these lawless acts; and was also in possession of proof amply sufficient to convict some of the persons before any impartial jury. He seemed to be amused at the idea that the names of the guilty parties were not known to the people, and asserted that he could furnish them, and could also have such persons arrested in a few hours. He expressed the belief that the reason why these parties persisted in such acts was the certainty they felt that no person would dare to testify against them; and, in this connection, he exonerated the civil officers at what would appear to be dereliction in the discharge of their duties, by not arresting and bringing to trial the guilty persons. For the reason that victims are afraid to make complaints, no warrants are issued, and consequently the sheriff or other proper officer is powerless to make arrests.

Major Merrill frankly stated that his sole object in asking a conference was that he might induce the influential citizens of the county to adopt prompt and decisive measures to suppress any further disturbance, and thereby avoid the consequences of military interference; that he much preferred that the civil authorities should regulate their own affairs; and that he was satisfied that if the people opposed to lawlessness would unite and sustain each other and the civil authorities in suppressing such acts, domestic disorder would cease at once. He referred to the fact that a large number of the laborers in the northeastern section of the county were afraid to sleep in their houses, and that such a state of affairs could not longer be tolerated; that he was daily expecting notice that the writ of *habeas corpus* had been suspended in this county, but still hoped, by the timely action of the people, the necessity of declaring martial law would be avoided.

It is now left with our people to say whether or not they intend to regulate their own civil affairs. To succeed in restoring quiet and order, men must no longer withhold their expressed and unequivocal disapprobation. Can we longer permit the best interests of society to be imperiled without a protest, when the remedy is so plain and obvious? All unlawful acts are wrong in principle, and the only difference can be as to the remedy. In this case that remedy lies in public opinion. Let public opinion condemn violent acts as wrong, and society will no longer be afflicted with domestic disorder.

Any further repetition of acts of violence in this county, we feel assured, will be regarded by the military authorities, under the Ku-Klux act, as a denial of the equal protection of law to all of our citizens. The military will proceed, by arresting the supposed guilty parties, to suppress acts of violence, as directed under the Ku-Klux act; and parties, when arrested, will be delivered over to the United States marshal, to be tried before the United States court at Columbia, Charleston or Greenville. Under such circumstances it will be next to impossible to procure bail. The innocent as well as the guilty are liable to be suspected, and the expense of trial in the United States court will necessitate costs in procuring witnesses, counsel fees, &c., that few of our citizens can meet.

The Ku-Klux act comprehends all persons found in disguise, or in unlawful assemblies on the highways, or on the premises of another. This act will be enforced, and rigidly enforced; and unless our people at once determine that there must be no further acts of violence in the county, we will soon have occasion to observe the practical operation of the law in its utmost severity and with all its unpleasant consequences.[1]

---

1 *Report of and Testimony*, vol. 5, Congress Joint Select Committee on the Condition of Affairs in the Late Insurrectionary States (1872), 1498. Available at http://books.google.com/books?id=stgNAQAAMAAJ.

THE RANGE OF HUMAN BEHAVIOR

The quotations below can help us understand the motivations of perpetrators and bystanders in episodes of group violence during Reconstruction.

Psychologist Philip Zimbardo describes the effects of dehumanization:

"Dehumanization occurs whenever some human beings consider other human beings to be excluded from the moral order of being a human person. . . . Under such conditions, it becomes possible for normal, morally upright, and even usually idealistic people to perform acts of destructive cruelty. Not responding to the human qualities of other persons automatically facilitates inhumane actions."[1]

Psychologist Philip Zimbardo describes the effects of anonymity:

"Anything, or any situation, that makes people feel anonymous, as though no one knows who they are or cares to know, reduces their sense of personal accountability, thereby creating the potential for evil action. This becomes especially true when a second factor is added: if the situation or some agency gives them *permission* to engage in antisocial or violent action against others."[2]

Psychologist Ervin Staub discusses the role that shame and humiliation play in violence:

"Individuals, groups, or nations that pride themselves on their power and superiority react strongly when events disconfirm their beliefs about themselves or their image in others' eyes. Shame and humiliation give rise to the motivation to reassert identity and dignity, often by violent means."[3]

Psychologist Ervin Staub discusses the role of bystanders in group violence:

"Bystanders, people who witness but are not directly affected by the actions of perpetrators, help shape society by their reactions. . . . Bystanders can exert powerful influences. They can define the meaning of events and move others toward empathy or indifference. They can promote values and norms of caring, or by their passivity of participation in the system, they can affirm the perpetrators."[4]

1 Philip Zimbardo, *The Lucifer Effect: Understanding How Good People Turn Evil* (New York: Random House, 2007), 307.

2 Zimbardo, *The Lucifer Effect*, 301.

3 Ervin Staub, *Overcoming Evil: Genocide, Violent Conflict, and Terrorism* (Oxford University Press, 2013), 113.

4 Ervin Staub, *The Roots of Evil: The Origins of Genocide and Other Group Violence* (Cambridge University Press, 1989), 86–87.

ANALYZING THE CAUSES OF KU KLUX KLAN VIOLENCE

LESSON 11   Shifting Public Opinion

ESSENTIAL QUESTIONS

Are laws enough to create and sustain change? What might cause the universe of obligation of a nation to shrink?

TRANSITION

In the previous lessons, students learned about Radical Reconstruction, the interracial democracy that grew out of its enactment, and the federal efforts to protect freedpeople from backlash by the Ku Klux Klan. The successes of Radical Reconstruction prompted many of its supporters to declare the process of Reconstruction complete by 1872, but the gains made in the movement for freedom and equality for black Americans were far from secure. In this lesson, students will learn about a variety of factors that influenced white Northern public opinion to shift against Reconstruction, paving the way for future violence against freedpeople and the toppling of Republican governments in the South.

RATIONALE

By 1870, with the passage of the Fifteenth Amendment and the readmission of the last Confederate states into the Union, many Americans were already proclaiming that Reconstruction was complete. Upon the passage of the Fifteenth Amendment, Frederick Douglass himself declared, "We can now breathe a new atmosphere; we have a new earth beneath and a new sky above." In 1872, as the federal government intervened to protect freedpeople from the Ku Klux Klan, Radical Republican Charles Sumner proclaimed:

> Reconstruction is now complete. Every State is represented in the Senate, and every District is represented in the House of Representatives. Every Senator and every Representative is in his place. There are no vacant seats in either Chamber; and among the members are fellow-citizens of the African race.[1]

The Radical Republican vision of freedom and political equality seemed to be coming to fruition. Yet, according to historian David Blight, the reality that Douglass and Sumner celebrated would soon prove to be only a dream.[2] In the 1870s, Northern public opinion shifted rapidly against Reconstruction in the South, enabling Southern white Democrats to perpetrate a new wave of violence without federal interference. According to Blight, the Radical Republican vision of American society would "crumble faster than it ever came into existence."[3] This lesson will help students understand the reasons for

---

1 From Charles Sumner, speech prepared for delivery at Faneuil Hall, Sept. 3, 1872, in Edmund C. Stedman and Ellen M. Hutchinson, eds., *A Library of American Literature*, vol. 7 (New York: Charles L. Webster & Company, 1889), 77–78.
2 David Blight, Lecture 25, "The 'End' of Reconstruction: Disputed Election of 1876, and the 'Compromise of 1877,'" Open Yale course HIST 119, http://oyc.yale.edu/history/hist-119/lecture-25.
3 David Blight, Lecture 24, "Retreat from Reconstruction: The Grant Era and Paths to 'Southern Redemption,'" Open Yale course HIST 119, http://oyc.yale.edu/history/hist-119/lecture-24.

the shift in Northern public opinion, and it will prompt them to consider what it takes to sustain progress toward freedom and equality in a democracy.

The shift in Northern sentiment was the result of myriad interdependent characteristics of the political, economic, and social life of the United States in the 1870s, but historians often point to the following as primary factors that led to the shift: (1) the dissipation of "war fever" following the Civil War, (2) the explosion of corruption in politics, (3) the Panic of 1873 and the economic depression that followed, and (4) the racism of white Northerners and Southerners and their tenuous opposition to the inclusion of African Americans in the identity of the nation.

Dissipation of War Fever

The Radical Republican coalition responsible for the laws and the amendments that sought to reshape Southern society was driven in part by passions and animosities that were left over from the Civil War. Andrew Johnson's goal to restore "the Union as it was" prompted many moderate Republicans to side with the more radical members of their party in the effort to remake the South and reaffirm the Northern victory. In time, those wartime passions diminished, and as Reconstruction policies were proving successful at establishing freedom and some measure of equality for freedpeople in the South, moderate Republicans turned to other priorities. Many of the leaders of the Radical Republican movement themselves shifted to other political priorities (such as ending corruption), while others died or left Congress. Historian Michael Fitzgerald writes:

> To some extent the popularity of Radical Republicanism had grown out of wartime patriotism. With the lapse of time, anger at white Southerners was likely to recede. New issues were moving to the fore, issues involving public and corporate malfeasance rather than slavery and its evils.[4]

CORRUPTION

The 1870s marked the beginning of the Gilded Age in the United States, a period characterized by both the massive creation of wealth and an explosion of corruption and patronage carried out by Republicans and Democrats alike at all levels of government and in all regions of the country. The Grant administration was beset by a series of corruption and patronage scandals that shook many Americans' faith in the federal government. As David Blight explains, "Financial corruption became rampant in the Grant years, and . . . [this was] a huge political distraction away from the issues of the South, the issues of the freedmen, the issues of Reconstruction."[5]

Corruption existed outside of the Grant administration, from the Tammany Hall political machine run by Democrat Boss Tweed in New York City to some of the Republican state governments in the South. Opponents of Reconstruction seized on the public outrage over corruption and accused Northern "carpetbaggers" and African Americans of tyranny and misrule over white Southern Democrats. While corruption did exist in these Southern governments, as it did everywhere, many of the accusations directed at Southern states were unfounded and intended to stoke racist fears of "Negro rule" over white Americans. Fitzgerald explains:

---

4 Michael Fitzgerald, *Splendid Failure: Postwar Reconstruction in the American South* (Chicago: Ivan R. Dee, 2007), 118.
5 Blight, Open Yale Lecture 25.

Whatever went wrong, black voters were likely to get blamed, given all the racial stereotypes in play. African-American leaders were not the main actors, or the major beneficiaries in corruption, but then they didn't need to be. Even behaving like their Gilded Age peers would do immense harm.[6]

The Panic of 1873

In the spring of 1873, the US economy collapsed, ushering in a depression that would last several years. Blight explains:

> A major economic depression had hit the country . . . that led to a great deal of labor strife and violence. It meant . . . that the issues now that politicians were most concerned about, and that voters were most concerned about, particularly in the North, were things like currency, tariffs, unemployment, railroad subsidies, labor strife, whether a union had the right to strike here or the right to strike there. And across the great Midwest, among farmers, the biggest issue was the price of wheat, which dropped from two dollars a barrel to fifty cents in a year and a half. Wages for manufacturing laborers in the United States, in a year and a half, dropped by fifty percent across the country; that's for those who kept their jobs. The Panic of 1873 shifted people's minds, to say the least.[7]

Several Southern states, most notably South Carolina, fell into enormous debt as their economies collapsed, and again racists attempted to shift the blame onto African American politicians and voters. This time the charge was incompetence instead of corruption. In South Carolina, there is evidence that Republican politicians did in fact mismanage the state's finances, but it was not the fault of African Americans. Fitzgerald explains: "Irresponsible behavior by Republican officials, much of it clandestine and virtually all by whites, imperiled the reputation of their African-American constituency."[8]

Racism

The shift in Northern public opinion was partially the result of the feeling that the war was in the past and Reconstruction was complete, and it was partially the result of Americans paying greater attention to corruption and economic concerns. Yet Northerners and Southerners alike also accepted racist caricatures of the corrupt, incompetent misrule of a supposedly inferior black race in the South. Several Northern reporters, some of whom were even Radical Republicans, traveled south in the 1870s, embraced the claims of white Southern Democrats, and then passed them along in their reports to the North. The most notable example is the series of reports of James Pike in the *New York Tribune*, eventually collected in the popular 1874 book on South Carolina entitled *The Prostrate State*. Pike reported: "The civilized and educated white race was under foot, prostrate, and powerless, and the black barbarian reigned in its stead."[9] Such accounts cemented the opposition of many Americans to land redistribution or other reparations to compensate for the labor provided to the United States by generations of the families of freedpeople. Now, in the views of many Americans by 1874, Reconstruction had gone too far, African Americans as a group had become too powerful, and the protection of freedpeople was no longer worth the cost of federal intervention.

---

6 Fitzgerald, *Splendid Failure*, 108.
7 Blight, Open Yale Lecture 25.
8 Fitzgerald, *Splendid Failure*, 113.
9 Quoted in Fitzgerald, *Splendid Failure*, 113.

Events in Louisiana between 1872 and 1874 would test the patience of a Northern public turning away from Reconstruction. While Republicans won the 1872 elections for governor and the majority of seats in the legislature, Democrats also declared victory and attempted to form their own government. The attempted coup touched off a vigilante war between Democrats and Republicans across the state that repeatedly required Grant to use the federal army to keep the peace. In 1874, Democrats attempted yet another coup by forcibly installing members of their party in five vacant seats in the Louisiana legislature. The army intervened, this time by entering the state capitol building and escorting the five Democrats out. Public opinion in the North aligned solidly against this intervention, and the idea of the military entering the capitol building of a state symbolized for many a too-powerful, untrustworthy federal government violating state sovereignty and putting too much effort into buttressing Reconstruction when it should be focused on other priorities. Historian Eric Foner writes: "Louisiana now came to represent the dangers posed by excessive federal interference in local affairs. The spectacle of soldiers 'marching into the Hall . . . and expelling members at the point of bayonet' aroused more Northern opposition than any previous federal action in the South."[10] The Northern public no longer had the patience to sustain Reconstruction and defend the rights of freedpeople in the South.

LEARNING GOALS

Understanding: Students will understand that:

- The changing priorities of both ordinary citizens and leaders can have a significant effect on how a democracy enforces its laws and protects the rights of individuals.

- Public opinion is one significant factor that shapes the priorities of elected officials in a democracy. The words and actions of leaders can also shape public opinion.

- Racism is a "convenient hatred" that changes to meet the needs of society and individuals to explain unpleasant political, economic, or social circumstances.

Knowledge: Students will know that:

- Northern public opinion started to shift against Reconstruction in the early 1870s.

- The shift in public opinion was the result of a variety of factors. Fading animosity from the war, concerns over government corruption, an economic depression, and racism were all factors that helped to shift Northerners' support from sustaining Reconstruction to other political priorities.

RESOURCE LIST

- "Reconstruction Is Now Complete" (document)

- "Scapegoating and Northern Racism" (document)

---

10 Eric Foner, *Reconstruction: America's Unfinished Revolution, 1863–1877*, Perennial Classics ed. (HarperCollins, 2002), 554.

- "Society Turned Bottom-side Up" (document)

- "Refuting Charges of Corruption and Incompetence" (document)

- "Bostonians Protest Federal Intervention in Louisiana" (document)

ACTIVITY SUGGESTIONS

Consider using the following activity ideas and strategies when you implement this lesson in your classroom.

- Begin the lesson with a journal reflection on the following prompt: *What does it mean for the universe of obligation of a nation or individual to shrink? What might cause that to happen?*

- Explain to the class that in the 1870s, public opinion among Northerners shifted against Reconstruction. Use the rationale for this lesson to create a mini-lecture that describes the following factors that helped cause this shift:

  - The dissipation of "war fever" following the Civil War

  - The explosion of corruption in politics

  - The Panic of 1873 and the economic depression that followed

  - Racism in both the North and South, and white Americans' tenuous commitment to the inclusion of African Americans in the identity of the nation

- Racism in the North is an especially important factor to examine with students. It can be easy to oversimplify the conflicts of Reconstruction, giving the impression that racism was a purely Southern phenomenon. Read the short document "Scapegoating and Northern Racism"(**Handout 11.2**) as a whole group. After reading, create a concept map for *scapegoating*. Ask students to consider this question: *What does Eric Foner mean when he states that racism offered a "convenient explanation for the alleged 'failure' of Reconstruction?*

- Use the "Save the Last Word for Me" strategy to structure a small-group discussion about one or more handouts in this lesson. This strategy requires all students to participate as active speakers and listeners. You might choose to have every trio of students read and discuss the same document, or you might assign different ones to different groups. Either way, students should select quotations for the activity that reflect reasons that public opinion in the North was shifting against Reconstruction. Group discussions should focus on the journal prompt above. For more information about this strategy, visit facinghistory.org/reconstruction-era/strategies.

  We recommend that when sharing **Handout 11.3**, "Society Turned Bottom-side Up," you accompany it with "Refuting Charges of Corruption and Incompetence" (**Handout 11.4**) so that students understand that Pike's virulently racist charges are unfounded.

- Consider staging a dramatic reading of Wendell Phillips's speech in **Handout 11.5**, "Bostonians Protest Federal Intervention in Louisiana." Either the teacher or a student can read Phillips's words while the rest of the class interjects with the interruptions of the crowd. After the reading, ask students to consider what they can conclude about the energy and emotion of the event. Why do they think Bostonians cared about what happened in Louisiana? What does this event reveal about the changing public opinion over Reconstruction policies?

You might explore this debate in Boston more deeply by asking students to work in pairs to imagine an individual conversation between Wendell Phillips and one of the Boston crowd members protesting during his speech. Students can use both the resolution written by the Boston citizens and the speech by Phillips to imagine a debate between the two individuals.

Have each pair write a dialogue for such a conversation that answers these questions:

- How would the pair begin a conversation about the federal intervention in Louisiana?

- What would be the tone of their conversation?

- How would each defend his or her position on the intervention? What arguments would they make?

- How would they respond to each other's arguments? Would they find any common ground?

- What would each believe to be the most important consequences of the federal intervention in Louisiana?

RECONSTRUCTION IS NOW COMPLETE

In the 1872 election, Charles Sumner, a former Radical Republican, opposed President Grant's reelection. The following is an excerpt from a speech Sumner gave in support of Horace Greeley, the candidate endorsed by liberal Republicans and Democrats.

And has not the time arrived when in sincerity we should accept the olive-branch? Is it not time for the pen to take the place of the sword? Is it not time for the Executive Mansion to be changed from a barrack cesspool to a life-giving fountain? Is it not time for a President who will show by example the importance of reform, and teach the duty of subordinating personal objects to the public service? Is it not time for the Head of the National Government to represent the idea of peace and reconciliation, rather than of battle and strife? Is it not time for that new era, when ancient enemies, forgetting the past, shall "clasp hands" in true unity with the principles of the Declaration of Independence as the supreme law? . . . Anxious for the Equal Rights of All, and knowing well that no text of Law or Constitution is adequate without a supporting sentiment behind, I cannot miss the opportunity afforded by the present election of obtaining this strength for our great guaranties.

Reconstruction is now complete. Every State is represented in the Senate, and every District is represented in the House of Representatives. Every Senator and every Representative is in his place. There are no vacant seats in either Chamber; and among the members are fellow-citizens of the African race. And amnesty nearly universal, has been adopted. In this condition of things I find new reason for change . . . The time for the soldier has passed, especially when his renewed power would once more remind fellow-citizens of their defeat . . . It is doubtful if such a presence can promote true reconciliation. Friendship does not grow where former differences are thrust into sight. There are wounds of the mind as of the body; these, too, must be healed. Instead of irritation and pressure, let there be gentleness and generosity. Men in this world get only what they give, — prejudice for prejudice, animosity for animosity, hate for hate. Likewise confidence is returned for confidence, good-will for good-will, friendship for friendship. On this rule, which is the same for the nation as for the individual, I would now act.[1]

---

1 Transcription of primary source available at http://archive.org/stream/charlessumnerhis20sumn/charlessumnerhis20sumn_djvu.txt.

SCAPEGOATING AND NORTHERN RACISM

Historian Eric Foner writes about the effect that racism in the North had on public opinion about Reconstruction in the 1870s:

> Racism, of course, had never been eliminated from northern life . . . Despite Reconstruction, the vast majority of African Americans remained trapped in poverty, confined to menial and unskilled jobs. Nonetheless, as a result of Reconstruction, the North's public life had been opened to blacks in ways inconceivable before the Civil War. In the 1860s, the Republican Party had not only given northern blacks the right to vote, but also sought to ensure their access to public schools, and in many places worked against discriminatory practices on streetcars and railroads, and in private businesses. In the economic crisis of the 1870s, however, as the nation looked for scapegoats, racism increasingly reasserted its hold on northern thought and behavior. Engravings in popular journals depicted freedpeople not as upstanding citizens harassed by violent opponents (as had been the case immediately after the Civil War) but as little more than unbridled animals. By the mid-1870s, it was quite common in the North to write, in the words of contemporary historian Francis Parkman, of "the monstrosities of Negro rule in South Carolina." Racism, in other words, offered a convenient explanation for the alleged "failure" of Reconstruction.[1]

---

1 Eric Foner, *Forever Free: The Story of Emancipation and Reconstruction* (Vintage Books, 2006), 192.

SOCIETY TURNED BOTTOM-SIDE UP

James Pike, a journalist and Radical Republican from Maine, changed his mind about Reconstruction in the 1870s. The following is an excerpt from his popular 1874 book The Prostrate State, *about the government of South Carolina.*

Here, then, is the outcome, the ripe, perfected fruit of the boasted civilization of the South, after two hundred years of experience. A white community, gradually risen from small beginnings, till it grew into wealth, culture, and refinement and became accomplished in all arts of civilization; . . . such a community is reduced to this. It lies prostrate in the dust, ruled over by this strange conglomerate, gathered from the ranks of its own servile population. It is the spectacle of a society suddenly turned bottom-side up.

In the place of this old aristocratic society stands the rude form of the most ignorant democracy that mankind ever saw, invested with the functions of government . . . It is barbarism overwhelming civilization by physical force. It is the slave rioting in the halls of this master, and putting that master under his feet . . .

. . . As things stand, the body [legislature] is almost literally a Black Parliament . . . The Speaker is black, the Clerk is black, the door-keepers are black, the little pages are black, the chairman of the Ways and Means is black, and the chaplain is coal-black. At some of the desks sit colored men whose types it would be hard to find outside of Congo . . . It must be remembered, also, that these men, with not more than half a dozen exceptions, have been themselves slaves, and that their ancestors were slaves for generations.

The rule of South Carolina should not be dignified with the name of government . . . The men who have had it in control, and who now have it in control, are picked villains of the community. They are the highwaymen of the State. They are professional legislative robbers. They are men who have studied and practiced the art of legalized theft. They are in no sense different from, or better than, the men who fill the prisons and penitentiaries of the world. They are, in fact, of precisely that class, only more daring and audacious. They pick your pockets by law. They rob the poor and rich alike, by law. They confiscate your estate by law. They do none of these things even under the tyrant's plea of the public good or the public necessity. They do all simply to enrich themselves personally . . .

Those who suppose that any thing short of a good government in the State of South Carolina, and, we may add, of any other State similarly situated in the South, is going to long stand, or be tolerated, may well take heed . . . The present government of South Carolina is not only corrupt and oppressive, it is insulting. It denies the exercise of rights of white communities, because they are white.[1]

---

1 Excerpted from James Pike, *The Prostrate State* (New York: D. Appleton and Company, 1874). Full text available at https://archive.org/details/prostratestates00pikegoog.

REFUTING CHARGES OF CORRUPTION AND INCOMPETENCE

In 1874, a group of white South Carolinians formed a group called the Taxpayers' Convention to protest corruption and incompetence in the state government. The Associated Press distributed their protests nationwide. Black legislator F. L. Cardozo wrote a detailed response to the accusations, excerpted here, but the Associated Press refused to print it.

Whatever corruption may exist in the Legislature is to be attributed to the Democrats as well as the Republicans. They never hesitate to offer bribes when they have a private bill [a bill for benefit of someone who has given them a financial contribution] to pass. But corruption existed long before the advent of the Republican party of this State into power, only it was carried on then with the artistic skill of more experienced operators, and not easily seen.

The gentlemen who have assembled in this Convention, constituting themselves . . . representatives of the so-called taxpayers, are not what they would have the country believe. They are the prominent politicians of the old regime—the former ruling element of the State—who simply desire to regain the power they lost by their folly of secession. They are not endorsed by the masses of the sober, thinking white Democrats of the State, who look upon their action as unwise and ill-timed . . .

The Republicans admit the existence of evils amongst them. They acknowledge they have committed mistakes and errors in the past, which they deeply regret. But those mistakes and errors are being daily corrected, and they see no necessity whatever to resort to the desperate remedies asked for by convention of the so-called taxpayers. There are enough able and good men among those who have the present charge of the government in their hands to right every existing wrong. They are determined to do so.

In this work the difficulties under which they have labored have been naturally great, and have been increased ten-fold by the determined hostility and opposition of the Democratic party ever since reconstruction . . .[1]

---

1 Excerpted in William E. Gienapp, ed., *The Civil War and Reconstruction: A Documentary Collection* (New York: W. W. Norton, 2001), 400–402.

BOSTONIANS PROTEST FEDERAL INTERVENTION IN LOUISIANA

In January 1875, Louisiana Democrats, with the help of the party's militia, attempted to take over the Republican-controlled legislature by force. Federal troops entered the Louisiana capitol building to remove the Democrats and protect the elected Republican legislature. This was only the latest in a series of interventions by the military to keep the peace in Louisiana. Most Northerners grew tired of such actions, believing that Southern states should have the right to settle their own affairs. Later in January, citizens assembled in Faneuil Hall in Boston to protest the Grant administration's intervention in Louisiana. They voted to send a formal protest to Washington that included the following statements:

We, citizens of Boston, assembled in Faneuil Hall, hereby resolve, —

- That we have heard with deep indignation, that five persons, occupying seats in the Legislature of Louisiana, were forcibly removed from the Hall of the House of Representatives on the 4th day of January, 1875, by the military forces of the United States.

- That we tender our sincere sympathy to the people of Louisiana, and appeal to them to continue the forbearance which they have shown under these trying circumstances, and assure them that we will do all that in us lies to secure to each and every State in the Union, and to all the people, the maintenance of their just and inalienable rights.

- That we fondly anticipate, with a better understanding between all parts of the country, the disappearance of sectional strife, being assured that the people of the country have cordially accepted the amendments to the Constitution, and intend to protect and maintain the civil and political rights which they guarantee to all.

- That we hail with gratitude and delight the fact that we are all under one Government and one flag, and we look forward with confidence to the prosperity, peace, and happiness which belong to a free people, who make and administer their own laws.

Only Wendell Phillips, an aging abolitionist, spoke at the assembly in opposition to the protest. His speech, excerpted here, was interrupted frequently by the shouts and heckles of the protestors. The interruptions are in italics.

If these resolutions are passed — (*Great uproar.*) Men of Boston, men of Boston, if these resolutions are passed, they will carry consternation and terror into the house of every negro in Louisiana. (*A voice, "We will pass them all!" Applause, hisses, groans, laughter, cheers and cries, loud and long.*) They will carry comfort to every assassin (*a voice, "Not a bit of it!"*) in New Orleans. (*"Oh!" and loud hisses and applause.*) My anxiety is not for Washington. I don't care who is President. My anxiety is for the hunted, tortured, robbed, murdered population, white and black, of the Southern States (*a voice, "That's played out!"*) whom you are going to consign to the hands of their oppressors. (*Hisses.*)

If you pass these resolutions — (*Cries of "We will!" "We will!"*) If you pass these resolutions — (*Renewed cries of "We will!" "We will!"*) If you pass these resolutions, gentlemen (*loud cries of "We will!" "We will!"*) — I say it in the presence of God Almighty (*cries of "Sh!" "Sh!" "Oh, ho!" "Oh, ho!" hisses and voices, "He don't know you!" "Whom you don't believe in!"*) — the blood of hundreds of blacks, and hundreds of whites, will be on your skirts before the first day of January next. (*Loud laughter and hisses.*) . . .

Gentlemen, you know perfectly well, every one of you, that this nation called four millions of negroes into citizenship to save itself. (*Applause.*) It never called them for their own sakes. It called them to save itself. (*Cries of "Hear!" "Hear!"*) And today, those resolutions, offered in Faneuil Hall, condemn the President of the United States (*a voice, "Sit down!"*), and would take from him the power to protect the millions you have just lifted into danger. (*Cries of "Played out!" "Sit down!" &c.*) You won't let him protect them. (*Cries of "No!"*) What more contemptible object than a nation which, for its own selfish purpose, summons four millions of negroes to such a position of peril, and then leaves them defenseless? What more pitiable object than the President of such a nation, vested with full power to protect these hunted men (and you will not let him protect them), if he yield to this contemptible clamor, and leave them defenseless? Well, gentlemen, I have done all I intended to do. I only wanted to record the protest of one citizen of Boston (*uproarious applause*) against that series of resolutions.[1]

---

1 Transcripts from Harvard University, Collection Development Department, Widener Library, HCL, digitized at http://nrs.harvard.edu/urn-3:FHCL:8493276.

LESSON 12 Reflections of Race in Nineteenth-Century Media

ESSENTIAL QUESTION

How do racial stereotypes in the media create and reinforce "in" groups and "out" groups in a society?

TRANSITION

In the last lesson, students learned about the shift in public opinion against Reconstruction that began among Northerners in the early 1870s, and they considered the challenges of sustaining progress toward equality in a democracy. In this lesson, they will deepen their thinking about public opinion by examining the nineteenth-century American media. In particular, they will examine four widely circulated images by a single political cartoonist, Thomas Nast, during the Reconstruction era. These images will help students understand the way the media can both shape and reflect public opinion about politics and race.

RATIONALE

The power of the media to shape public opinion grew enormously in the middle of the nineteenth century. "The American press mobilized the entire electorate, tying readers together as they read and responded to a variety of printed views," writes historian Heather Cox Richardson.[1] Americans were informed about current affairs from a variety of print media, including essays, stories, novels, and travelogues, but newspapers had the largest audience. Both daily and weekly newspapers typically identified themselves with particular political parties and delivered the news to Americans through a partisan lens. The *New York World*, one of the most widely read daily newspapers, supported the Democratic Party and had a readership of about 500,000. *Harper's Weekly*, perhaps the most influential weekly newspaper, supported the Republican Party and was read by 100,000 Americans each week. Such widespread, politically filtered reporting had a profound effect on the opinions and arguments of both ordinary citizens and elected officials. Even members of Congress regularly cited newspaper reports as evidence for their arguments.[2]

With the growth of print media also came the advent of printed images in newspapers. Weekly newspapers such as *Harper's Weekly* and *Frank Leslie's Illustrated* depicted the news for their readers through wood-block engravings, line drawings, and increasingly elaborate political cartoons. (It was not yet feasible to print photographs in newspapers.) Perhaps no one popularized the art of newspaper drawings and editorial cartoons more than *Harper's Weekly*'s Thomas Nast. Richardson writes:

> *Harper's Weekly* added another dimension to popular debate by publishing
> Thomas Nast's line drawings, which, the paper editorialized, "are of an

---

1 Heather Cox Richardson, *The Death of Reconstruction: Race, Labor, and Politics in the Post-Civil War North, 1865–1901* (Cambridge, MA: Harvard University Press, 2001), x–xi.
2 Ibid.

allegorico-political character, at once poems and speeches. They argue the case to the eye, and conclusively. A few lines does the work of many words, and with the force of eloquence which no words can rival." Even the illiterate could follow a story in Nast's pictures.[3]

More than the printed word, the images created by artists such as Nast mounted powerful visual arguments that swayed the opinions of thousands. Nast depicted a variety of events and issues of his time, from politics to popular culture (he is often credited with creating the modern image of Santa Claus). The politics and realities of Reconstruction were among his most common topics. He opposed Andrew Johnson and Presidential Reconstruction with a scathing editorial cartoon in *Harper's Weekly*, and he was initially an ardent supporter of President Grant and Radical Reconstruction.

Throughout the Civil War and the Reconstruction era, freedpeople were common subjects of drawings and cartoons by newspaper artists such as Nast, and their depictions varied widely. Historian David Blight suggests that the ways in which white Northerners imagined African Americans had a profound impact on public support for Reconstruction in the South. Would white Northerners imagine freedpeople as diligent workers and students? As responsible voters and lawmakers? Or would they imagine freedpeople as inherently lazy, dependent, and childlike? As violent and dangerous? As better off under slavery or some comparable form of white domination? In the enormous number of Reconstruction-era images, black Americans were depicted in all of these contradictory ways. Therefore, the conflict over the meaning of freedom and equality for African Americans was not fought only in voting booths, statehouses, courts, plantation fields, backwoods, and town squares. It was also fought in the pages of newspapers and other media.

Nast's body of work provides a case study of the variety of often-contradictory ways that African Americans were portrayed in Reconstruction-era media. Nast's visual commentary also sheds light on the changing attitudes of many white Northerners during the 1870s and provides examples of the power of media to shape those opinions. His cartoons from the late 1860s include positive, realistic depictions of freedpeople celebrating the opportunities made possible by Emancipation. Some images even argue that black soldiers should be honored for their crucial role in winning the Civil War. However, Nast was not immune to demeaning stereotypes and misinformation. His work frequently depicted Irish immigrants as apes and Catholics and Mormons as vicious reptiles. By the mid-1870s, Nast was also employing negative racial stereotypes in his images of freedpeople. Biographer Fiona Deans Halloran explains:

> Nast never adopted an entirely positive view of black Americans. Like everyone else of his generation, he grew to maturity in a world where race usually determined destiny. The same sensitivity to cultural norms that helped the cartoonist respond to public tastes and tickle a reader's fancy made him vulnerable to stereotyping.[4]

Stereotypes of blacks as lazy, shiftless, and childlike were common in Nast's world. A new stereotype emerged during the Reconstruction era, as well: the image of the free black man as a violent and dangerous brute. It is important to have students consider what needs all of these stereotypes served and what actions by individuals and society they justified. Nast employed these stereotypes as he tempered his support for Reconstruction in the 1870s, appearing to believe the unfounded assumption that

---

3 Richardson, *The Death of Reconstruction*, xi.
4 Fiona Deans Halloran, *Thomas Nast: The Father of Modern Political Cartoons* (Chapel Hill: University of North Carolina Press, 2012), 111.

African Americans were responsible for corruption and incompetence in Southern Republican governments. As a result, Nast helped reinforce ideas about the "black race" being inferior and society being better off when African Americans were enslaved or controlled by a social and economic system similar to slavery. The images in this lesson provide powerful examples of how the media's use of stereotypes can create or reinforce "in" groups and "out" groups in the political, economic, and social life of a nation.

LEARNING GOALS

Understanding: Students will understand that:

- The media plays a powerful role in shaping people's explicit actions and unconscious beliefs about society, membership, and equality.

- The media's use of stereotypes can create or reinforce "in" groups and "out" groups in the political, economic, and social life of a nation.

Knowledge: Students will know that:

- Images of African Americans during Reconstruction document the ways that stereotypes change based on the needs of society.

- Images of African Americans reflected changing stereotypes and beliefs about the need to enforce laws protecting the rights of freedpeople.

RESOURCE LIST

- "Douglass on Media Images of African Americans" (document)

- "'Emancipation' (1865)" (image)

- "'Franchise' (1865)" (image)

- "'Colored Rule in a Reconstructed(?) State' (1874)" (image)

- "'He Wants a Change Too' (1876)" (image)

ACTIVITY SUGGESTIONS

Consider using the following activity ideas and strategies when you implement this lesson in your classroom.

- Before analyzing this lesson's images, ask students to reflect on and discuss the meaning of the term *stereotype*. You might begin this discussion with the class by sharing the following quotation by psychologist Deborah Tannen:

  > We all know we are unique individuals, but we tend to see others as representatives of groups. It's a natural tendency, since we must see the world in patterns in order to make sense of it; we wouldn't be able to deal with the daily onslaught of people and objects if we couldn't predict a lot about them and feel that we know who or what they are.[5]

---

5 Deborah Tannen, *You Just Don't Understand* (New York: Morrow, 1990), 16.

Ask students to respond to Tannen in their journals. Do they agree? What is the benefit of seeing the world in patterns and viewing others as representatives of groups? What gets lost when we categorize our experiences in this way? What kinds of stories do we attach to categories we create for people? When is it offensive or harmful to see others as representatives of groups?

Finally, ask students to write a working definition for the word *stereotype*. In their definitions, they might reflect on the word's connotation. Is it positive or negative? Does the connotation of the word imply that stereotypes are useful or harmful? When does a judgment about an individual based on the characteristics of a group become offensive? Give students the opportunity to share and refine their definitions with one or more classmates.

- Share the quotation by Frederick Douglass from **Handout 12.1**, "Douglass on Media Images of African Americans." After reading the quotation together, ask students to read it again silently and then write a short reflection in their journals, answering these questions: *What is Douglass suggesting about the power of stereotypes? How can stereotypes affect the way we think about others? How do you think stereotypes can affect how we treat others?*

- To help students look closely at and analyze the images by Thomas Nast in this lesson, try the "Crop It" strategy. This strategy requires students to notice, identify, and respond to specific portions of an image before interpreting the image's overall meaning and impact.

  To prepare for this activity, you will need to make a copy of all four images from this lesson for each student. You will also need to create cropping tools for students to use, or have students create them. Each tool consists of two *L*-shaped strips of paper (cut from the border of a blank sheet of 8 ½ x 11-inch paper). During the activity, students will use the two *L*-shaped strips to create a rectangle shape, pushing the corners together or pulling them apart to change its size. Each student should have two cropping tools to work with.

  To conduct the activity, ask students to look at each image closely. Call out some or all of the prompts below, giving students time in between to use their cropping tools to frame a portion of the image independently and then discuss their choice with a classmate or small group:

  - Identify the part of the image that first caught your eye.

  - Identify a part of the image that shows what this image is about.

  - Identify a part of the image that shows a tension, problem, or dilemma.

  - Identify a part of the image that captures an idea about membership or universe of obligation.

  - Identify a part of the image that either perpetuates or challenges a negative stereotype about African Americans.

  - Identify a part of the image that you think would have influenced the audience's opinion about whether or not freedpeople deserved protection for the freedoms and rights they gained during Reconstruction.

  As you reach the end of the prompts for each image, you might also ask students to write and explain a new title or caption for the image.

- Finish the lesson by having students reflect in their journals on the following prompt: *What examples of stereotypes have you noticed in the media today? How do racial stereotypes in the media create and reinforce "in" groups and "out" groups in a society?* Please preview these images before use as they contain stereotypical imagery of African Americans.

DOUGLASS ON MEDIA IMAGES OF AFRICAN AMERICANS

Frederick Douglass wrote the following in 1849, published in his abolitionist newspaper North Star:

Negroes can never have impartial portraits, at the hands of white artists. It seems next to impossible for white men to take likenesses of black men without most grossly exaggerating their distinctive features. Artists, like all other white persons, have adopted a theory respecting the distinctive features of Negro physiognomy. We have heard many white persons say that "Negroes look all alike," and that they could not distinguish between the old and the young. They associate with the Negro face, high cheek bones, distended nostril, depressed nose, thick lips, and retreating foreheads. This theory impressed strongly upon the mind of an artist exercises a powerful influence over his pencil, and very naturally leads him to distort and exaggerate those peculiarities, even when they scarcely exist in the original.[1]

---

1 Quoted in Joshua Brown, "True Likenesses," in Eric Foner, *Forever Free: The Story of Emancipation and Reconstruction* (Vintage Books, 2006), 35.

IMAGE

"EMANCIPATION" (1865)

Wood engraving by Thomas Nast (1865), Library of Congress

"FRANCHISE" (1865)

A previous Thomas Nast image entitled "Amnesty" depicts Columbia (the woman who represents the nation) with a group of former Confederates. She asks, "Shall I trust these men?" In the caption to this image, she continues, "And not this man?"

Wood engraving by Thomas Nast (1865), Library of Congress

"COLORED RULE IN A RECONSTRUCTED(?) STATE" (1874)

How do racial stereotypes in the media create and reinforce "in" groups and "out" groups in a society?

Wood engraving by Thomas Nast (1874), Library of Congress

"HE WANTS A CHANGE TOO" (1876)

How do racial stereotypes in the media create and reinforce "in" groups and "out" groups in a society?

Wood engraving by Thomas Nast (1876), The Newberry Digital Collection

Connecting to the Writing Prompt

Because of the number of documents and the quantity of evidence in Section 5, we recommend providing students with the opportunity to work on their evidence logs before continuing to Lesson 13. How are the documents from Lessons 10, 11, and 12 relevant to the prompt? What helpful information do they provide?

Ask students to reflect on the new evidence they have recorded. Does it confirm or conflict with their thinking about the question posed in the prompt? Has what they have learned about backlash, public opinion, and the influence of the media changed their thinking about the prompt? Have students record their thoughts in their journals.

LESSON 13 Violence, Race, and "Redemption"

ESSENTIAL QUESTIONS

What makes democracy fragile? What can be done to protect and strengthen democracy?

TRANSITION

In previous lessons, students learned about challenges to the achievements of Radical Reconstruction, including the first wave of violent backlash in Southern states and the factors that led many Northerners to turn against federal policies that protected freedpeople. In this lesson, students will confront a new, more decisive period of violence that spread across the South between 1873 and 1876. Students will reflect on the factors that led to the success of this violence in precipitating the defeat of Republican governments in the former Confederacy, and they will consider the choices available to individual citizens and government officials who did not support this campaign of violence and intimidation.

RATIONALE

From 1873 to 1876, a campaign of violence and intimidation, organized by the Democratic Party, swept across several Southern states with the goal of toppling Republican-controlled state governments and removing federal officeholders from power. Democrats at the time claimed that they were "redeeming" the South, a word that imbued their actions with a sense of religious significance. They argued that they were saving the South from evil—the "evil" of being controlled by Republicans, Northerners, and blacks. Historians continue to refer to this campaign to return the South to Democratic Party control as "Redemption," even though most agree that the literal meaning of the word is not consistent with the way that they interpret the events of this period.

By learning about the violent methods that opponents of Reconstruction used to reestablish "home rule" in the former Confederate states, students will have the opportunity to deepen their thinking about a variety of important themes in this unit. These include:

- The corrosive effects of violence and intimidation on the ability of citizens to vote their consciences and speak their minds in a democracy

- How "in" groups and "out" groups that result from racism and other socially constructed divisions in society weaken a democracy, leave some groups of citizens vulnerable, and encourage other groups to either perpetuate or accept ostracism, intimidation, and violence

- The fragility of democracy and the difficulties of responding effectively to those who desire to undermine it

Early Democratic Victories in the South

While pinpointing the end of the Reconstruction era is a topic debated by historians today, there is no dispute in dating when each state of the former Confederacy returned to Democratic Party control in the 1870s:

Year	State
1870	Tennessee
1871	Georgia
1873	Texas
1873	Virginia
1874	Alabama
1874	Arkansas
1875	Mississippi
1876	Florida
1876	Louisiana
1876	North Carolina
1876	South Carolina[1]

While violence and intimidation toward freedpeople and their white Republican allies occurred in every Southern state, by 1873 four states were already in the hands of a Democratic governor and legislature. In fact, the efforts to roll back the effects of Radical Reconstruction began as soon as those laws and policies took hold. For states in which blacks comprised small minorities of the population, "Redemption" came earliest. Tennessee and Virginia Democrats never lost control of their state legislatures, and they elected Democratic governors in 1870 and 1873, respectively. Georgia Democrats regained control of their state's legislature in 1870 and the governorship in 1871. All of these states pioneered the implementation of poll taxes and similar measures, not forbidden by the Fifteenth Amendment, to further diminish the power of the African American voting bloc.[2] Meanwhile, Texas returned to Democratic rule in 1873, largely as a result of an influx of white immigrants who generally voted Democratic.[3] These trends, combined with discontent with Republican governance in the face of the economic depression that began in 1873, enabled Democrats to regain control of the US House of Representatives in a historic landslide in 1874.

"Redemption" Violence

All of these factors combined to complicate efforts by the Grant administration to enforce Reconstruction policies and protect freedpeople; Grant no longer had the support of Congress or the public in such endeavors. As a result, a new wave of violence

---

1 Eric Foner, *Freedom's Lawmakers: A Directory of Black Officeholders during Reconstruction*, revised ed. (Baton Rouge, LA: Louisiana State University Press, 1996), xi–xxxii.

2 Eric Foner, *Reconstruction: America's Unfinished Revolution, 1863–1877*, Perennial Classics ed. (HarperCollins, 2002), 422–423.

3 Foner, *Reconstruction*, 549.

erupted in the South, and, unchecked, it spread from Louisiana to Alabama, Mississippi, and South Carolina.

The violence that swept several Southern states between 1873 and 1876 is notable for the following characteristics:

- It was planned and perpetrated by paramilitary groups allied with the Democratic Party in the South.

- These Democratic groups publicly and explicitly stated their intentions to "redeem" their states—to restore them to Democratic Party rule—by using violence and intimidation to affect elections.

- Unlike with Ku Klux Klan violence, perpetrators were not masked and often attacked political rallies and other public gatherings in broad daylight.[4]

- Perpetrators primarily targeted African American Republican voters and candidates. White Republicans were sometimes attacked and murdered, but more often they were singled out for social ostracism in their communities.

- The Democratic Party and associated paramilitary groups in the South explicitly used racism to divide their allies from their enemies.[5] They said that Democrats belonged to the "white party" while Republicans belonged to the "Negro party." White Republicans were called "traitors to their race."

The White Line and the Red Shirts

In Mississippi and Louisiana, the White Line, a paramilitary arm of the Democratic Party, instigated much of the violence. Two of the most brazen White Line attacks occurred in Louisiana in 1873 and 1874. The murder of some 100 freedmen in Colfax, Louisiana, in April 1873 constituted perhaps the greatest loss of life from any racial incident in American history. The next year at Coushatta, Louisiana, White Line members ambushed and murdered six white Republican leaders and several African American witnesses, striking a significant blow against the Republican leadership in the state. Many White Line attacks followed a similar pattern, as described by historian Michael Perman: "Whites would provoke a public racial incident, and, after the brawl or riot that ensued, white men would scour the nearby countryside in search of blacks to beat up and kill." Specific examples of incidents that followed this pattern are described in handouts in this lesson. In 1875, White Line violence resulted in Democrats winning elections for governor and a majority of seats in the legislature in Mississippi.[6]

The success of the White Line in Mississippi in 1875 inspired another Democratic paramilitary group to use violence during political campaigns the following year. This group, the Red Shirts, was mostly associated with South Carolina, but they were also active in North Carolina. Red Shirts murdered scores of African Americans and threatened still others during political campaigns in both states. Like the White Line, this group disrupted Republican political rallies and massacred black state militia members, most notably at Hamburg on July 4, 1876. Instructions circulated to Red Shirt members stated that murder was preferable to threats: "A dead Radical is very

---

4 "Illegitimacy and Insurgency in the Reconstruction South," in Michael Perman and Amy M. Taylor, eds., *Major Problems in the Civil War and Reconstruction: Documents and Essays*, 3rd ed. (Boston: Wadsworth/Cengage Learning, 2011), 459.
5 Ibid., 459.
6 Ibid., 460.

harmless—a threatened Radical is often troublesome, sometimes dangerous, and always vindictive."[7]

The goal of the White Line and Red Shirt campaigns was twofold: to intimidate African Americans from voting and to encourage more white Southerners to go to the polls. Perman points out the irony of using violence to commandeer the machinery of democracy: "Lawless and utterly undemocratic means were employed to secure the desired outcome, which was to win a lawful, democratic election."[8] While these groups succeeded at returning their state governments to the Democratic Party, one aspect of their strategy may have failed. According to election records, the number of voters from African American communities actually rose at the height of the violence. However, the violent campaigns were so successful at driving more white Southerners to the polls that "home rule" was restored across the South by the late 1870s.[9]

Pleas for Federal Intervention

In response to the "Redemption" campaign of violence, Southern Republican governors again called for the assistance of the federal government, as they did in response to Ku Klux Klan violence a few years before. This time Grant's options were limited. Since Democrats controlled the US House of Representatives after 1874, any effort by Grant to intervene would be in defiance of Congress. Additionally, in 1876 the Supreme Court overturned the federal convictions of two perpetrators of the Colfax massacre and declared parts of the Enforcement Acts of the early 1870s unconstitutional. The court ruled that under these laws, the federal government only had the right to stop *states* from denying the rights of citizens. If *individuals* acted to deprive other individuals of their rights, only states, not the federal government, could prosecute them. Freedpeople would have to rely on the governments of their own states, increasingly violent and increasingly Democratic, to protect them.

Therefore, despite Grant's stated desire to protect the black citizens of the South, his authority to do so was diminished. In response to Mississippi governor Adelbert Ames's plea for intervention, Grant famously responded, "The whole public are tired out with these annual autumnal outbreaks in the South, and the great majority are ready now to condemn any interference on the part of the Government."[10] After sympathetically responding to South Carolina governor Daniel Chamberlain's plea, Grant nevertheless asserted that any protection for freedpeople there would have to be provided "without aid from the Federal government."

The Disputed 1876 Election

The 1876 election spelled the end of Republican governments in the former Confederacy and their protection for freedpeople. The presidential contest between Republican Rutherford B. Hayes and Democrat Samuel Tilden came down to the election results of South Carolina, Florida, and Louisiana; the candidate that received the electoral votes from those three states would win. Widespread violence, intimidation, and fraud helped Tilden and Democratic governors win the vote counts in all three states. Amidst

---

7 In Dorothy Sterling, ed., *The Trouble They Seen: The Story of Reconstruction in the Words of African Americans* (Da Capo Press, 1994), 465.

8 Perman, *Major Problems in the Civil War and Reconstruction*, 461.

9 Ibid., 460–461.

10 Michael Fitzgerald, *Splendid Failure: Postwar Reconstruction in the American South* (Chicago: Ivan R. Dee, 2007), 191

the controversy following the disputed results in three states, both parties claimed victory and inaugurated separate governors in South Carolina and Louisiana (while Florida's supreme court settled the dispute there). Congress appointed a 15-member commission to decide the presidential election, and its members voted for Hayes by an 8-to-7 vote. The state elections in South Carolina and Louisiana remained unresolved, and with the two Southern states each having inaugurated two opposing governments, fears of a new civil war spread. To defuse the situation, President Hayes agreed to remove federal troops in South Carolina and Louisiana, leaving no protection for the Republican governments and thus ending them. "Home rule" now prevailed, and Democratic governments now controlled all Southern states. Historians commonly cite Hayes's removal of the few remaining federal troops from the South as the end of the Reconstruction era.[11]

While the return of the former Confederate states to Democratic Party rule was the result of a variety of political, social, and economic factors, the role of violence and intimidation by Democratic paramilitary groups in bringing about this outcome is unquestionable. By confronting the violence of this period of American history, students can reflect more deeply on the fragility of democracy and the constant struggle of maintaining a healthy democratic society.

LEARNING GOALS

Understanding: Students will understand that:

- The "in" groups and "out" groups that result from racism and other socially constructed divisions in society can leave citizens vulnerable to ostracism, intimidation, and violence.

- Violence and intimidation often silence the voices and votes of citizens on which democracy depends.

Knowledge: Students will know that:

- Paramilitary violence swept across the South in the 1870s, helping to restore the Democratic Party to power in every Southern state and removing protections for the freedom and equality of freedpeople.

- Federal protection for freedpeople was hampered by Northern public opposition, Democratic victories in Congress, and limits placed on federal power by the Supreme Court.

- The disputed 1876 election led to a compromise in which Rutherford B. Hayes, a Republican, would become president, but Democrats would be allowed to take control of the remaining Republican-controlled Southern states.

RESOURCE LIST

The following resources are included or referenced in this lesson. The handouts are grouped into four sets for the lesson plan that follows.

---

11 Eric Foner, *Forever Free: The Story of Emancipation and Reconstruction* (Vintage Books, 2006), 198–199.

Document Set 1: Platforms, Plans, and Patterns of Violence

- "Louisiana White League Platform (1874)" (document)

- "Democratic Party Platform of Pike County, Alabama (1874)" (document)

- "The White Line Instigates Violence (1874)" (document)

- "White Line Violence Spreads to Mississippi (1875)" (document)

- "South Carolina 'Red Shirts' Battle Plan (1876)" (document)

Document Set 2: Reports of Violence

- "White League Massacre at Coushatta (1874)" (document)

- "'Worse Than Slavery' (1874)" (image)

- "Election Violence in Mississippi (1875)" (document)

- "A Black Republican Leader Asks for Protection (1875)" (document)

- "A Teacher Describes Violence and Intimidation (1875)" (document)

- "'Shall We Call Home Our Troops?' (1875)" (image)

- "Election Day in Clinton, Mississippi (1875)" (document)

- "Massacre in Hamburg (1876)" (document)

- "'Of Course He Votes the Democratic Ticket' (1876)" (image)

Document Set 3: Responses to "Redemption"

- "A Republican Switches Parties (1874)" (document)

- "Speech by Senator Charles Hays Reaffirming the Rights of African Americans (1874)" (document)

- "Black South Carolinians Form a Militia for Protection (1874)" (document)

- "Blood and Treasure Spent in Vain (1875)" (document)

- "South Carolina's Governor Requests Federal Intervention (1876)" (document)

- "President Grant Replies to the South Carolina Governor (1876)" (document)

Document Set 4: The End of Republican Rule in the South

- "President Hayes Removes the Remaining Troops (1877)" (document)

- "Chamberlain Decries the End of Republican Rule (1877)" (document)

LESSON PLAN

Note that a detailed Common Core–aligned close reading protocol for the handout "Speech by Senator Charles Hays Reaffirming the Rights of African Americans" (**Handout 13.16***)
follows this lesson. The Common Core standards recommend that students begin a close
reading activity with little, if any, prior knowledge of the text at the heart of the activity.
Therefore, if you plan to include a close reading of this handout in your unit, we recommend
that you either complete the activity prior to implementing this lesson plan or omit the
handout from the activities outlined below.*

ESTIMATED DURATION: 2 CLASS PERIODS

SKILLS ADDRESSED:

- **Literacy:** Drawing evidence from informational texts to support analysis, reflection, and research

- **Historical thinking:** Interpretation—establishing why a past event is significant for our historical understanding of a particular time period by analyzing primary source documents

- **Social-emotional:** Responsible decision making—reflecting on choices made by people in history and the cumulative effect of their choices

DAY ONE

I. Opener: Journal Reflection on the Fragility of Democracy

Give students a few minutes to reflect on the essential questions for this lesson and record their thoughts in their journals: *What makes democracy fragile? What can be done to protect and strengthen democracy?*

Explain to students that in this lesson, they will be looking at the years 1874 to 1876 to see how white supremacists and the Democratic Party in the South used violence to reverse the gains made in the earlier years of Reconstruction. After students examine this history, they might want to modify or reaffirm their answer to this prompt. Therefore, have them leave room in their journals after their responses so they can add additional thoughts at the end of the lesson.

II. Examining Platforms, Plans, and Patterns of Violence

The goal of this activity is to help students recognize some important characteristics of the "Redemption" violence that was instrumental in overthrowing Republican state governments throughout the South in the mid-1870s. In order to discover these characteristics, students will read and analyze documents in which the Democratic Party and the White Line explicitly state their goals, as well as firsthand accounts that show a recurring pattern to the violence perpetrated by these groups. Students will read, annotate, and discuss these documents using the "Little Paper" strategy. For information on the "Little Paper" strategy, visit facinghistory.org/reconstruction-era/strategies.

PROCEDURE

1. Explain to students that the goal of this activity is to examine several documents to discover how the Democratic Party and two affiliated groups, known as the White Line and the Red Shirts, planned to use violence and intimidation to defeat Republican state governments in the South.

2. Divide the class into groups of five, and provide each group member with one of the handouts from "Document Set 1: Platforms, Plans, and Patterns of Violence" (**Handouts 13.1** to **13.5**).

3. Give students time to read and annotate their document in silence. They should highlight portions of the text and write comments in the margins that describe strategies and tactics that the Democratic Party, the White Line, and the Red

Shirts used to weaken or overthrow Republican state governments. In particular, students should highlight the role of race and racism in what they read. What purposes did it seem to serve?

4. Continuing to work in silence, have students pass their documents to the classmates next to them in their groups. They can then repeat the previous step, reading and commenting on the new document. However, this time they should also respond to the comments the previous reader added. Repeat this step at least once more so that every student has read at least three documents. If time permits, repeat so that each student has read all five documents.

5. Now have the groups break their silence and discuss the documents aloud. Remind them of the essential questions for this lesson: *What makes democracy fragile? What can be done to protect and strengthen democracy?* Ask students to use their documents to respond to these questions.

6. Finally, help students see how similar strategies for instigating violence against African Americans spread across Southern states between 1874 and 1876. Ask the students holding **Handout 13.3** ("The White Line Instigates Violence") to raise their hand, and then ask one of those students to identify the state and year in which the events described in this document took place. Record the state and year (Louisiana, 1874) on the board. Repeat this step with the documents "White Line Violence Spreads to Mississippi" (**Handout 13.4**) and "South Carolina 'Red Shirts' Battle Plan"(**Handout 13.5**), adding additional states and years to the board (Mississippi, 1875, and South Carolina, 1876). Ask the class what story this data tells about the violence in the South in the mid-1870s.

III. Confronting "Redemption" Violence

The goal of this activity is for students to learn about and respond to individual incidents of violence against freedpeople and white Republicans in the mid-1870s and to begin to understand why this wave of terror was so decisive in ending Republican control of Southern state governments. Students will debrief their work in this activity at the beginning of the second day of this lesson.

PROCEDURE

1. Explain to students that they will now analyze individual reports of violence in Louisiana, Mississippi, and South Carolina in the years 1874 to 1876, and they will consider the effects of this violence on the health of democracy in these states.

2. Give each student one document from "Document Set 2: Reports of Violence" (**Handouts 13.6** to **13.14**). Documents of a variety of lengths and formats are included in this set so that you can accommodate a variety of learning styles in your class.

3. Explain to students that their task is to read the document they have been assigned and to record the following in their journals:

   • One to three phrases or sentences from the document that capture the essence of the events it describes

- A brief description of a choice that an individual made during the events described in the document and the consequences of that choice

- A color that represents how they think the events described in the document impacted the health of democracy (a choice that they will need to be able to explain in the next class period)

DAY TWO

IV. Debriefing Reports of Violence

Begin the second day of this lesson by asking students to work in pairs or small groups to discuss the individual reports of violence they analyzed in the previous activity. Students can share with their classmates the words, phrases, and sentences they identified from their documents, discuss the choices they observed, and then explain the color they chose to represent the event's impact on the health of democracy.

After students have had sufficient time to share their work with each other, you might share the following quotation from historian Michael Perman with the whole group: "Lawless and utterly undemocratic means were employed to secure the desired outcome, which was to win a lawful, democratic election."[12]

Discuss as a class how the documents that students examined support or refute Perman's claim. Make sure that students use specific evidence from their documents in the discussion.

V. Analyzing Responses to "Redemption" Violence

Individuals, groups, governors, members of Congress, and President Grant responded in a variety of ways to the violence perpetrated by the paramilitary groups associated with the Democratic Party in the 1870s. In this activity, students will use the "Thought Museum" strategy (introduced in Lesson 7) to examine some of the choices that were made.

PROCEDURE

1. Post the six documents in "Document Set 3: Responses to 'Redemption'" (**Handouts 13.15** to **13.20**) around the room; each document will make up one "exhibit."

2. Before students leave their seats, ask them to reflect briefly on the choices that were available to those who did not support "Redemption" violence. You might ask students to reflect together in small groups, assigning each of the following sets of people to a different group of students:

- Black Southern Republicans/freedpeople

- White Southern Republicans

- State governors

- Members of Congress

- President Grant

Perman, *Major Problems in the Civil War and Reconstruction*, 461.

3. Explain that the "Thought Museum" represents the choices made by some of these individuals and groups, but afterward students might imagine different situations and additional options beyond those represented in this activity.

4. Give each student several self-stick notes and then provide sufficient time for them to visit and respond to as many exhibits as possible. Explain that their task is to observe and analyze the choices described in each exhibit. After reading the document at each exhibit, students can add a note with a comment or question it raises for them. They might also post a connection between the quotation and another historical event, current event, or personal experience.

5. Once students have spent sufficient time exploring the exhibits, assign one student to "curate" each exhibit. This means going to the assigned exhibit and choosing two to three notes that seem particularly important or clarifying.

6. While the curators are working, everyone else should return to their seats. Students can discuss the following questions in pairs:

   • What story do these exhibits tell?

   • What can we learn from the choices made in response to "Redemption" violence?

7. When the curators are finished, they should each share the notes they chose and explain their choices. After each curator finishes his or her report, allow time for discussing the following question: *What do the choices made by individuals, groups, governors, members of Congress, and the president reveal about the dilemmas of the time?*

VI. Mini-Lecture on the Compromise of 1877

Following the "Thought Museum" activity, give a brief lecture on the Compromise of 1877. Make sure to point out that many historians consider this compromise as marking the end of the Reconstruction era.

Information on which to base your mini-lecture can be found in this lesson's rationale or in the document "President Hayes Removes the Remaining Troops" (**Handout 13.21**). As part of your mini-lecture, read aloud this document as well as the document "Chamberlain Decries the End of Republican Rule" (**Handout 13.22**).

VII. Revisiting the Fragility of Democracy

Conclude this lesson by prompting students to review their journal entry from the beginning of Day One. Give them a few minutes to reflect in their journals on what they have learned from studying the "Redemption" violence of 1874 to 1876 and how it has affected their thinking about the fragility of democracy. You might have them extend their thinking by answering the following question in their journals: *Why would Americans resort to extremism and murder to prevent citizens from exercising their freedom of speech and right to vote?*

It is also important to give students an opportunity to reflect on their own experience of learning about the intense violence and hatred described in this lesson. A quotation from Václav Havel, the former president of the Czech Republic, might help to facilitate this reflection. Before he became president, Havel led the opposition to the Soviet Union's occupation and oppression of his country. He said of those difficult times: "Mostly what we needed was hope, an orientation of the spirit, a willingness to sometimes be in hopeless places and be a witness."

Ask students to reflect on Havel's statement and answer the following questions in their journals or in a brief discussion:

- What is a witness? What effect might a witness have on hopeless places?

- How does this quotation relate to your experience learning about violence and hatred in this lesson? In what sense have you become a witness?

LOUISIANA WHITE LEAGUE PLATFORM (1874)

The White League was a paramilitary group that was allied with the Democratic Party in the South. In 1874 and 1875, the White League was responsible for widespread violence against black and white Republicans in Louisiana and Mississippi. The group's platform from 1874 stated the following:

Disregarding all minor questions of principle or policy, and having solely in view the maintenance of our hereditary civilization and Christianity menaced by a stupid Africanization, we appeal to men of our race, of whatever language or nationality, to unite with us against that supreme danger. A league of whites is the inevitable result of that formidable, oath-bound, and blindly obedient league of the blacks, which, under the command of the most cunning and unscrupulous negroes in the State, may at any moment plunge us into a war of races . . . It is with some hope that a timely and proclaimed union of the whites as a race, and their efficient preparation for any emergency, may arrest the threatened horrors of social war, and teach the blacks to beware of further insolence and aggression, that we call upon the men of our race to leave in abeyance all lesser considerations; to forget all differences of opinions and all race prejudices of the past, and with no object in view but the common good of both races, to unite with us in an earnest effort to re-establish a white man's government in the city and the State.[1]

---

1 Quoted in Glenn M. Linden, *Voices from the Reconstruction Years 1865–1877* (Harcourt Brace/Cengage, 1998), 205.

DEMOCRATIC PARTY PLATFORM OF PIKE COUNTY, ALABAMA (1874)

As the 1874 campaign for governor and state legislature began in Alabama, the Pike County Democratic Party's platform gave supporters this guidance for how to treat white Republicans:

> [Nothing] is left to the white man's party but social ostracism of all those who act, sympathize or side with the negro party, or who support or advocate the odious, unjust, and unreasonable measure known as the civil rights bill; and that from henceforth we will hold all such persons as enemies of our race, and we will not in the future have intercourse with them in any of the social relations of life.[1]

---

1 Quoted in Glenn M. Linden, *Voices from the Reconstruction Years, 1865–1877* (Harcourt Brace/Cengage 1998), 201.

THE WHITE LINE INSTIGATES VIOLENCE (1874)

Louisiana freedman Henry Adams testified before Congress in 1874 about how members of the White Line instigated confrontations with African Americans with the intention of committing murder. The following is an excerpt from his testimony.

They raise a little disturbance with some of the colored people. They come to a place where there is a kind of little gathering. One will take a drink—he won't drink enough to get drunk—then comes out and commences to meddle with one of the colored men. Maybe the colored man will say something sort of rash like. If he does [the white] will haul out a revolver and strike him and maybe, perhaps, shoot him. As soon as [the whites] hear that firing, many come with guns and revolvers, and the first colored man they see, they beat him or shoot him. Then a passel of them will commence firing on them colored men who haven't got anything to fight with. Now if one of them colored men will show fight, if he hurts one of them, his life ain't no more than a chicken's. He may go home but he won't stay for a passel will come after him that night . . .

Q: Why do not the colored people arm themselves? Cannot they get arms?

A: They can buy arms if they have the money till the riot come. If there is a riot started, [the whites] go down by fifties and hundreds in a gang to watch us to see whether the colored men were going to buy arms. At the time a riot is going on, the colored men cannot buy no ammunition.

If the colored men are attacked, they call it a riot, because they are killing the colored men. You never hear of the colored man raising a riot, because he never gets the chance. If he shoots at a white man they kill fifty colored men for the one white man that was shot.[1]

---

1 In Dorothy Sterling, ed., *The Trouble They Seen: The Story of Reconstruction in the Words of African Americans* (Da Capo Press, 1994), 437–438.

WHITE LINE VIOLENCE SPREADS TO MISSISSIPPI (1875)

Eugene B. Welborne, a prosperous black farmer and state representative, explained in this way how a White Line attack began in Clinton, Mississippi, in 1875:

They had a barbecue and there were speakers invited. It was a kind of joint discussion. Amos R. Johnston [a Democrat] spoke first. After he got through Capt. H. T. Fisher, who was a Republican, was called upon to speak. There were a couple of young fellows standing in front of me—Sivley and Thompson. These gentlemen were a committee sent from Raymond. In the event that the Republican speakers told anything that they thought was not so, they had a right to contradict them. Captain Fisher had spoke two or three minutes when this Sivley says, "Come down out of there, you God damned radical, you. We don't want to hear any more of your lies."

I spoke to Aleck Wilson who was one of our officers there to keep the peace. We had about thirty men that we got the magistrate to deputize. I saw Wilson and said, "I want you to stand here and prevent anything. I see a difficulty brewing." Thompson had a bottle of whisky in his hand. He was drinking, and every now and then they would holler, "Come down! Stop your damned lying there, and come down."

Wilson went up to Mr. Thompson and said, "Mr. Thompson, we listened very quietly to your speaker and you must not go on in that way." He told him he was an officer and that he would have to arrest him if he did not stop. When Wilson said that, they all got right together around Thompson. He said, "Get away from here." Then Wilson attempted to arrest him and Thompson pulled his pistol out and shot him down. When Wilson fell, every [white] man in the line pulled out their pistols and began to fire on the crowd.

On Sunday—that was on Saturday—they just hunted the whole county clean out. Every man they could see they were shooting at him just the same as birds. I mean colored men, of course. A good many they killed and a good many got away. The men came into Jackson, two or three thousand of them. They were running in all day Sunday, coming in as rapidly as they could. We could hear the firing all the time.[1]

---

1 In Dorothy Sterling, ed., *The Trouble They Seen: The Story of Reconstruction in the Words of African Americans* (Da Capo Press, 1994), 442–443.

SOUTH CAROLINA "RED SHIRTS" BATTLE PLAN (1876)

Democratic Party paramilitary groups also emerged in South Carolina during the 1876 state and national campaigns. There, members of these groups called themselves the "Red Shirts." Their official battle plan, which called for Democratic clubs armed with rifles and pistols, stated in part:

Every Democrat must feel honor bound to control the vote of at least one Negro, by intimidation, purchase, keeping him away.

We must attend every Radical meeting. Democrats must go in as large numbers as they can, and well armed, behave at first with great courtesy and as soon as their speakers begin tell them that they are liars and are only trying to mislead the ignorant Negroes.

In speeches to Negroes you must remember that they can only be influenced by their fears, superstitions and cupidity. Treat them so as to show them you are the superior race and that their natural position is that of subordination to the white man.

Never threaten a man individually. If he deserves to be threatened, the necessities of the times require that he should die. A dead Radical is very harmless—a threatened Radical is often troublesome, sometimes dangerous, and always vindictive.

Every club must be uniformed in a red shirt and they must be sure and wear it upon all public meetings and particularly on the day of election.[1]

---

1 In Dorothy Sterling, ed., *The Trouble They Seen: The Story of Reconstruction in the Words of African Americans* (Da Capo Press, 1994), 465.

WHITE LEAGUE MASSACRE AT COUSHATTA (1874)

In August 1874, the White League murdered six white Republicans and as many as 20 black witnesses in Coushatta, Louisiana. Following the massacre, Louisiana governor William Kellogg issued the following statement.

Having felt it my duty to issue my proclamation offering a large reward for the apprehension and conviction of the murderers in the Coushatta outrage, and to the end that the law-abiding citizens of the State may fully comprehend the magnitude of the crime committed and be induced to render more active assistance to the officers of the law, I deem it proper to make the following statement :

These facts are gathered from reliable information received at the executive department :

On or about the 28th day of August, 1874, a body of persons, belonging to a semi-military organization known as the White League of Louisiana, assembled in the town of Coushatta, parish of Red River, in this State, *for the purpose of compelling by force of arms the State officers of that parish to resign their positions.*

These officers were men of good character, most of them largely interested in planting and mercantile pursuits. They held their positions with the full consent of *an admittedly large majority of the legal voters of the parish*, this being a largely republican parish, as admitted even by the fusion returning-boards.

The only known objection to them was *that they were of republican principles*. Frank S. Edgerton, the duly-qualified sheriff of the parish, in strict compliance with the laws of this State and of the United States, summoned a *posse comitatus* of citizens, white and colored, to assist him in protecting the parish officers in the exercise of their undoubted rights and duties from the threatened unlawful violence of the White Leagues. His posse, consisting of sixty-five men, *was overpowered by a superior force assembled from the adjacent parishes, and finally, after several colored and white men had been killed, surrendered themselves prisoners with the explicit guarantee that their lives would be spared* if the more prominent republicans would agree to *leave the parish* and those holding office would *resign their positions*.

These stipulations, though unlawfully exacted, *were complied with* on the part of the republican officials, who were then locked up in the jail for the night.

The following-named persons were among those so surrendering and resigning:

Homer J. Twitchell, planter and tax-collector of Red River, and deputy United States postmaster in charge of the post-office at Coushatta; Robert A. Dewees, supervisor of registration, De Soto Parish; Clark Holland, merchant and supervisor of registration, Red River Parish; W. J. Howell, parish attorney and United States commissioner; Frank S. Edgerton, sheriff of Red River Parish; M. C Willis, merchant and justice of the peace.

On the following morning, Sunday, the 30th day of August, these persons *were bound and conducted by an armed guard* to the McFarland plantation, just over the parish-line of Red River, within the boundaries of Bossier Parish, about forty miles east of the Texas line. *There they were set upon and deliberately murdered in cold blood*. Their bodies were buried near where they fell, without inquest or any formality whatever.

On the night preceding the surrender a body of forty members of the White League of Caddo Parish, mounted and armed, left the city of Shreveport, and were seen riding in the direction of the place where the murder was subsequently committed.

WILLIAM P. KELLOGG, Governor.[1]

---

1 From Index to Reports of Committees of the House of Representatives for the Second Sessions of the Forty-Third Congress, 1874–1875, 1003, http://books.google.com/books?id=pKUFAAAAQAAJ.

"WORSE THAN SLAVERY" (1874)

Wood engraving by Thomas Nast from Harper's Weekly (1864), *Library of Congress*

ELECTION VIOLENCE IN MISSISSIPPI (1875)

Robert Gleeds, an African American candidate for sheriff in Lowndes County, Mississippi, described the violence in his county that occurred on the eve of the 1875 election this way:

> In the latter part of the canvas the young men had a cannon and pistols, very much like an army. The election was wound up on the 2nd of November and on the night before in our city three buildings were set on fire and four men killed. Most of the colored people were run out of their houses during the night. It was the worst time we have ever had as far as an election was concerned.
>
> The first fire broke out near my house. I went to work to get my family and as many of my things out as I could. Then a young man came to me and said, "They will kill you when this fire burns low." The next morning a man told me that he did not think it would be safe to go back and I went out in the country and stayed until Saturday after the election. Prior to the election we had a meeting at the courthouse. Dr. Lipscomb and Judge Simms, the candidate on the Democratic side were invited to speak and I had a few words to say myself. I asked, "What could we do? Was there any concession we could make that would secure peace and a quiet election?" Dr. Lipscomb said the way we would have it was by abstaining from voting altogether. Of course I couldn't concede that for others but I was willing to forego any sacrifice as far as I was individually concerned. I told him we used to ask for life and liberty but now if we could just be spared our lives so we could go peacefully along as men and human beings we would be satisfied . . .
>
> It was the most violent time that ever we have seen.[1]

---

1 In Dorothy Sterling, ed., *The Trouble They Seen: The Story of Reconstruction in the Words of African Americans* (Da Capo Press, 1994), 447–448.

A BLACK REPUBLICAN LEADER ASKS FOR PROTECTION (1875)

Bolton, [Mississippi,] October 13, 1875

Gov. Ames:

I am here in Jackson and cannot leave. The white peoples is looking for me on every train and have got men on every road watching for me. They have sworn to take my life because I am president of the club at Bolton. I wish you would, if please, protect me. I am in a bad fix, with about 6 bales of cotton in the field and 150 bushel of corn to gather; no one to tend to it when I am gone. Tell me what to do, if you please.

Lewis McGee

President of Bolton's Republican Club[1]

---

1 In Dorothy Sterling, ed., *The Trouble They Seen: The Story of Reconstruction in the Words of African Americans* (Da Capo Press, 1994), 444.

A TEACHER DESCRIBES VIOLENCE AND INTIMIDATION (1875)

We have chosen to include certain racial epithets in this handout in order to honestly communicate the bigoted language of the time. We recommend that teachers review the section "Addressing Dehumanizing Language from History" on page xiv before using this material.

J. L. Edmonds, an African American schoolteacher, gave this account of the murder and intimidation before the 1875 election in Clay County, Mississippi:

Where we appointed a meeting [the Democrats] would go there and speak as they pleased. They would take a cannon and load it up with chains and leave it with the mouth pointing toward the crowd of colored people. When they fired they had nothing in it more than powder, but when they were going to speak they would have it turned around and chains hanging around it.

They had a parade at West Point. I was standing on the corner talking and some of the colored men came up, and a colored man says, "I do not care how many are riding around, I am a Republican and expect to vote the ticket." Just then a man walked up with a pistol and shot him. Pretty soon another colored man made some expression and he was shot at.

They had flags—red, white, and crimson flags. The whole street was covered. You could not hear your ears hardly for the flags waving and flapping over your head. They had one United States [flag] at the courthouse but most of the flags were just the old Confederate flags.

They said they were going to beat at this election. They said that at the meetings, on the stumps and at schoolhouses around the county. They said they would carry the county or kill every nigger. They would carry it if they had to wade in blood.[1]

---

1 In Dorothy Sterling, ed., *The Trouble They Seen: The Story of Reconstruction in the Words of African Americans* (Da Capo Press, 1994), 450.

"SHALL WE CALL HOME OUR TROOPS?" (1875)

As Northerners debated how to respond to the growing violence in Mississippi, Harper's Weekly *printed this political cartoon. The caption reads: "Shall We Call Home Our Troops? 'We intend to beat the Negro in the battle of life, and defeat means one thing—EXTERMINATION.'"*

SHALL WE CALL HOME OUR TROOPS?
"We intend to beat the Negro in the battle of life, and defeat means one thing—EXTERMINATION."—*Birmingham (Alabama) News.*

Wood engraving by C. S. R. from Harper's Weekly *(1875), Library of Congress*

ELECTION DAY IN CLINTON, MISSISSIPPI (1875)

We have chosen to include certain racial epithets in this handout in order to honestly communicate the bigoted language of the time. We recommend that teachers review the section "Addressing Dehumanizing Language from History" on page xiv before using this material.

State Senator Charles Caldwell was a former slave who had led a company of African American soldiers, earlier in 1875, in a state militia formed to protect freedpeople from the White Line. The militia was later disbanded by the governor as part of a "peace agreement" with the White Line, but attacks and intimidation continued, and Caldwell himself was assassinated later that year. Eugene Welborne, who served as Caldwell's first lieutenant in the militia, gave this account of election day in November 1875 in Clinton, Mississippi, and Caldwell's efforts to ensure a fair vote.

We could hear in the morning, the cannons commencing to shoot in every direction, just a firing. You could see men with their sixteen-shooters buckled on them charging all through the country. They went in squads.

One crowd would come in from Raymond and say, "One hundred and fifty niggers killed in Raymond; one white man slightly wounded." The guns were firing continually. Word came from Jackson, "The white men have whipped the niggers and run them out."

We did not know what in the world to do. Senator Caldwell was there and I said, "Senator, I think we might just as well give up. We can't do anything here. These men are riding all about the county with their sixteen-shooters." He says, "No. We are going to stay right here. I don't care what they say to you, don't you say a word." We voted as rapidly as we could.

Our votes were pretty strong all day and we would have polled our usual vote, even with all the intimidation, if they would have let us. But our Republicans that were appointed by the board of registration were told that it would not be healthy for them to serve and they made the whole thing Democratic. So when a Republican would come in to vote this fellow looked on the book and said, "I cannot find your name here. Stand aside." They turned off 80 Republicans, one after the other, that way.

I saw Senator Caldwell standing at the door. Said I, "What are you going to do about these registration papers?" "I think," says he, "we will go in and see these fellows." So we went in and spoke to one of the officers. When Mr. Caldwell said, "I know that this man's name was on that book," they said it didn't make any difference what he knew and that he was not going to vote.[1]

---

1 In Dorothy Sterling, ed., *The Trouble They Seen: The Story of Reconstruction in the Words of African Americans* (Da Capo Press, 1994), 452.

MASSACRE IN HAMBURG (1876)

We have chosen to include certain racial epithets in this handout in order to honestly communicate the bigoted language of the time. We recommend that teachers review the section "Addressing Dehumanizing Language from History" on page xiv before using this material.

The Hamburg massacre occurred on July 4, 1876, in South Carolina. The Republican governor raised a state militia to stem the spreading violence in the state. An all-black regiment of the militia, led by Dock Adams, was stationed in Hamburg, angering white paramilitary groups, known as the Red Shirts, in nearby towns. Hundreds of Red Shirts surrounded and eventually attacked the 84-member black militia regiment, killing seven. The following is testimony by Adams before a congressional committee describing what he witnessed while hiding near his house.

I could look right into my bedroom and sitting room window. I saw them taking down my pictures and breaking up the furniture. They took all my clothes, my mattresses and feather-bed and cut it in pieces, destroying everything I had. They took all my wife's clothes and everything.

By that time they commenced getting very thick in the [town] square. I jumped over a little fence and went up in the postmaster's house . . . Right on the street, there were over a thousand men. They had their headquarters there. Every time the party would bring a colored man that they had captured they would bring him to what they called the "dead-ring." Every time they would come in general Butler would yell, "Good boys! Goddamnit! Turn your hounds and bring the last one in," and they would ask, "Can you find that Dock Adams? We want to get him." Some asked what kind of man I was and some would agree—"man with side-whiskers and a moustache." One man said, "We'll have him before day." And I was standing right there looking at him through the blinds. That was between two and three o'clock. So finally they said, "Well we had better go to work and kill all the niggers we have. We won't be able to find that son of a bitch." They called them out one by one and would carry them off across the railroad, and stand them up there and shoot them. M. C. Butler was telling them what men to kill. They were shot, I guess, about four o'clock in the morning. The moon was shining very bright—about as bright as ever you seen it. I remained in the house until you could just discover day. I went out through the back way and got on the South Carolina Railroad and came to Aiken.

Q: When they were killing those colored men, was anything said about politics?

A: Yes, sir. You could hear it all the time. "By God! We will carry South Carolina now. About the time we kill four or five hundred men we will scare the rest." Even before it begun you could hear, "We are going to redeem South Carolina today!" You could hear them singing it on the streets, "This is the beginning of the redemption of South Carolina."[1]

---

1 In Dorothy Sterling, ed., *The Trouble They Seen: The Story of Reconstruction in the Words of African Americans* (Da Capo Press, 1994), 463–464.

IMAGE

"OF COURSE HE VOTES THE DEMOCRATIC TICKET" (1876)

This image appeared in Harper's Weekly in 1876. The caption reads:

"Of course he wants to vote the Democratic ticket!"

Democratic "Reformer": "You're as free as air, ain't you? Say you are or I'll blow yer black head off!"

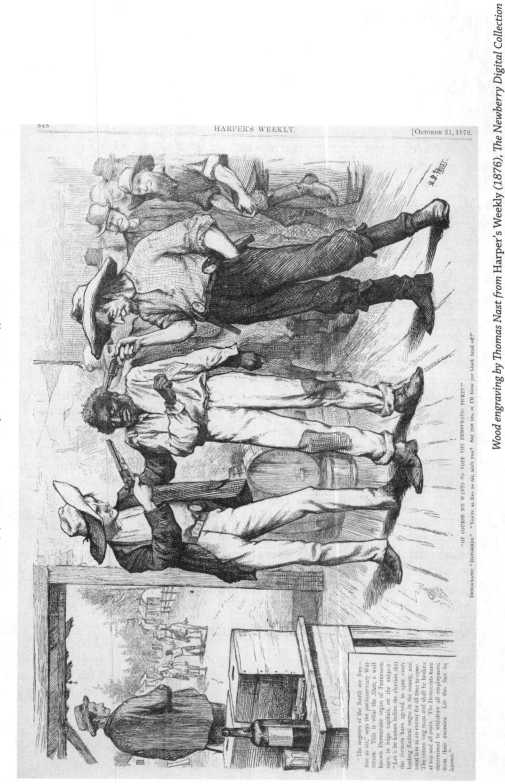

Wood engraving by Thomas Nast from Harper's Weekly (1876), The Newberry Digital Collection

A REPUBLICAN SWITCHES PARTIES (1874)

James Lusk, a white man from Alabama, abandoned the Republican Party in 1874. He gave this explanation to a former political associate:

No white man can live in the South in the future and act with any other than the Democratic party unless he is willing and prepared to live a life of social isolation and remain in political oblivion. While I am somewhat advanced in years, I am not so old as to be devoid of political ambition. Besides I have two grown sons. There is, no doubt, a bright, brilliant and successful future before them if they are Democrats; otherwise, not. If I remain in the Republican party,—which can hereafter exist at the South only in name,—I will thereby retard, if not mar and possibly destroy, their future prospects. Then, you must remember that a man's first duty is to his family. My daughters are the pride of my home. I cannot afford to have them suffer the humiliating consequences of the social ostracism to which they may be subjected if I remain in the Republican party.

The die is cast. I must yield to the inevitable and surrender my convictions upon the altar of my family's good,—the outgrowth of circumstances and conditions which I am powerless to prevent and cannot control. Henceforth I must act with the Democratic party or make myself a martyr; and I do not feel that there is enough at stake to justify me in making such a fearful sacrifice as that. It is, therefore, with deep sorrow and sincere regret, Henry, that I am constrained to leave you politically, but I find that I am confronted with a condition, not a theory. I am compelled to choose between you, on one side, and my family and personal interests, on the other. That I have decided to sacrifice you and yours upon the altar of my family's good is a decision for which you should neither blame nor censure me. If I could see my way clear to pursue a different course it would be done; but my decision is based upon careful and thoughtful consideration and it must stand.[1]

---

1 In William E. Gienapp, ed., *The Civil War and Reconstruction: A Documentary Collection* (New York: W. W. Norton, 2001), 411.

SPEECH BY SENATOR CHARLES HAYS REAFFIRMING THE RIGHTS OF AFRICAN AMERICANS (1874)

In 1874, Congress was debating a new civil rights bill that would end segregation of public transportation and public accommodations (such as hotels). Charles Hays of Alabama, a former slaveholder turned Republican congressman, supported the bill despite growing opposition, threats, and violence in his state. He addressed Congress as follows:

I am aware, sir, that the hate of the ignorant and the scorn of the untutored will be invoked against me. All these things are sources of profound regret; but they shall not deter me from the faithful discharge and sacred observance of a duty which God, reason, and conscience tell me is right.

Coming from the far South, being once the owner of a large number of slaves, thoroughly conversant with their history in the past and present, I feel that I have some idea of what should be accorded them now. Set free by the strong arm of Federal power, cut adrift upon the cold charities of an inhuman world in ignorance and penury that they did not bring upon themselves, struggling against adverse winds and storms of hate, in my opinion, sir, the colored race have set an example that fairly entitles them to the plaudit of "Well done, ye good and faithful servants."

The discussion of this question of "civil rights" has brought about a state of feeling in the South which is to be deplored. Fancies have taken the place of facts. Imagination has been called upon to paint pictures which reality could not do. Newspapers, politicians, demagogues, and inciters of sectional hate preached to the white masses of the south that Congress was upon the verge of enacting a law enforcing "social equality" and blotting out the lines between knowledge and ignorance. You and I know better . . .

The appeal is made that such an undying antipathy exists between the races as will render this law dangerous to be passed. I believe no such twaddle. Thousands of the most intelligent men of the South were born and raised upon the old plantations. Childhood's earlier days were passed listening to the lullaby song of the Negro nurse, and budding manhood found them surrounded by slave association. Was there prejudice then? Was cry against "social equality" raised then? Never, sir; but now that they are free and receiving the enlightenment of education, for the first time the fact is discovered that the Negro, who molded our fortunes, built our railroads, erected our palatial mansions, and toiled for our bread, is a curse upon the face of the earth, and not entitled to the protection of society.

Sir, for one, as a Southern man, I feel a debt of gratitude to them. I remember that when the tocsin of war called Southern men to the field of battle; when our whole country, from Virginia to Texas, was populated by none other than women and children, and when "insurrection" and "revolt" could have butchered those that were near and dear to us, the poor Negro toiled on and toiled well; protected our defenseless homes, and fed our destitute widows and starving children. In that hour of bondage and slavery they proved true to me and mine, and now that it lies in my power to pay the debt, the instincts of honor tell me to do it willingly and cheerfully, "as best becomes a man."

No possible harm can come to the white man by the passage of this law. Get upon the cars tomorrow morning and start South; take your seat in the finest palace car, and you will find southern women traveling and sitting side-by-side with colored women as nurses and servants. Is objection raised to this? Not at all. Does anyone feel debased by the Negro there? Not at all. Why then should the case be changed when the Negro buys a first-class ticket and travels alone? Have not Southern men associated with them for ages? Has any great conflict arisen heretofore? If "social equality" has been practiced it has been voluntary.

Sir, this talk about "social equality" will not bear the scrutiny of reason and common sense. It is the cry of the oldest time office-holder and cod-fish aristocrat, who uses the Negro now as he once did the poor white man—to make capital of. Who brought about the state of affairs? When the 13th Amendment was offered to the South was it accepted? No, sir; the very men who today are deluding the people by the specious cry of "social equality" caused the South to reject that proposition. Andrew Johnson and his providential provisional governors dictated the policy of the South. That move failed. Then came the 14th Amendment, and, last of all, the 15th Amendment. If, then, anyone is responsible for the present state of affairs it is the southern democracy [Democratic Party] themselves, who would not listen to reason, but rushed blindly on in the wanted paths of prejudice and hate.

This new issue is upon us and must be met. There is no ground for retreat. The past is gone, and the present is upon us. True-hearted patriots cannot swerve from the past, but, guided by the logic of events, must cheerfully accord to our colored fellow citizens every right that belongs to a "freeman," and every privilege that is guaranteed them by the Constitution of the country. "The world moves;" and a vindication of our course will come as sure as the waters flow or the stars shine.[1]

1 In Glenn M. Linden, *Voices from the Reconstruction Years, 1865–1877* (Harcourt Brace/Cengage 1998), 241–242.

BLACK SOUTH CAROLINIANS FORM A MILITIA FOR PROTECTION (1874)

Hamburg, South Carolina, was an all-black town on the border with Georgia, an area that was a stronghold for the Democratic Party. Hearing news of white militias forming in surrounding towns, the intendant (or mayor) of Hamburg, John Gardner, formed an all-black militia of 84 men and, with the following letter, asked the governor to arm them as part of the state's National Guard.

Town Hall, Town of Hamburg, August 19, 1874

His Excellency F. J. Moses, Jr., Governor of South Carolina

I respectfully recommend to your immediate and favorable consideration the application of 75 of the Citizens of this Town who have formed themselves into a Company and wish to be received into the National Guards and be armed as such. I have several reasons for urging this matter, but will only allude to one. We are situated on the banks of the Savannah River, a bridge connecting us with the City of Augusta [Georgia]. We call your attention to the paper of last Tuesday and today which show the danger the poor colored and few white Republicans of this town are in when 50 men or more leave their State to come to ours for the purpose of aiding a riot. In our rear some 6 or 8 miles we hear of two well-organized cavalry companies (whites) fully armed, ready for any purpose. We are entirely unarmed.

Therefore I pray your Excellency to receive the Company of which I am a member, commission the officers and use your authority in immediately arming them. The Citizens have for the last three nights been guarding this Town as the rumors are that those men would pay us a call with their Sharps rifles. Hoping your Excellency will assist us. I am your Obedient Servant,

John Gardner, Intendant (Mayor) of Hamburg[1]

---

1 In Dorothy Sterling, ed., *The Trouble They Seen: The Story of Reconstruction in the Words of African Americans* (Da Capo Press, 1994), 459–461.

BLOOD AND TREASURE SPENT IN VAIN (1875)

In February 1875, Alabama's black Republican legislators sent the following petition to the US Congress:

The Democratic Party of Alabama has made, and is now making, a deliberate and persistent attempt, as shown by their leaders in the present general assembly, to change the penal code and criminal laws of Alabama so as to place the liberty and legal rights of the poor man, and especially of the poor colored man, who is generally a Republican in politics, in the power and control of the dominant race who are, with few exceptions, the landholders, and Democratic in politics.

We need not remind you how such a policy is at variance with all the results intended to be wrought out by the war for the preservation of the Union. That was a conflict of ideas as well as of armies. The issue was free-labor institutions and principles against slave-labor institutions and principles. It was a conflict between these two types of civilization. And yet, while the slave-labor system did not triumph at Appomattox, they are thus seen to be practically triumphant in Alabama. After the war came reconstruction, by which the free-labor type of civilization was believed to have been firmly established throughout the entire South . . . But no sooner does the Democratic Party accede to power in Alabama than its leaders propose to forget not only all that has been done and promised, but to undo, as fast as possible, that which was wrought out by the war, and all that has since been promised in connection therewith. It would practically reverse the verdict wrought out at the point of the bayonet, reverse the policy of Reconstruction, and strike out of existence not only our free-State constitutions, but the laws made in pursuance thereof, thus violating the fundamental conditions of the readmission of Alabama into the Union. If this is allowed to be done, it is not difficult to perceive that the war for the Union was a grand mistake, and the blood and treasure of the people spent in vain.[1]

---

1 American Social History Project, *Who Built America? Working People and the Nation's History*, vol. 1, 3rd ed. (Bedford/St. Martin's, 2007), 509.

SOUTH CAROLINA'S GOVERNOR REQUESTS FEDERAL INTERVENTION (1876)

South Carolina governor Daniel Chamberlain sent the following letter to President Grant in 1876:

STATE OF SOUTH CAROLINA,
EXECUTIVE CHAMBER,
Columbia, July 22, 1876.

SIR: The recent massacre at Hamburgh, in this State, is a matter so closely connected with the public peace of this State that I desire to call your attention to it for the purpose of laying before you my views of its effect and the measures which it may become necessary to adopt to prevent the recurrence of similar events.

. . . It is not to be doubted that the effect of this massacre has been to cause widespread terror and apprehension among the colored race and the republicans of this State. There is as little doubt, on the other hand, that a feeling of triumph and political elation has been caused by this massacre in the minds of many of the white people and democrats. The fears of the one side correspond with the hopes of the other side.

. . . It is certainly true that most, though not all, of those who have spoken, through the newspapers or otherwise, here, on the white or democratic side, upon this matter, have condemned the massacre. Their opposition to such conduct has not, however, sufficed to prevent this massacre, nor do I see any greater reason for believing that it will do so in the future. That class which now engage in this cruel work certainly disregard the express sentiments of those who assume to speak, for the most part, for their communities, and go forward without fear of public opinion or punishment.

. . . [S]uch occurrences as this at Hamburgh have generally resulted in what is thought to be political advantage to the democratic party here. From this fact it results that the white people here are induced, to a considerable extent, to overlook the naked brutality of the occurrence, and seek to find some excuse or explanation of conduct which ought to receive only unqualified abhorrence and condemnation, followed by speedy and adequate punishment.

In this way it often happens that a few reckless men are permitted or encouraged to terrorize a whole community and destroy all freedom of action on the part of those who differ from them in political opinions. The more respectable portion of the white people here content themselves with verbal perfunctory denunciations, and never adopt such measures or arouse such a public sentiment as would here, as elsewhere, put a stop to such occurrences.

In respect to the Hamburgh massacre, as I have said, the fact is unquestionable that it has resulted in great immediate alarm among the colored people, and all republicans in that section of the State. Judging from past experience, they see in this occurrence a new evidence of a purpose to subject the majority of the voters of that vicinity to such a degree of fear as to keep them from the polls on election-day, and thus reverse, or stifle, the true political voice of the majority of the people . . .

. . . [W]ill the [federal] Government exert itself vigorously to repress violence in this State during the present political campaign on the part of persons belonging to either political party, whenever that violence shall be beyond the control of the State authorities? Will the [federal] Government take such precautions as may be suitable, in view of the feeling of alarm already referred to, to restore confidence to the poor people of both races and political parties in this State . . . ?

. . . I understand that an American citizen has a right to vote as he pleases; to vote one ticket as freely and safely as another; to vote wrong as freely and safely as to vote right; and I know that whenever, upon whatever pretext, large bodies of citizens can be coerced by force or fear into absenting themselves from the polls, or voting in a way contrary to their judgment or inclination, the foundation of every man's civil freedom is deeply if not fatally shaken . . .

I have the honor to be, your obedient servant,

D. H. CHAMBERLAIN,
Governor of South Carolina[1]

---

1 *Congressional Series of United States Public Documents*, vol. 1729 (US Government Printing Office, 1877), 480–483, available at http://books.google. com/books?id=MFFHAQAAIAAJ.

PRESIDENT GRANT REPLIES TO THE SOUTH CAROLINA GOVERNOR (1876)

Executive Mansion,
Washington, D. C., July 26, 1876.

Dear Sir: I am in receipt of your letter of the 22d of July . . . giving an account of the late barbarous massacre at the town of Hamburgh, S. C. . . . The scene at Hamburgh, as cruel, blood-thirsty, wanton, unprovoked, and uncalled for as it was, is only a repetition of the course which has been pursued in other Southern States within the last few years, notably in Mississippi and Louisiana. Mississippi is governed to-day by officials chosen through fraud and violence, such as would scarcely be accredited to savages, much less to a civilized and Christian people. How long these things are to continue, or what is to be the final remedy, the Great Ruler of the universe only knows; but I have an abiding faith that the remedy will come, and come speedily, and I earnestly hope it will come peacefully. There has never been a desire on the part of the North to humiliate the South. Nothing is claimed for one State that is not fully accorded to all others, unless it may be the right to kill negroes and republicans without fear of punishment and without loss of caste or reputation. This has seemed to be a privilege claimed by a few States. . . . I will give every aid for which I can find law or constitutional power. A government that cannot give protection to life, property, and all guaranteed civil rights (in this country, the greatest is an untrammeled ballot) to the citizen is, in so far, a failure, and every energy of the oppressed should be exerted, always within the law and by constitutional means, to regain lost privileges and protection. Too long denial of guaranteed rights is sure to lead to revolution, bloody revolution, where suffering must fall upon the innocent as well as the guilty.

Expressing the hope that the better judgment and co-operation of citizens of the State over which you have presided so ably may enable you to secure a fair trial and punishment of all offenders, without distinction of race or color or previous condition of servitude, and without aid from the Federal Government, but with the promise of such aid on the conditions named in the foregoing, I subscribe myself, very respectfully, your obedient servant,

U. S. GRANT[1]

---

1 *Congressional Series of United States Public Documents*, vol. 1729 (US Government Printing Office, 1877), 480–483, available at http://books.google. com/books?id=MFFHAQAAIAAJ.

PRESIDENT HAYES REMOVES THE REMAINING TROOPS (1877)

The 1876 presidential race between Republican Rutherford B. Hayes and Democrat Samuel Tilden was extremely close. Amidst violence, intimidation, and voter fraud, the winner of the election for president and governor in three Southern states—South Carolina, Florida, and Louisiana—was disputed. These states were the last three former Confederate states governed by Republicans.

Congress set up a special commission to decide the election, and a compromise was reached. According to the Compromise of 1877, the three Southern states would give their electoral votes for president to Republican Rutherford B. Hayes, but Democrats would be allowed to take control of the governments of those states.

Hayes was inaugurated on March 5, 1877. Among his first acts was to end Northern occupation of the states still under military control. He also appointed Frederick Douglass as marshal in the District of Columbia and a Southerner, D. M. Key of Tennessee, as postmaster general. Hayes wrote:

> April 22. — We have got through with the South Carolina and Louisiana problems. At any rate, the troops are ordered away, and I now hope for peace, and what is equally important, security and prosperity for the colored people. The result of my plans to get from those states and by their governors, legislatures, press, and people pledges that the 13th, 14th, and 15th amendments shall be faithfully observed; that the colored people shall have equal rights to labor, education, and the privileges of citizenship. I am confident this is a good work. Time will tell . . .[1]

---

1 Quoted in Glenn M. Linden, *Voices from the Reconstruction Years, 1865–1877* (Harcourt Brace/Cengage 1999), 316.

CHAMBERLAIN DECRIES THE END OF REPUBLICAN RULE (1877)

The following is excerpted from Daniel Chamberlain's address to the Republicans of South Carolina after President Hayes removed federal troops from the state, allowing Democrats to take over the state government.

Today—April 10, 1877—by order of the President whom your votes alone rescued from overwhelming defeat, the government of United States abandons you, and by the withdrawal of troops now protecting the state from domestic violence abandons the lawful government of the state to a struggle with insurrectionary forces too powerful to be resisted.[1]

---

1 In Dorothy Sterling, ed., *The Trouble They Seen: The Story of Reconstruction in the Words of African Americans* (Da Capo Press, 1994), 475–476.

Speech by Senator Charles Hays Reaffirming the Rights of African Americans

*Close reading is carefully and purposefully **rereading** a text. It's an encounter with the text in which we closely focus on what the author has to say, what the author's purpose is, what the words mean, and what the structure of the text tells us. Close reading ensures that we truly understand what we've read. At Facing History and Ourselves, we use this careful investigation of text to make connections to essential questions about history, human behavior, and ourselves. This protocol can be used to implement a close reading for select documents during the Reconstruction unit. Adapt this procedure to meet your goals and the needs of your students.*

FIRST READ: Read aloud. Either the teacher or an extremely fluent student can read the text aloud. Ask students to circle unfamiliar words as they listen. After the read-aloud, as students share these words with the class, decide which words to define immediately to limit confusion and which definitions you want students to uncover through careful reading.

SECOND READ: Individual read. Ask students to read silently to get a feel for the text. They can note specific words or phrases that jump out at them for any number of reasons: because they are interesting, familiar, strange, confusing, funny, troubling, difficult, etc. Share some of these as a class. Particular questions to ask students at this stage of the reading are:

- What can you already infer about the author of this text?

- How is the text structured?

- Does this structure make it easy or difficult to make meaning?

- Does this structure tell us anything about the author's style or purpose?

THIRD READ: Text-dependent questions. In small groups, have students read the text in chunks and answer a set of text-dependent questions. These questions are included with each closereading exemplar. Sample answers are provided to help guide the teacher. See the "Close Reading D: Student Handout" form for a student version of the document. See "Close Reading D: Teacher Guide" for the teacher's version.

FOURTH READ: Visual image. In small groups, have students create a visual image on paper that captures the essence of the text. You may also ask them to include three words or a sentence summary of each section of text. Groups can be assigned either the entire text or sections of text for this portion of the close reading.

FIFTH READ: Gallery read. Ask students to do a "gallery read" of the images that have been created.

TRANSITION TO DISCUSSION

At this point, we recommend organizing a class discussion so that students can make connections beyond the text. This discussion can be informal or can use the format of the "Socratic Seminar" or "Save the Last Word for Me" strategy (see the "Teaching Strategies" section of our website at facinghistory.org/reconstruction-era/strategies for details).

DISCUSSION SUGGESTIONS

As mentioned earlier, this unit includes two writing prompts. Both prompts can be used to launch a discussion after a close reading. Examples include:

- To connect to the argumentative writing prompt (*Support, refute, or modify the statement: Laws are the most important factor in overcoming discrimination*):

  - What does Hays say about his own personal evolution with regard to racism? More specifically, how does he reflect on his days as a slaveholder? Why does he say he has changed his mind?

  - How does Hays's description of his change of heart impact your answer to the prompt?

  - How does his argument supporting a bill in Congress impact your answer to the prompt?

- To connect to the informative writing prompt: *Historian Eric Foner calls Reconstruction "America's unfinished revolution." What debates and dilemmas from the Reconstruction era remain unresolved? After researching informational texts on Reconstruction, write an essay in which you explain one debate that was central to this period that remained unresolved. Explain why the debate was significant to the history of Reconstruction. In your conclusion, discuss the legacy of the debate not being resolved.*

  - Ask students to find connections between Hays's appeal for social equality and contemporary examples of social structures in the United States today. What aspects of Hays's plea to both end segregation and find justice for previously oppressed groups remains "unfinished" in the twenty-first century?

  - Ask students to find connections between Hays's change of heart and contemporary issues surrounding identity and change. What aspects of Hays's story still resonate today?

- To connect to more general Facing History and Ourselves themes:

  - How does Hays's speech connect to issues of "we" and "they"? What does his speech teach us about the different divisions in American society during Reconstruction? How does it connect to issues of belonging and exclusion in American communities today?

  - What makes democracy fragile? What can be done to protect and strengthen democracy? How do you think Hays would answer that question? How do you answer that question?

- It's also possible to have students themselves create the questions for a discussion. To do this, you might guide students by asking them to find connections between the essential questions and the text or to write questions based on what resonates for them. They might choose to make connections to the author's purpose, the structure of the text, the tone of the text, or the main messages of the text. Alternatively, they may want to make connections to issues related to the individual and society, to examples of discrimination, to the role of laws in a democracy, and beyond.

Text of Charles Hays's Speech

I am aware, sir, that the hate of the ignorant and the scorn of the untutored will be invoked against me. All these things are sources of profound regret; but they shall not deter me from the faithful discharge and sacred observance of a duty which God, reason, and conscience tell me is right.

Coming from the far South, being once the owner of a large number of slaves, thoroughly conversant with their history in the past and present, I feel that I have some idea of what should be accorded them now. Set free by the strong arm of Federal power, cut adrift upon the cold charities of an inhuman world in ignorance and penury that they did not bring upon themselves, struggling against adverse winds and storms of hate, in my opinion, sir, the colored race have set an example that fairly entitles them to the plaudit of "Well done, ye good and faithful servants."

1. **Given the opening sentence, what kind of reception does Hays anticipate for his speech? What signals are there in the first paragraph as to how he will react to and address that attitude?**

   Students should note that Hays believes his speech with be received unfavorably—"the hate of the ignorant and the scorn of the untutored will be invoked against [him]." However, given the way he describes those who will disagree with him (using words like ignorant and untutored), it is clear that he does not value these differing opinions. In addition, it should be noted that at the end of the opening paragraph, he states that a hostile response to his message will "not deter" him because he believes that conveying this message is the right thing to do, a conviction supported by "God, reason, and conscience."

2. **What do we learn about Hays in the second paragraph that makes his position unique?**

   Hays notes that he is not just a Southerner—he is a former "owner" of a large number of slaves." Students should recognize that given his position as a senator, his personal history is surprising, yet he feels that it puts him in a position to know and understand the history of African Americans "in the past and present."

Guided Close Reading
with Text-Dependent Questions

3. Paraphrase in your own words the reasons why Hays believes that African Americans deserve to be told, "Well done, ye good and faithful servants."

Hays recognizes that African Americans have endured difficult circumstances after the abolition of slavery. They were cast adrift after being freed without financial support into a world that was ignorant of all that they had endured, and they had to constantly struggle against widespread negative sentiment. Hays is saying that in the face of such obstacles, they have "set an example" that merits praise.

4. In the third paragraph, what action does Hays attribute to media and political leaders?

Hays calls out "newspapers" and "politicians" for misrepresenting facts in order to incite strong feelings among whites in the South, likening these figures to "demagogues" and "inciters of sectional hate." He goes on to invite to his side those listeners who know better than opponents who claim that with the passage of this law, the lines between knowledge and ignorance would become blurred and "social equality" (his quotes) would become the new norm.

5. Given the context in which it appears, what is the meaning of the phrase "undying antipathy"? What is Hays's view of the situation described by this phrase?

Students should know from the background to Hays's speech that the relationship "between the races" is assumed to be negative by those making the "appeal" to block the law. The information from the passage discussing possible "dangerous" implications of the law is an added clue to the meaning of the phrase. Therefore, students should contextually define "undying antipathy" as "permanent ill will" or "perpetual hostility." Students should recognize that Hays does not agree with this assessment of the relationship between blacks and whites. He knows from his background as a slave owner and from growing up in the South that this has not always been the situation, and he believes that the races can peacefully coexist.

Text of Charles Hays's Speech

The discussion of this question of "civil rights" has brought about a state of feeling in the South which is to be deplored. Fancies have taken the place of facts. Imagination has been called upon to paint pictures which reality could not do. Newspapers, politicians, demagogues, and inciters of sectional hate preached to the white masses of the south that Congress was upon the verge of enacting a law enforcing "social equality" and blotting out the lines between knowledge and ignorance. You and I know better . . .

The appeal is made that such an undying antipathy exists between the races as well render this law dangerous to be passed. I believe no such twaddle. Thousands of the most intelligent men of the South were born and raised upon the old plantations. Childhood's earlier days were passed listening to the lullaby song of the Negro nurse, and budding manhood found them surrounded by slave association. Was there prejudice then? Was cry against "social equality" raised then? Never, sir; but now that they are free and receiving the enlightenment of education, for the first time the fact is discovered that the Negro, who molded our fortunes, built our railroads, erected our palatial mansions, and toiled for our bread, is a curse upon the face of the earth, and not entitled to the protection of society.

Text of Charles Hays's Speech

Sir, for one, as a Southern man, I feel a debt of gratitude to them. I remember that when the tocsin of war called Southern men to the field of battle; when our whole country, from Virginia to Texas, was populated by none other than women and children, and when "insurrection" and "revolt" could have butchered those that were near and dear to us, the poor Negro toiled on and toiled well; protected our defenseless homes, and fed our destitute widows and starving children. In that hour of bondage and slavery they proved true to me and mine, and now that it lies in my power to pay the debt, the instincts of honor tell me to do it willingly and cheerfully, "as best becomes a man."

No possible harm can come to the white man by the passage of this law. Get upon the cars tomorrow morning and start South; take your seat in the finest palace car, and you will find southern women traveling and sitting side-by-side with colored women as nurses and servants. Is objection raised to this? Not at all. Does anyone feel debased by the Negro there? Not at all. Why then should the case be changed when the Negro buys a first-class ticket and travels alone? Have not Southern men associated with them for ages? Has any great conflict arisen heretofore? If "social inequality" has been practiced it has been voluntary.

Guided Close Reading with Text-Dependent Questions

6. **How does Hays's assertion that African Americans "molded our fortunes, built our railroads, erected our palatial mansions, and toiled for our bread" contribute to his argument?**

Students should note that with this line in his speech, Hays is recognizing the great contributions that African Americans made to this country. He sees it as disingenuous for those who oppose the law to have benefited from the contributions of African Americans in the past only to miraculously discover—now that former slaves are receiving an education—that they are "a curse" and not entitled to the protections of society.

7. **In addition to the evidence from the previous paragraph, in paragraph five, why does Hays say that he personally feels "a debt of gratitude" toward African Americans?**

Students should recognize that in the fifth paragraph, Hays is referring to the time of the Civil War. He explains that during a period when most white men in the South were away fighting, slaves continued to work the land and defend the homes and families of their masters. In this time when Southerners were most vulnerable, slaves did not "revolt" or cause harm, and Hays argues that these actions are reason to believe further, African Americans deserve the same rights as he does. Further, because of their loyalty, Hays feels that it is his duty to "pay the debt" and argue for their civil rights.

8. **Paraphrase in your own words Hays's logic in the sixth paragraph. How does the example he provides add to his overall argument?**

Students should understand how Hays uses the current situation and facts to explain why passing the debated civil rights law would not cause any harm. Students should outline his argument in two parts: First, he notes that if one were to take a train trip tomorrow, he or she would find black people in the same coach as white people, serving as nurses or servants accompanying their white employers. Second, Hays notes that this current state of affairs does not cause harm to anyone, including Southern males. Therefore, he does not believe that African Americans riding in that same car after purchasing the ticket on their own would cause conflict.

Text of Charles Hays's Speech

Sir, this talk about "socially equality" will not bear the scrutiny of reason and common sense. It is the cry of the oldest time office-holder and cod-fish aristocrat, who uses the Negro now as he once did the poor white man—to make capital of. Who brought about the state of affairs? When the 13th Amendment was offered to the South was it accepted? No, sir; the very men who today are deluding the people by the specious cry of "social equality" caused the South to reject that proposition. Andrew Johnson and his providential provisional governors dictated the policy of the South. That move failed. Then came the 14th Amendment, and, last of all, the 15th Amendment. If, then, anyone is responsible for the present state of affairs it is the southern democracy [Democratic Party] themselves, who would not listen to reason, but rushed blindly on in the wanted paths of prejudice and hate.

This new issue is upon us and must be met. There is no ground for retreat. The past is gone, and the present is upon us. True-hearted patriots cannot swerve from the past, but, guided by the logic of events, must cheerfully accord to our colored fellow citizens every right that belongs to a "freeman," and every privilege that is guaranteed them by the Constitution of the country. "The world moves," and a vindication of our course will come as sure as the waters flow or the stars shine.

Guided Close Reading
with Text-Dependent Questions

9. **Explain why Hays believes that the "social equality" argument against the civil rights legislation will not pass the "scrutiny of reason and common sense."**
   Students should use the information contained in this paragraph to tease out an explanation. At the beginning of the seventh paragraph, Hays claims that the people who are on the other side of the argument are really just trying to deny African Americans their rights in order to use them for their own gain, in the same way that aristocrats previously used the "poor white man." In addition, he references the Thirteenth Amendment later in the paragraph to call attention to the fact that the people arguing against civil rights are the same people who did not want to abolish slavery. Rather than believing that this is a question about "social equality," Hays is trying to make it clear that his opponents are driven by prejudice against African Americans.

10. **Who does Hays blame for the current situation? Why?**
    Near the end of the paragraph, Hays makes it clear that he blames the current Democratic Party for "the present state of affairs." He believes that the Democratic point of view is not valid and well reasoned but rather is based on "prejudice and hate."

11. **In the final paragraph, how does Hays make the issue of time central to his argument?**
    In this paragraph, Hays repeatedly stresses that the past is over and the present calls for new thinking. While the past is important, there is no returning to it, and the "logic" of current events must guide "true-hearted patriots."

12. **What document does Hays believe gives African Americans the rights that he is arguing for?**
    Students should recognize that Hays believes that the rights outlined in the debated law should be "guaranteed" to every man in the United States as outlined in the Constitution.

Text of Charles Hays's Speech

13. **How does Hays's statement that "a vindication of our course will come as sure as the waters flow or the stars shine" fit into the final paragraph? What is his final argument?**

Hays ends his speech by calling for progress, noting that "the world moves" (implicitly suggesting that it moves forward). Students should understand that Hays believes that recent history has outlined a path toward guaranteeing these civil rights for all men, and it will become clear that reaffirming the rights of African Americans through this law is the right course of action—as right as the natural processes he refers to in the quote.

Text of Charles Hays's Speech

I am aware, sir, that the hate of the ignorant and the scorn of the untutored will be invoked against me. All these things are sources of profound regret; but they shall not deter me from the faithful discharge and sacred observance of a duty which God, reason, and conscience tell me is right.

Coming from the far South, being once the owner of a large number of slaves, thoroughly conversant with their history in the past and present, I feel that I have some idea of what should be accorded them now. Set free by the strong arm of Federal power, cut adrift upon the cold charities of an inhuman world in ignorance and penury that they did not bring upon themselves, struggling against adverse winds and storms of hate, in my opinion, sir, the colored race have set an example that fairly entitles them to the plaudit of "Well done, ye good and faithful servants."

1. **Given the opening sentence, what kind of reception does Hays anticipate for his speech? What signals are there in the first paragraph as to how he will react to and address that attitude?**

2. **What do we learn about Hays in the second paragraph that makes his position unique?**

Guided Close Reading
with Text-Dependent Questions

3. **Paraphrase in your own words the reasons why Hays believes that African Americans deserve to be told, "Well done, ye good and faithful servants."**

4. **In the third paragraph, what action does Hays attribute to media and political leaders?**

5. **Given the context in which it appears, what is the meaning of the phrase "undying antipathy"? What is Hays's view of the situation described by this phrase?**

Text of Charles Hays's Speech

The discussion of this question of "civil rights" has brought about a state of feeling in the South which is to be deplored. Fancies have taken the place of facts. Imagination has been called upon to paint pictures which reality could not do. Newspapers, politicians, demagogues, and inciters of sectional hate preached to the white masses of the south that Congress was upon the verge of enacting a law enforcing "social equality" and blotting out the lines between knowledge and ignorance. You and I know better . . .

The appeal is made that such an undying antipathy exists between the races as well render this law dangerous to be passed. I believe no such twaddle. Thousands of the most intelligent men of the South were born and raised upon the old plantations. Childhood's earlier days were passed listening to the lullaby song of the Negro nurse, and budding manhood found them surrounded by slave association. Was there prejudice then? Was cry against "social equality" raised then? Never, sir; but now that they are free and receiving the enlightenment of education, for the first time the fact is discovered that the Negro, who molded our fortunes, built our railroads, erected our palatial mansions, and toiled for our bread, is a curse upon the face of the earth, and not entitled to the protection of society.

Guided Close Reading
with Text-Dependent Questions

6. How does Hays's assertion that African Americans "molded our fortunes, built our railroads, erected our palatial mansions, and toiled for our bread" contribute to his argument?

7. In addition to the evidence from the previous paragraph, in paragraph five, why does Hays say that he personally feels "a debt of gratitude" toward African Americans?

8. Paraphrase in your own words Hays's logic in the sixth paragraph. How does the example he provides add to his overall argument?

Text of Charles Hays's Speech

Sir, for one, as a Southern man, I feel a debt of gratitude to them. I remember that when the tocsin of war called Southern men to the field of battle; when our whole country, from Virginia to Texas, was populated by none other than women and children, and when "insurrection" and "revolt" could have butchered those that were near and dear to us, the poor Negro toiled on and toiled well; protected our defenseless homes, and fed our destitute widows and starving children. In that hour of bondage and slavery they proved true to me and mine, and now that it lies in my power to pay the debt, the instincts of honor tell me to do it willingly and cheerfully, "as best becomes a man."

No possible harm can come to the white man by the passage of this law. Get upon the cars tomorrow morning and start South; take your seat in the finest palace car, and you will find southern women traveling and sitting side-by-side with colored women as nurses and servants. Is objection raised to this? Not at all. Does anyone feel debased by the Negro there? Not at all. Why then should the case be changed when the Negro buys a first-class ticket and travels alone? Have not Southern men associated with them for ages? Has any great conflict arisen heretofore? If "social inequality" has been practiced it has been voluntary.

Guided Close Reading
with Text-Dependent Questions

9. Explain why Hays believes that the "social equality" argument against the civil rights legislation will not pass the "scrutiny of reason and common sense."

10. Who does Hays blame for the current situation? Why?

11. In the final paragraph, how does Hays make the issue of time central to his argument?

12. What document does Hays believe gives African Americans the rights that he is arguing for?

Text of Charles Hays's Speech

Sir, this talk about "socially equality" will not bear the scrutiny of reason and common sense. It is the cry of the oldest time office-holder and cod-fish aristocrat, who uses the Negro now as he once did the poor white man—to make capital of. Who brought about the state of affairs? When the 13th Amendment was offered to the South was it accepted? No, sir; the very men who today are deluding the people by the specious cry of "social equality" caused the South to reject that proposition. Andrew Johnson and his providential provisional governors dictated the policy of the South. That move failed. Then came the 14th Amendment, and, last of all, the 15th Amendment. If, then, anyone is responsible for the present state of affairs it is the southern democracy [Democratic Party] themselves, who would not listen to reason, but rushed blindly on in the wanted paths of prejudice and hate.

This new issue is upon us and must be met. There is no ground for retreat. The past is gone, and the present is upon us. True-hearted patriots cannot swerve from the past, but, guided by the logic of events, must cheerfully accord to our colored fellow citizens every right that belongs to a "freeman," and every privilege that is guaranteed them by the Constitution of the country. "The world moves;" and a vindication of our course will come as sure as the waters flow or the stars shine.

253

Text of Charles Hays's Speech

13. How does Hays's statement that "a vindication of our course will come as sure as the waters flow or the stars shine" fit into the final paragraph? What is his final argument?

LESSON 14 The Coming of Segregation

ESSENTIAL QUESTIONS

What does it mean to be free? Can one have freedom without safety?

TRANSITION

In the last lesson, students learned about the violence perpetrated by paramilitary groups in order to influence elections and return Southern states to rule by the Democratic Party. This lesson seeks to bridge the gap between the ascendency of the Democratic Party in the former Confederacy in the late 1870s and the creation of a racially segregated Southern society by the first decades of the twentieth century. In particular, students will learn about some of the ways that white-supremacist state governments, with eventual backing from the Supreme Court, circumvented the Fourteenth and Fifteenth Amendments to deny African Americans the vote and create an unequal society divided by race. Students will revisit questions about the meaning of freedom and consider the limited choices available to African Americans as their rights were significantly curtailed.

RATIONALE

Black political participation and the remnants of interracial democracy in the South did not disappear immediately after the "Redemption" campaign of violence restored control of the former Confederate states to the Democratic Party. African Americans continued to vote and hold office in Southern states for another decade or more. In the wake of the Compromise of 1877, which awarded the presidency to Rutherford B. Hayes in exchange for the removal of the few remaining federal soldiers from the South, some Democratic leaders agreed to appoint African Americans to posts in Southern state governments, even if they were usually positions of little power. Nevertheless, in the 1870s and 1880s the federal government continued to retrench policies that protected the rights of freedpeople, and by the 1890s, many Southern states had devised legal methods of disenfranchising blacks and legislating racial segregation.

While a deeper, more nuanced look at the institutionalization of segregation is warranted in a unit about the Jim Crow South and the civil rights movement, the goal of this lesson is for students to understand the consequences of the politics of violence and intimidation that ended the Reconstruction era. In time, the rights of black Southerners were curtailed and their participation in the political, economic, and social life of the South was denied. Under these circumstances, African Americans had few choices, and their physical safety was often pitted against their claims for citizenship and equal rights. By learning about the coming of segregation at the end of the nineteenth century, students will once again reflect on what one needs in order to be truly free, and they will evaluate the extent to which black Southerners were free as the promise of Reconstruction faded.

Courts Weaken the Reconstruction Amendments

As it became clear that paramilitary violence had succeeded in undermining Republican rule in the South, the legal framework that buttressed the policies of Radical Reconstruction was also weakened. Two Supreme Court decisions, in particular, diminished the power of the federal government to protect the rights of black Southerners. In *United States v. Cruikshank* in 1876, the court overturned the convictions of three perpetrators of the Colfax massacre in 1873. In doing so, the court declared that, contrary to the Enforcement Act and Ku Klux Klan Act of the early 1870s, only states could prosecute individuals for crimes, not the federal government. Therefore, the federal government became powerless to bring charges against perpetrators of violence against black Southerners. Targets of violence could only turn to state governments, run by white Democrats, for protection.

Seven years later, the Supreme Court invalidated the 1875 Civil Rights Act—which required that citizens of all races be granted equal privileges with regard to inns, restaurants, public facilities, and transportation—in a decision on what became known as the Civil Rights Cases. In this decision, the court argued that the Fourteenth Amendment only prohibited discrimination by the states and not by private individuals. Therefore, Congress could only pass legislation that corrected state laws that conflicted with the Fourteenth Amendment— and Congress would not have the will to do so for several decades.

States Begin Segregation

By 1890, many Southern states had begun to erect legal barriers to voting for African Americans. They did so by creating requirements that were not expressly forbidden by the Fifteenth Amendment. Historian Eric Foner explains:

> Since the Fifteenth Amendment prohibited the use of race as a qualification for suffrage, these new measures were ostensibly color-blind. The most popular devices included poll taxes, without payment of which a voter lost the franchise; literacy tests and requirements that a prospective voter demonstrate an "understanding" of the state constitution; and stringent residency requirements. . . . [T]he aim, as a Charleston, South Carolina, newspaper declared, was to "reduce the colored vote to insignificance in every county in the state" and to make clear that the white South "does not desire or intend ever to include black men among its citizens."[1]

Because such voting requirements did not explicitly target African Americans—they prevented many poor whites from voting, as well—the Supreme Court upheld their legality under the Fifteenth Amendment in 1898. As a result, not long after the turn of the century, the black vote in the South was nearly eliminated entirely. In Louisiana, for instance, the number of black voters was reduced from over 130,000 to about 1,000.

At the same time, Southern states began to pass an increasing number of laws separating whites and blacks in schools, streetcars, restaurants, and other public accommodations. When these segregation laws were challenged under the Fourteenth Amendment's equal protection clause in 1896, the Supreme Court issued its landmark decision in *Plessy v. Ferguson*. In an 8–1 decision, the court declared that segregation was legal, as long as the facilities provided to whites and blacks were "separate but equal." The lone dissenter, Justice John Marshall Harlan, argued that the purpose of segregation was not

---

1 Eric Foner, *Forever Free: The Story of Emancipation and Reconstruction* (Vintage Books, 2006), 206.

separation but domination, and that Jim Crow laws were designed expressly to maintain the dominance of the white race over the black race in the South. Therefore, according to Harlan, segregation laws violated the principle of equality before the law.

Segregation, nevertheless, was a reality of life in the South shortly after the turn of the twentieth century. African Americans' survival in the South depended on their learning to live by strict racial codes. Some blacks responded by moving north or west; a trickle of migrants in the late nineteenth century would become a flood in the twentieth century as more than six million blacks left the South in the Great Migration between 1915 and 1970. Some other African Americans sought to create Southern communities that existed entirely apart from white society. These communities perhaps embodied the preference expressed in 1865 by Garrison Frazier at the Savannah Colloquy when he stated, "I would prefer to live by ourselves, for there is a prejudice against us in the South that will take years to get over."

Mound Bayou in Mississippi was one such community, founded by Isaiah Montgomery in 1887 as a "paradise for black landowners." An autonomous city of homes, streets, and storefronts owned and governed entirely by African Americans, Mound Bayou was a place where residents found themselves safe from the violence and intimidation of white-supremacist groups. Representing the town, Montgomery was the only black delegate to a state constitutional convention in 1890. At the convention, surprisingly, he voted in favor of literacy tests as a requirement for voting, knowing that the measure would disenfranchise most of the residents of Mound Bayou. His hope was that by willingly removing himself and his constituents from the political process, he would guarantee the safety of the residents of Mound Bayou and the community would thrive. Indeed, the white citizens of Mississippi left the town alone. In the documentary *The African Americans*, historian Thavolia Glymph wrestles with Montgomery's calculation that "by giving up some of your freedom, you could become free."[2] Students might also wrestle with Montgomery's compromise and reflect on the fragility of democracy when the rights and safety of society's "out" groups are not protected.

LEARNING GOALS

Understanding: Students will understand that:

Democracy is fragile, especially when the rights and safety of some groups in a society are threatened.

Knowledge: Students will know that:

- The federal government continued to withdraw from laws and policies designed to protect the rights of Southern African Americans throughout the 1880s and 1890s.

- By the 1890s, Southern states had effectively disenfranchised that vast majority of their African American citizens through measures such as poll taxes and literacy tests, which were not outlawed by the Fifteenth Amendment.

As Southern states increasingly segregated their societies by race, some African Americans tested out the idea that withdrawing from white society altogether could enable their communities to thrive.

---

2 "Into the Fire (1861–1896)" (Episode 3) of *The African Americans: Many Rivers to Cross* (PBS documentary film), 2014.

RESOURCE LIST

- "'Long View: Negro' by Langston Hughes" (poem)

- "Restricting the Vote and Dividing Society" (document)

- "Into the Fire," Episode 3 of *The African Americans* (PBS documentary) (video)

  (Available from the Facing History and Ourselves library.)

ACTIVITY SUGGESTIONS

Consider using the following activity ideas and strategies when you implement this lesson in your classroom.

- Begin the lesson with the Langston Hughes poem "Long View: Negro" (**Handout 14.1**). Read it aloud as a class multiple times, choosing a different reader each time. Then ask students to reflect in their journals on the metaphor Hughes employs:

  - What is the difference between looking through one end of a telescope and looking through the other? What is different about the way objects appear?

  - By using this image, what might Hughes be suggesting about how African Americans perceived the promise of Emancipation in 1865 and how their expectations changed after Reconstruction?

  Debrief students' reflections using the "Think-Pair-Share" strategy. (For more information on this strategy, visit facinghistory.org/reconstruction-era/strategies.)

- Review the concept map the class created for *freedom* in Lesson 3. Then read together **Handout 14.2** ("Restricting the Vote and Dividing Society") for a brief overview of how Jim Crow segregation emerged in the decades after the Compromise of 1877.

  Have the class reflect on the concept map and the document in their journals or participate in a brief class discussion centered around the following questions:

  - Which aspirations for freedom did not become a reality for black Americans during Reconstruction?

  - Which aspirations became a reality during Reconstruction and then were lost? Which were achieved and sustained?

  - What choices were left for black Southerners by the 1890s?

- Play a clip from the video *The African Americans* (41:25 to 47:15) after explaining to the class that they are about learn about some of the choices and dilemmas that were still present for black Southerners in the 1880s and 1890s. As students watch the clip, have them keep a list in their journals of the dilemmas faced and the choices made by Isaiah Montgomery, the founder of the all-black community of Mound Bayou. (To borrow the video from the Facing History resource library, visit facinghistory.org/library.)

  One way for students to process their reactions to the choices made by Isaiah Montgomery is through the "Learn to Listen/Listen to Learn" strategy. (Visit facinghistory.org/reconstruction-era/strategies to learn more about this strategy.)

This format helps students develop their discussion skills—particularly their ability to listen to one another. It is especially useful when trying to discuss controversial topics and difficult dilemmas. The strategy begins with five to ten minutes of journal writing. Have students reflect on the following questions:

- What choices did Isaiah Montgomery make in order to establish Mound Bayou and protect its citizens? What were the advantages and disadvantages of those choices? What is your reaction to them?

- What do the choices and dilemmas faced by Montgomery say about the state of freedom and democracy in Mississippi, and the entire United States, in the 1890s?

"LONG VIEW: NEGRO" BY LANGSTON HUGHES

Emancipation: 1865
Sighted through the
Telescope of dreams
Looms larger,
So much larger,
So it seems,
Than truth can be.

But turn the telescope around,
Look through the larger end—
And wonder why
What was so large
Becomes so small
Again.[1]

---

1 In *The Collected Works of Langston Hughes: The Poems, 1951–1967*, vol. 3 (University of Missouri, 2001), 152.

RESTRICTING THE VOTE AND DIVIDING SOCIETY

Historian Eric Foner explains some of the changes that took place in the South after the Democratic Party took control of state governments in all of the former Confederate states:

For nearly a generation after the end of Reconstruction, despite fraud, violence, and redistricting, most black southerners continued to cast ballots. Beginning in 1890, however, every southern state enacted laws or constitutional provisions designed to eliminate the black vote entirely. Since the Fifteenth Amendment prohibited the use of race as a qualification for suffrage, these new measures were ostensibly color-blind. The most popular devices included poll taxes, without payment of which a voter lost the franchise; literacy tests and requirements that a prospective voter demonstrate an "understanding" of the state constitution; and stringent residency requirements . . . . [T]he aim, as a Charleston, South Carolina, newspaper declared, was to "reduce the colored vote to insignificance in every county in the state" and to make clear that the white South "does not desire or intend ever to include black men among its citizens."

The result was the virtual elimination of black voting in the South. And although sympathetic election officials often allowed whites who did not meet the new qualifications to register, the number of eligible white voters declined as well. Louisiana, for example, reduced the number of black voters from 130,000 to 1,000. But 80,000 white voters also lost the franchise . . .

Along with disenfranchisement, the 1890s saw the widespread imposition of racial segregation in the South. Of course, . . . racial separation had existed in Reconstruction schools and many other institutions, and among the first acts of the Redeemers had been to institutionalize in the law the principle of separate schools for white and black students. But it was not until the 1890s that the Supreme Court, in the landmark decision *Plessy v. Ferguson*, gave its approval to state laws requiring separate facilities for blacks and whites. The case arose in Louisiana, where the legislature enacted a law requiring railroad companies to maintain a separate car for black passengers . . . [Opponents of the law argued that] the state's requirement that blacks be separated from whites violated the Fourteenth Amendment's guarantee of equal protection before the law. But in an 8–1 decision, the court upheld the law, arguing that separate facilities were not discriminatory so long as they were "separate but equal" . . .

[T]he *Plessy* decision was quickly followed by state laws mandating racial segregation in every aspect of life, from schools to hospitals, waiting rooms to toilets, drinking fountains to cemeteries.[1]

---

1 Eric Foner, *Forever Free: The Story of Emancipation and Reconstruction* (Vintage Books, 2006), 206–208.

Connecting to the Writing Prompt

This is an appropriate time to return to the writing prompt for this unit. Students will need time both to continue their evidence logs and to start developing a thesis for their essays.

GATHERING EVIDENCE

Give students the opportunity to review the documents they encountered in Lessons 13 and 14. What information, arguments, and other perspectives have they encountered in the documents from these lessons that connect to the prompt? Provide students with the opportunity to continue their evidence logs.

Also consider using the "Give One, Get One" activity, described in the "Teaching Strategies" section of our website at facinghistory.org/reconstruction-era/strategies, to give students the opportunity to share the evidence they have collected and identify questions they have about what they are learning. You can focus the activity with the question: *Who do you think was most responsible for the defeat of Reconstruction governments in Southern states in the 1870s?*

After the activity, have students reflect in their journals on the following questions:

- How has what you have learned about the effects of violence on democracy changed your thinking about the prompt?

- What did you learn today? How does this information relate to the essay prompt?

- What else do you want to know?

DEVELOPING A THESIS

Although students will continue to gather evidence throughout the final two lessons of this unit, this is an appropriate time for them to begin the process of developing their position in response to the writing prompt and crafting a thesis to express it. The "Writing Strategies" section suggests a variety of activities to help students begin this process. Consider using the following strategies from the guide:

- "Taking a Stand on Controversial Issues"

- "Building Arguments Through Mini-Debates"

SECTION 6
MEMORY AND LEGACY

This section contains the following lessons:

LESSON 15 The Power of Myth and the Purpose of History

ESSENTIAL QUESTION

How does our experience and memory of the past affect our choices and beliefs in the present?

TRANSITION

In the last lesson, students learned about the transition from a more inclusive democracy to a segregated society as Reconstruction ended. In this lesson, students will learn about the misrepresentations of the history of Reconstruction that emerged at the same time. They will reflect on how the way a society understands its history can reinforce the existence of "in" groups and "out" groups in the present. They will also consider the relationship between the study of history and the creation and maintenance of a just, democratic society.

RATIONALE

Perhaps one of the most enduring legacies of Reconstruction is its historiography—the very way that the history of the era has been remembered over the past 140 years. As Southern states dismantled the interracial democracy of the Reconstruction era, history itself became one of the most powerful tools they used in justifying and establishing a racially segregated society. By the turn of the twentieth century, a historical narrative about Reconstruction had emerged that claimed that "Negro rule" had ruined the South and that white supremacy and segregation were necessary to restore the noble society that white Southerners believed had existed there before the Civil War. That narrative dominated history books until the 1960s, and as a result, few other periods of American history have been as contested or misunderstood as Reconstruction.

By examining some of the ways that Reconstruction has been remembered and misremembered, students will gain a deeper understanding of what is at stake when we study history. They will reflect on the power of history to shape the attitudes and beliefs of citizens and affect their political, economic, and social choices. They will also consider the consequences for individuals and for democracy when history is manipulated to serve political goals. Finally, learning about the historiography of Reconstruction can help students understand that studying history, learning and using the skills needed to be an effective historical thinker, and challenging persistent misconceptions with well-substantiated arguments can together be a powerful means of participating in democracy.

The Dunning School and the "Lost Cause"

The view of Reconstruction that prevailed throughout at least the first half of the twentieth century is known as the "Dunning School," named after Columbia historian William A. Dunning. Although the Dunning School's version of Reconstruction has been discredited by historians for several decades, its influence on twentieth-century politics and popular culture was significant. Even today, this version of Reconstruction's history is the only one known by many Americans. Contemporary historian Eric Foner describes the central tenets of this school of thought:

> According to this view, the vindictive Radical wing of the Republican Party, motivated by hatred of the South, overturned the lenient plans for national reunion designed by Abraham Lincoln and his successor, Andrew Johnson, and imposed black suffrage on the defeated Confederacy. There followed a sordid period of corruption and misrule, the argument went, presided over by unscrupulous political opportunists from the North (derisively termed "carpetbaggers"), southern whites who had abandoned their racial and regional loyalties to cooperate with the Radical Republicans (the "scalawags"), and the former slaves, who were allegedly unprepared for the freedom that had been thrust upon them and unfit to participate in government. Eventually, organizations such as the Ku Klux Klan, deemed patriotic by proponents of this interpretation, overthrew this "misgovernment" and restored "home rule" (a euphemism for white supremacy) to the South.[1]

The Dunning School is closely related to the persistent mythology surrounding the Civil War and Reconstruction known as the "Lost Cause" that emerged shortly after the war. The Lost Cause takes a nostalgic view of the antebellum South, holding that disagreement over states' rights rather than slavery was the central cause of the war, that slave society was a harmonious one (even for enslaved people) and that Southerners, a brave and noble people, were defeated in what amounted to an unfair fight because of the numbers and resources of the Union military. Thus, according to the Dunning School and some Lost Cause mythology, groups like the Ku Klux Klan were heroes in the Reconstruction era for fighting to restore a noble society destroyed by the war.

The Dunning School played in important role in sustaining the system of racial segregation in the South that emerged after Reconstruction because it gave scholarly justification for those who resisted calls for racial justice. Such resisters cited this version of history when arguing that protecting the political and civil rights of Southern blacks would cause the "horrors of Reconstruction" to be repeated. Therefore, the Dunning School offers us a powerful example of the influence that a society's collective understanding of the past has on the present.[2]

The Influence of The Birth of a Nation

The misconceptions of the Dunning School and the Lost Cause were embodied in some of the most significant works of American popular culture in the twentieth century. Perhaps most influential film of that century's first half, The Birth of a Nation was steeped in the Dunning School's interpretation of Reconstruction. Based on the novel The Clansman by Thomas Dixon (a university classmate of Woodrow Wilson's), the three-hour silent film glorified the Ku Klux Klan as the saviors of the South from freedpeople, portrayed as brutish and bestial. Describing his novel, Dixon wrote:

> My object is to teach the North, the young North, what it has never known— the awful suffering of the white man during the dreadful Reconstruction period. I believe that Almighty God anointed the white men of the South by

---

1 Eric Foner, *Forever Free: The Story of Emancipation and Reconstruction* (Vintage Books, 2006), xx.
2 Communication between Eric Foner and Daniel Sigward, May 28, 2014.

their suffering during that time . . . to demonstrate to the world that the white man must and shall be supreme.[3]

The Birth of a Nation was a sensation after its release in 1915. Describing the Reconstruction era, the film adapts quotations from a history book written by Woodrow Wilson, an adherent of the Dunning School. One such quotation went, "The white men were roused by a mere instinct of self-preservation . . . until at last there had sprung into existence a great Ku Klux Klan, a veritable empire of the South, to protect the Southern country." Wilson praised the movie and made it the first film ever to be screened at the White House. In New York City, *The Birth of a Nation* promoters sent white-robed horsemen riding through the city to advertise the new film about heroic Klansmen. Civil rights organizations such as the recently formed National Association for the Advancement of Colored People challenged the film's portrayal of African Americans and unsuccessfully attempted to have it banned or censored.[4] The most ambitious film ever made at the time, *The Birth of a Nation* was a popular success. African American writer James Weldon Johnson wrote in 1915 that *The Birth of a Nation* did "incalculable harm"[5] to black Americans by creating a justification for prejudice, racism, and discrimination for decades to follow. That same year, the Ku Klux Klan, inactive since the trials of 1872, reemerged across the country to terrorize African Americans and immigrants.

Challenges to the Dunning School

While the vast majority of historians in the early 1900s adhered to the Dunning School's version of Reconstruction, a few individuals challenged the prevailing view. In 1913, John Lynch, a black former congressman from South Carolina, published his book *The Facts of Reconstruction*, providing a challenge to misconceptions about African Americans' preparedness for freedom from someone who actively participated in the era's politics.

A milestone in the historiography of Reconstruction arrived in 1935 with W. E. B. Du Bois's book *Black Reconstruction in America*. With the book, Du Bois not only sought to set the historical record straight but also took his fellow historians of the era to task. In a chapter entitled "The Propaganda of History," he questions the motives behind Dunning School histories, and he then states: "Nations reel and stagger on their way; they make hideous mistakes; they commit frightful wrongs; they do great and beautiful things. And shall we not best guide humanity by telling the truth about all this, so far as the truth is ascertainable?"[6]

Although Du Bois's work provided a powerful refutation of Dunning School mythology, its influence on the American public paled in comparison to *Gone With the Wind*, the novel and movie released during the same decade as *Black Reconstruction*. Shaped by Dunning School misconceptions and Lost Cause mythology, Margaret Mitchell's story is still well known to many Americans today. Nevertheless, Du Bois's work influenced

---

3 Quoted in "'Art [and History] by Lightning Flash': *The Birth of a Nation* and Black Protest," Roy Rosenzweig Center for History and New Media website, http://chnm.gmu.edu/episodes/the-birth-of-a-nation-and-black-protest/ (accessed Jan. 7, 2014).
4 Ibid.
5 James Weldon Johnson, March 1915, quoted in introduction to "*Birth of a Nation*, the NAACP, and the Balancing of Rights," EDSITEment! website, National Endowment for the Humanities project, http://edsitement.neh.gov/lesson-plan/birth-nation-naacp-and-balancing-rights.
6 W. E. B. Du Bois, *Black Reconstruction in America, 1860–1880* (Free Press, 1999), 714.

a new generation of historians who, beginning in the 1960s, would dismantle the Dunning School just as segregation was being dismantled in the South.

While the history of Reconstruction has been corrected by historians in academia, myths about the era from the Dunning School narrative persist among many Americans today. Eric Foner laments this misunderstanding of history: "The period of Reconstruction is probably the least well known and the least well understood era of American history. Most people know nothing about Reconstruction, or if they do think they know something, it is generally misguided, [rooted in] misconception, or a very out of date historical interpretation."[7] This lesson, like this broader unit, seeks to empower students to challenge the misconceptions Americans hold about this essential era in the history of the United States.

LEARNING GOALS

Understanding: Students will understand that:

- The way individuals understand history shapes their beliefs about the present and affects their political, economic, and social choices.

- History can be used as a powerful tool to reinforce the existence of "in" groups and "out" groups in the present.

- Challenging misconceptions about history with accurate and well-substantiated claims can be a powerful means of contributing to a healthier democracy.

Knowledge: Students will know that:

- Until the 1960s, most US history books, films, and other works of popular culture told an incorrect story of Reconstruction that was used to justify segregation in society.

- Even though historians have established a more accurate version of Reconstruction's history, many Americans still hold misconceptions created by the outdated narrative from the early twentieth century.

RESOURCE LIST

- "Movie Poster for *The Birth of a Nation* (1915)" (image)
- "*The Birth of a Nation* Summarizes Reconstruction" (document)
- "The Importance of Getting History Right" (document)
- "W. E. B. Du Bois Reflects on the Purpose of History" (document)
- "*The Birth of a Nation* Depicts the South Carolina Legislature": 1:53:45–1:56:45 (film clip)
- "*The Birth of a Nation* Depicts Klansmen as Heroes": 2:45:50–2:59:00 (film clip)

To stream clips from *The Birth of a Nation*, visit facinghistory.org/reconstruction-era/videos.

---

7 "Eric Foner on Reconstruction and Its Legacy," video presented by the Gilder-Lehrman Institute of American History (2009), http://www.youtube.com/watch?v=NmEcPCiiDjs (accessed Jan 7, 2014).

ACTIVITY SUGGESTIONS

*Note that a detailed Common Core–aligned close reading protocol for the document "W. E. B. Du Bois Reflects on the Purpose of History" (**Handout 15.4**) follows this lesson. The Common Core standards recommend that students begin a close reading activity with little, if any, prior knowledge of the text at the heart of the activity. Therefore, if you plan to include a close reading of this document in your unit, we recommend that you complete the activity prior to any activities in this lesson that include it.*

Consider using the following activity ideas and strategies when you implement this lesson in your classroom.

- Begin with a journal reflection on the following prompt: *Why is history important? How does our experience and memory of the past affect our choices and beliefs in the present?*

- Explain that the story of Reconstruction told by many famous works of popular culture from the twentieth century is considered by most historians today to be inaccurate, racist, and obsolete. Introduce the film *The Birth of a Nation* using context from the rationale for this lesson. There are a variety of ways that you can help students critically observe this film's version of Reconstruction, in which Ku Klux Klan members are portrayed as heroes saving white Southerners from the supposed danger and tyranny of black political participation. Consider using one or all of the following approaches:

  - Use the "Analyzing Visual Images" strategy with **Handout 15.1** ("Movie Poster for *The Birth of a Nation*") to help students reflect on the film's portrayal of the Ku Klux Klan as heroic.

  - Use the "Big Paper" silent-conversation strategy with **Handout 15.2** ("*The Birth of a Nation* Summarizes Reconstruction") to invite students to critique the brief introduction of the era that appears on-screen in the movie.

  - Watch a short clip from the film (suggestions and links are listed in the resource list above), having students apply the "Two-Column Note-taking" strategy in their journals as they watch. In the left column, they can record a running list of notable images and words they see in the clip. In the right column, they can comment on their observations, using what they have learned in this unit to identify stereotypes and inaccurate or questionable depictions of the era. Students will likely need a few minutes after watching the clip to complete the right column. Please preview these clips as they contain racist and disturbing images to determine if they are appropriate for your class.

  To learn more about all three teaching strategies mentioned above, visit facinghistory.org/reconstruction-era/strategies.

- Give students the opportunity to reflect on the inaccuracies and stereotypes they identify in *The Birth of a Nation*:

  - The document "The Importance of Getting History Right" (**Handout 15.3**) briefly and directly makes the connection between the story of Reconstruction told by sources such as *The Birth of a Nation* and the reality of segregated Southern society during the twentieth century.

  - In the document "W. E. B. Du Bois Reflects on the Purpose of History" (**Handout 15.4**). Du Bois argues powerfully that seeking accuracy in history can lead to a more just society. The close-reading activity for this text that follows the lesson will help students reach a deeper understanding of Du Bois's ideas about the connection between history and democracy.

- Conclude this lesson by asking students to write a one-page letter to D. W. Griffith, the director of *The Birth of a Nation*. In the letter, students should identify a scene or portrayal in the film that is not accurate and use what they have learned in this unit to explain why it is inaccurate. They should then argue why it is important that Griffith's portrayal of Reconstruction be corrected.

MOVIE POSTER FOR *THE BIRTH OF A NATION* (1915)

The following poster was used to advertise the movie The Birth of a Nation *in 1915.*

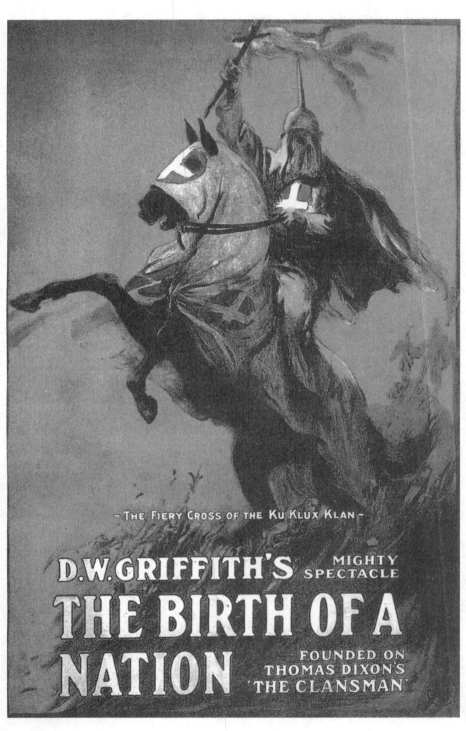

Film poster via Wikimedia Commons

THE BIRTH OF A NATION SUMMARIZES RECONSTRUCTION

The following summary of Reconstruction, which quotes heavily from a history textbook written by President Woodrow Wilson, appears screen by screen to introduce part two of the silent film The Birth of a Nation.[1]

Second part—Reconstruction.
The agony which the South endured that a nation might be born.

The blight of war does not end when hostilities cease.

This is an historical presentation of the Civil War and Reconstruction Period, and is not meant to reflect on any race or people of today.

Excerpts from Woodrow Wilson's "History of the American People:"

" . . . . . Adventurers swarmed out of the North, as much the enemies of one race as of the other, to cozen, beguile, and use the negroes . . . . . In the villages the negroes were the office holders, men who knew none of the uses of authority, except its insolences."

" . . . . The policy of the congressional leaders wrought . . . a veritable overthrow of civilization in the South . . . . . in their determination to 'put the white South under the heel of the black South.'"

"The white men were roused by a mere instinct of self-preservation . . . . . until at last there had sprung into existence a great Ku Klux Klan, a veritable empire of the South, to protect the Southern country."

---

1 Transcribed from the film *The Birth of a Nation* (1915), available to stream at https://archive.org/details/dw_griffith_birth_of_a_nation.

THE IMPORTANCE OF GETTING HISTORY RIGHT

Misconceptions about the history of Reconstruction persist today. Historian James Grossman describes the importance of establishing an accurate history of Reconstruction:

It is important to get Reconstruction right because for nearly a century, especially in the South, white Americans denied African Americans the vote. White Americans denied the possibility [and] the implications of full citizenship for African Americans by pointing to Reconstruction as a failure, by saying, "Look what happened. We gave these people the vote and these states were run in a corrupt fashion and everything went to hell in a handbasket." Well, it's not true. In fact, Reconstruction governments were successful for their time—they were clean, they were progressive—and as W. E. B. Du Bois said back in the 1930s, what white Southerners feared far more than black failure was black success. Reconstruction governments were successful, and that's why they had to be taken down.[1]

---

1 Transcribed from video interview related to the film *Slavery by Another Name* (PBS), available at http://www.pbs.org/tpt/slavery-by-another-name/themes/reconstruction/video-getting-reconstruction-right/ (accessed April 12, 2013).

W. E. B. DU BOIS REFLECTS ON THE PURPOSE OF HISTORY

The following is an excerpt from a chapter titled "The Propaganda of History" in W. E. B. Du Bois's influential 1935 book Black Reconstruction in America.

How the facts of American history have in the last half century been falsified because the nation was ashamed. The South was ashamed because it fought to perpetuate human slavery. The North was ashamed because it had to call in the black men to save the Union, abolish slavery and establish democracy.

What are American children taught today about Reconstruction? . . . [A]n American youth attending college today would learn from current textbooks of history that the Constitution recognized slavery; that the chance of getting rid of slavery by peaceful methods was ruined by the Abolitionists; that after the period of Andrew Jackson, the two sections of the United States "had become fully conscious of their conflicting interests. Two irreconcilable forms of civilization . . . [with] the democratic . . . in the South, a more stationary and aristocratic civilization." He would read that Harriet Beecher Stowe brought on the Civil War; that the assault on Charles Sumner was due to his "coarse invective" against a South Carolina Senator; and that Negroes were the only people to achieve emancipation with no effort on their part. That Reconstruction was a disgraceful attempt to subject white people to ignorant Negro rule . . .

In other words, he would in all probability complete his education without any idea of the part which the black race has played in America; of the tremendous moral problem of abolition; of the cause and meaning of the Civil War and the relation which Reconstruction had to democratic government and the labor movement today . . .

War and especially civil strife leave terrible wounds. It is the duty of humanity to heal them. It was therefore soon conceived as neither wise nor patriotic to speak of all the causes of strife and the terrible results to which national differences in the United States had led. And so, first of all, we minimized the slavery controversy which convulsed the nation from the Missouri Compromise down to the Civil War. On top of that, we passed by Reconstruction with a phrase of regret or disgust.

But are these reasons of courtesy and philanthropy sufficient for denying Truth? If history is going to be scientific, if the record of human action is going to be set down with the accuracy and faithfulness of detail which will allow its use as a measuring rod and guidepost for the future of nations, there must be set some standards of ethics in research and interpretation.

If, on the other hand, we are going to use history for our pleasure and amusement, for inflating our national ego, and giving us a false but pleasurable sense of accomplishment, then we must give up the idea of history as a science or as an art using the results of science, and admit frankly that we are using a version of historic fact in order to influence and educate the new generation along the way we wish.

It is propaganda like this that has led men in the past to insist that history is "lies agreed upon"; and to point out the danger in such misinformation. It is indeed extremely doubtful if any permanent benefit comes to the world through such action. Nations reel and stagger on their way; they make hideous mistakes; they commit frightful wrongs; they do great and beautiful things. And shall we not best guide humanity by telling the truth about all this, so far as the truth is ascertainable?[1]

---

1 W. E. B. Du Bois, *Black Reconstruction in America, 1860–1880* (Free Press, 1999), 711–714.

Excerpt from "The Propaganda of History" by W. E. B. Du Bois

*Close reading is carefully and purposefully **rereading** a text. It's an encounter with the text in which we closely focus on what the author has to say, what the author's purpose is, what the words mean, and what the structure of the text tells us. Close reading ensures that we truly understand what we've read. At Facing History and Ourselves, we use this careful investigation of text to make connections to essential questions about history, human behavior, and ourselves. This protocol can be used to implement a close reading for select documents during the Reconstruction unit. Adapt this procedure to meet your goals and the needs of your students.*

FIRST READ: Read aloud. Either the teacher or an extremely fluent student can read the text aloud. Ask students to circle unfamiliar words as they listen. After the read-aloud, as students share these words with the class, decide which words to define immediately to limit confusion and which definitions you want students to uncover through careful reading.

SECOND READ: Individual read. Ask students to read silently to get a feel for the text. They can note specific words or phrases that jump out at them for any number of reasons: because they are interesting, familiar, strange, confusing, funny, troubling, difficult, etc. Share some of these as a class. Particular questions to ask students at this stage of the reading are:

- What can you already infer about the author of this text?

- How is the text structured?

- Does this structure make it easy or difficult to make meaning?

- Does this structure tell us anything about the author's style or purpose?

THIRD READ: Text-dependent questions. In small groups, have students read the text in chunks and answer a set of text-dependent questions. These questions are included with each closereading exemplar. Sample answers are provided to help guide the teacher. See the "Close Reading E: Student Handout" form for a student version of the document. See "Close Reading E: Teacher Guide" for the teacher's version.

FOURTH READ: Visual image. In small groups, have students create a visual image on paper that captures the essence of the text. You may also want them to include three words or a sentence summary of each section of text. Groups can be assigned either the entire text or sections of text for this portion of the close reading.

FIFTH READ: Gallery read. Ask students to do a "gallery read" of the images that have been created.

TRANSITION TO DISCUSSION

At this point, we recommend organizing a class discussion so that students can make connections beyond the text. This discussion can be informal or can use the format of the "Socratic Seminar" or "Save the Last Word for Me" strategy (see the "Teaching Strategies" section of our website at facinghistory.org/reconstruction-era/strategies for details).

DISCUSSION SUGGESTIONS

As mentioned earlier, this unit includes two writing prompts. Both prompts can be used to launch a discussion after a close reading. Examples include:

- To connect to the argumentative writing prompt (*Support, refute, or modify the statement: Laws are the most important factor in overcoming racism and prejudice*):

  - What is the role of history in creating a just democracy? What is the role of education and history textbooks in creating a society that overcomes racism and prejudice? How does Du Bois answer this question about the history of Reconstruction? How do you answer that question?

- To connect to the informative writing prompt: *Historian Eric Foner calls Reconstruction "America's unfinished revolution." What debates and dilemmas from the Reconstruction era remain unresolved? After researching informational texts on Reconstruction, write an essay in which you explain one debate that was central to this period that remained unresolved. Explain why the debate was significant to the history of Reconstruction. In your conclusion, discuss the legacy of the debate not being resolved.*

  - Ask students to find connections between Du Bois's statements and this prompt. What does Du Bois say is left "unfinished" about the history of Reconstruction?

  - Ask students to find connections between Du Bois's arguments about history education and their schooling today. What other histories feel "unfinished" to students today? What do they want to learn more about? What parts of Reconstruction do they think should be included in textbooks today?

- To connect to more general Facing History and Ourselves themes:

  - How does our experience and memory of the past affect our choices and beliefs in the present?

  - What is the goal of learning history? How do we uncover the histories that are not in our textbooks?

  - How do the legacies of Reconstruction impact our understanding of society today? How might not knowing the true history of Reconstruction impact others' understanding of society today?

  - What is your role in creating a society that values "truth" in history?

  - How can you help educate others about what you have learned about Reconstruction?

  - How can you be a critical consumer of media today so that you are not swayed by propaganda but instead are able to investigate the complexity of a situation?

- It's also possible to have students themselves create the questions for a discussion. To do this, you might guide students by asking them to find connections between the essential questions and the text or to write questions based on what resonates for them. They might choose to make connections to the author's purpose, the structure of the text, the tone of the text, or the main messages of the text. Alternatively, they may want to make connections to issues related to memory and legacy, to examples of histories not yet fully told, to the role of education in a democracy, and beyond.

CLOSE READING E Teacher Guide

Excerpt from "The Propaganda of History" by W. E. B. Du Bois

How the facts of American history have in the last half century been falsified because the nation was ashamed. The South was ashamed because it fought to perpetuate human slavery. The North was ashamed because it had to call in the black men to save the Union, abolish slavery and establish democracy.

What are American children taught today about Reconstruction? . . . [A]n American youth attending college today would learn from current textbooks of history that the Constitution recognized slavery; that the chance of getting rid of slavery by peaceful methods was ruined by the Abolitionists; that after the period of Andrew Jackson, the two sections of the United States "had become fully conscious of their conflicting interests. Two irreconcilable forms of civilization . . . [with] the democratic . . . in the South, a more stationary and aristocratic civilization." He would read that Harriet Beecher Stowe brought on the Civil War; that the assault on Charles Sumner was due to his "coarse invective" against a South Carolina Senator; and that Negroes were the only people to achieve emancipation with no effort on their part. That Reconstruction was a disgraceful attempt to subject white people to ignorant Negro rule . . . .

Guided Close Reading with Text-Dependent Questions

1. **According to Du Bois, why have "the facts of American history" been changed? Based on what you can you infer, who does Du Bois believe is responsible for providing the misinformation?**

   A good close reading starts with some "easy wins" for students. They should answer this question by noting that American history is not being represented truthfully because Americans feel "ashamed." Students should recognize that Du Bois attributes the falsification of information to Americans in both the South and the North because he claims that Southerners and Northerners feel embarrassed by their history, although for different reasons.

2. **Paraphrase in your own words what Du Bois claims that American students are taught about Reconstruction as it relates to slavery and the experience of African Americans.**

   Students should be able to list a number of facts from the second paragraph. Their paraphrase should include ideas such as the claims that slavery was recognized by the Constitution and that abolitionists are to blame for the nation's inability to solve the conflict over slavery peacefully. They should also note that during the period before the Civil War, the North and the South developed into two very different societies—the North being "democratic" and the South being "aristocratic." Lastly, they should note that historically, students have been taught that African Americans were the only group of people to be emancipated "with no effort on their part."

3. **Based on what you can infer, what did Du Bois want readers to take away from his list of "facts" about slavery and the African American experience?**

   Students should recognize that the facts presented in the second paragraph are very one-sided, telling only a portion of the truth. The information does not reflect the African American experience and seems to be a list of excuses for the events of the Civil War and Reconstruction rather than an accurate description of what transpired. Du Bois's heightened language in describing these so-called facts reflects

Excerpt from "The Propaganda of History" by W. E. B. Du Bois

In other words, he would in all probability complete his education without any idea of the part which the black race has played in America; of the tremendous moral problem of abolition; of the cause and meaning of the Civil War and the relation which Reconstruction had to democratic government and the labor movement today. . . .

War and especially civil strife leave terrible wounds. It is the duty of humanity to heal them. It was therefore soon conceived as neither wise nor patriotic to speak of all the causes of strife and the terrible results to which national differences in the United States had led. And so, first of all, we minimized the slavery controversy which convulsed the nation from Missouri Compromise down to the Civil War. On top of that, we passed by Reconstruction with a phrase of regret or disgust.

Guided Close Reading with Text-Dependent Questions

his dissatisfaction with this litany of claims, such as the idea that abolitionists "ruined" chances for peace and that Reconstruction was a "disgraceful attempt" to foist "ignorant" Negro leadership on white Americans. Leading into the next paragraph, students should infer from the way the list is presented that Du Bois wants his audience to pick up on what is left out of this version of history.

4. **In the third paragraph, what does Du Bois argue that an American student would not learn about during the course of his or her education? What clues are there to his feelings about these omissions?**
After reading the paragraph, students should recognize several elements that Du Bois argues are omitted from the history of Reconstruction found in textbooks and described in the paragraph above, including any description of the contributions of African Americans to the history of America, "the tremendous moral problem of abolition," a discussion of the real "cause and meaning of the Civil War," and an accurate portrayal of the relationship between Reconstruction and "democratic government" or the present-day labor movement. Students should understand that Du Bois finds such omissions troubling and serious. The language he uses in this paragraph, such as the phrases "the tremendous moral problem of abolition" and "without any idea of the part which the black race has played in America," makes it clear that he believes that these facts need to be taught in schools and understood by American students.

5. **Based on information from the third and fourth paragraphs, what can you infer that Du Bois thinks was the cause of the Civil War?**
Students should link the fact that Du Bois lists "the cause and meaning of the Civil War" as something that American students do not learn about to his reference to the "slavery controversy" in the fourth paragraph. The juxtaposition of these points in his argument should point to his belief that slavery was the real cause of the war.

Guided Close Reading
with Text-Dependent Questions

6. **What duty does Du Bois believe humanity has in the wake of war and violence?**

   Students should answer this question by referring to the first two sentences of the fourth paragraph, where Du Bois states that "the duty of humanity" is to "heal" the "terrible wounds" that have been left by "war and especially civil strife."

7. **According to Du Bois, why did Americans minimize the historical controversy over slavery?**

   In the fourth paragraph, Du Bois recognizes the "terrible wounds" caused by war and "civil strife." Because of the pain and suffering and the damage to the nation, after the Civil War, people did not care to discuss the differences that led to the conflict. Students should note that Americans generally believed that the best way to heal was to ignore the issue of slavery. It should be noted that in this paragraph, Du Bois makes a point of using the pronoun "we." The change in this paragraph is important for two reasons: first, Du Bois is recognizing that the recovery from the Civil War and Reconstruction is something that everyone in the nation, all "humanity," needs to confront together. Further, he is not placing blame on one group in particular for the way that the "slavery controversy" has been ignored. Instead, he understands that Northerners and Southerners, white Americans and black Americans, have all allowed this omission to occur, and it is everyone's responsibility to confront history together. (This is quite similar to Lincoln's way of discussing slavery in his Second Inaugural Address.)

8. **Paraphrase in your own words the question that opens the fifth paragraph: "But are these reasons of courtesy and philanthropy sufficient for denying Truth?" What are the "reasons of courtesy and philanthropy" that Du Bois is referring to? What "Truth" does he believe is being denied?**

   Students should begin to answer this question by understanding the surface meaning of Du Bois's words. The important point for students to tease out is the fact that he is questioning whether or not presenting false

But are these reasons of courtesy and philanthropy sufficient for denying Truth? If history is going to be scientific, if the record of human action is going to be set down with the accuracy and faithfulness of detail which will allow its use as a measuring rod and guidepost for the future of nations, there must be set some standards of ethics in research and interpretation.

information is acceptable in order to make others feel better. Students should know that the phrase "courtesy and philanthropy" refers to the nation's response to dealing with the legacy of the Civil War, and that the "Truth" that is being denied in this case is the history of slavery in this country.

9. **Explain the two competing visions of history that Du Bois presents. How does each version differ from the other, and what are the implications of each?**

Du Bois claims that there are two possible ways to think about the subject of history. On the one hand, he says, history can be treated as a science, or as an "art using the results of science." If treated this way, history should be "the record of human action" truthfully and meticulously documented in order for the nation to use the past as a way to move forward. In this case, there should be "standards of ethics" put forth in order to ensure that facts are being recorded faithfully and accurately. On the other hand, he says, history can be stripped of facts and details or manipulated, meant purely to be used for "pleasure and amusement" or "inflating our national ego." In that case, he says, we must understand that what we are representing is not the truth but rather a version of the facts used simply to "influence and educate the new generation along the way we wish."

10. **Based on clues from the surrounding text and paragraph, define the word propaganda. Which vision of history that Du Bois presents in the previous two paragraphs is he referring to with the phrase "lies agreed upon"?**

Students should recognize that Du Bois uses the word propaganda to describe the type of history that he outlines in the previous paragraph—the use of historical facts that are not completely truthful or accurate to influence others. Therefore, propaganda can be contextually defined as "misinformation." Students should also understand that he is referring to the same type of propaganda-based history when he describes that version as "lies agreed upon."

Excerpt from "The Propaganda of History" by W. E. B. Du Bois

If, on the other hand, we are going to use history for our pleasure and amusement, for inflating our national ego, and giving us a false but pleasurable sense of accomplishment, then we must give up the idea of history as a science or as an art using the results of science, and admit frankly that we are using a version of historic fact in order to influence and educate the new generation along the way we wish.

It is propaganda like this that has led men in the past to insist that history is "lies agreed upon"; and to point out the danger in such misinformation. It is indeed extremely doubtful if any permanent benefit comes to the world through such action. Nations reel and stagger on their way; they make hideous mistakes; they commit frightful wrongs; they do great and beautiful things. And shall we not best guide humanity by telling the truth about all this, so far as the truth is ascertainable?

[From W. E. B. Du Bois, *Black Reconstruction in America, 1860–1880* (Free Press, 1999), 711–714.]

Guided Close Reading
with Text-Dependent Questions

11. **What additional concern does Du Bois raise in the final paragraph about the difference between scientific and non-scientific history?**

Students should reference Du Bois's point about the danger of "misinformation" and accepting a history that is little more than "lies agreed upon." As students should note, Du Bois says that it is "extremely doubtful" that this perpetuation of misinformation for the purpose of influencing others carries any benefits. This point of view should be contrasted with the idea that omitting things from history, such as ignoring the issue of slavery, is necessary for genuine healing to occur. Du Bois is arguing that treating history this way causes more harm than good.

12. **What is the significance of Du Bois ending his argument with a question?**

Students should recognize that by ending with a question, Du Bois is asking his audience to reflect on whether or not they agree that history should be a presentation of all the facts rather than the shaping of some information to change perceptions of it. Given that Du Bois earlier suggests that history is meant to serve as a "measuring rod or guidepost" for nations moving forward, he clearly believes that we are best served by "telling the truth about all this"—both the "hideous mistakes" and the "beautiful things."

13. **Based on what you can infer, what does Du Bois believe is missing from the way that historians manage the subject of Reconstruction? How do these omissions fit into Du Bois's larger arguments about the treatment of history?**

It should be clear to students that Du Bois does not believe that the African American experience is sufficiently included in the history of Reconstruction. Rather than recording all of the facts "with the accuracy and faithfulness of detail," as he argues that history should, his contemporaries' understanding of Reconstruction is limited and selective. Du Bois, it can be inferred, believes that because only one side of the story is being told, this history is not being treated as a science with "standards of ethics in research and interpretation." Instead, he thinks it is a false representation of fact designed to give the nation a "pleasurable sense of accomplishment."

Excerpt from "The Propaganda of History" by W. E. B. Du Bois

How the facts of American history have in the last half century been falsified because the nation was ashamed. The South was ashamed because it fought to perpetuate human slavery. The North was ashamed because it had to call in the black men to save the Union, abolish slavery and establish democracy.

What are American children taught today about Reconstruction? . . . [A]n American youth attending college today would learn from current textbooks of history that the Constitution recognized slavery; that the chance of getting rid of slavery by peaceful methods was ruined by the Abolitionists; that after the period of Andrew Jackson, the two sections of the United States "had become fully conscious of their conflicting interests. Two irreconcilable forms of civilization . . . [with] the democratic . . . in the South, a more stationary and aristocratic civilization." He would read that Harriet Beecher Stowe brought on the Civil War; that the assault on Charles Sumner was due to his "coarse invective" against a South Carolina Senator; and that Negroes were the only people to achieve emancipation with no effort on their part. That Reconstruction was a disgraceful attempt to subject white people to ignorant Negro rule. . . .

Guided Close Reading with Text-Dependent Questions

1. According to Du Bois, why have "the facts of American history" been changed? Based on what you can you infer, who does Du Bois believe is responsible for providing the misinformation?

2. Paraphrase in your own words what Du Bois claims that American students are taught about Reconstruction as it relates to slavery and the experience of African Americans.

3. Based on what you can infer, what did Du Bois want readers to take away from his list of "facts" about slavery and the African American experience?

Excerpt from "The Propaganda of History"
by W. E. B. Du Bois

In other words, he would in all probability complete his education without any idea of the part which the black race has played in America; of the tremendous moral problem of abolition; of the cause and meaning of the Civil War and the relation which Reconstruction had to democratic government and the labor movement today . . .

War and especially civil strife leave terrible wounds. It is the duty of humanity to heal them. It was therefore soon conceived as neither wise nor patriotic to speak of all the causes of strife and the terrible results to which national differences in the United States had led. And so, first of all, we minimized the slavery controversy which convulsed the nation from Missouri Compromise down to the Civil War. On top of that, we passed by Reconstruction with a phrase of regret or disgust.

4. In the third paragraph, what does Du Bois argue that an American student would *not* learn about during the course of his or her education? What clues are there to his feelings about these omissions?

5. Based on information from the third and fourth paragraphs, what can you infer that Du Bois thinks was the cause of the Civil War?

Excerpt from "The Propaganda of History"
by W. E. B. Du Bois

6. What duty does Du Bois believe humanity has in the wake of war and violence?

7. According to Du Bois, why did Americans minimize the historical controversy over slavery?

8. Paraphrase in your own words the question that opens the fifth paragraph: "But are these reasons of courtesy and philanthropy sufficient for denying Truth?" "What are the "reasons of courtesy and philanthropy" that Du Bois is referring to? What "Truth" does he believe is being denied?

But are these reasons of courtesy and philanthropy sufficient for denying Truth? If history is going to be scientific, if the record of human action is going to be set down with the accuracy and faithfulness of detail which will allow its use as a measuring rod and guidepost for the future of nations, there must be set some standards of ethics in research and interpretation.

Excerpt from "The Propaganda of History"
by W. E. B. Du Bois

If, on the other hand, we are going to use history for our pleasure and amusement, for inflating our national ego, and giving us a false but pleasurable sense of accomplishment, then we must give up the idea of history as a science or as an art using the results of science, and admit frankly that we are using a version of historic fact in order to influence and educate the new generation along the way we wish.

9. **Explain the two competing visions of history that Du Bois presents. How does each version differ from the other, and what are the implications of each?**

It is propaganda like this that has led men in the past to insist that history is "lies agreed upon"; and to point out the danger in such misinformation. It is indeed extremely doubtful if any permanent benefit comes to the world through such action. Nations reel and stagger on their way; they make hideous mistakes; they commit frightful wrongs; they do great and beautiful things. And shall we not best guide humanity by telling the truth about all this, so far as the truth is ascertainable?

[From W. E. B. Du Bois, *Black Reconstruction in America, 1860–1880* (Free Press, 1999), 711–714.]

10. **Based on clues from the surrounding text and paragraph, define the word *propaganda*. Which vision of history that Du Bois presents in the previous two paragraphs is he referring to with the phrase "lies agreed upon"?**

Excerpt from "The Propaganda of History"
by W. E. B. Du Bois

11. What additional concern does Du Bois raise in the final paragraph about the difference between scientific and non-scientific history?

12. What is the significance of Du Bois ending his argument with a question?

13. Based on what you can infer, what does Du Bois believe is missing from the way that historians manage the subject of Reconstruction? How do these omissions fit into Du Bois's larger arguments about the treatment of history?

LESSON 16 The Unfinished Revolution

ESSENTIAL QUESTIONS

Why has democracy been called a "work in progress"? What can individuals do to help bring about a more just and equal society?

TRANSITION

In the previous lesson, students examined the way that Reconstruction has been remembered and mythologized over the past 150 years, and they reflected on how history can be used to reinforce the existence of "in" groups and "out" groups in society. In this lesson, students will identify and research contemporary debates that echo those of the Reconstruction era, and they will reflect on the idea of democracy as a continuous process rather than a fixed achievement. Finally, students will consider how they can best participate in the ongoing work of strengthening our democracy.

RATIONALE

So many of the debates at the heart of the Reconstruction era are also central to the entire sweep of American history, and many are still being debated today, including these key questions:

- What does it mean to be free?

- What is equality, and how can it be measured?

- What is the role of laws and government in creating a more just and equal society?

- Who can be a citizen, to what rights are citizens entitled, and under what conditions can those rights be denied?

- Who is entitled to vote, and under what circumstances can voting rights be denied?

- What is the proper relationship between the federal government, state governments, and individuals?

These questions contain some of the fundamental issues and problems of a democracy. They were at the core of the debates surrounding the writing of United States Constitution, and there have been a number of times in American history when they have been illuminated and challenged. In a single lesson, it is not possible for a class to investigate deeply all of the ways that these questions continue to fuel debates in contemporary society. The goal of this lesson is to provide students with the opportunity to identify how one or more of these questions that were central to the dilemmas of Reconstruction are still being debated today. In doing so, students can gain a deeper understanding of democracy as a continuous process rather than a finished product, and they can begin to understand why Eric Foner has referred to Reconstruction as "America's unfinished revolution."

"I Have a Dream"

An excellent starting point for these investigations is for the class to look together at a portion of Martin Luther King Jr.'s famous "I Have a Dream" speech. The civil rights movement is the direct historical legacy of Reconstruction; some historians, in fact, have referred to it as the Second Reconstruction. This social and political movement of the twentieth century is an essential topic in any student's study of American history, and it deserves its own in-depth investigation (visit facinghistory.org/reconstruction-era/links for a collection of resources pertaining to the civil rights movement). King's 1963 speech was one of the defining moments of the movement. As part of the March on Washington, King spoke from the steps of the Lincoln Memorial to between 200,000 and 300,000 marchers in the centennial year of the Emancipation Proclamation. The march was organized to rally support for a new civil rights bill proposed by the Kennedy administration that was being debated in Congress. King's speech tied the civil rights movement to the ideals of freedom and equality expressed during the nation's founding and reaffirmed in the laws and amendments of Reconstruction. In referring to those ideals as a promissory note, a check to be cashed by future Americans, King has provided a powerful framework for an investigation of the realities of American life in relation to these ideals.

Contemporary Echoes

Even after the many successes of the civil rights movement, Americans continue to debate the extent of the progress we have made and whether or not our society lives up to its ideals of freedom and equality. The principle of equality was enshrined in the Constitution for the first time through the Fourteenth Amendment's equal protection clause. Yet, like the meaning of the Fourteenth Amendment itself, the true meaning of equality has been a source of debate and conflict in American society ever since.

This lesson offers teachers and students the opportunity to explore the ways in which debates over freedom and equality are continuing to take place in our contemporary society. The first question the class might consider is how we might go about measuring freedom and equality in the first place. What evidence might we look for that would show that all of the members of our society are both free and equal? This lesson will then prompt teachers and students to review some of the nineteenth-century debates about freedom and equality that they learned about in this unit and consider the ways that these debates are still alive today. Teachers might provide students with some of the resources suggested in this lesson as a springboard into a deeper research project about one or more of the ongoing debates about the meaning of freedom and equality.

For some students, there is a potential risk in discovering that questions about equality and justice at the core of the Reconstruction era are still at the center of contemporary political debates in the United States: their emotional reactions to some realities of American society and their own place in it can lead them to feel disempowered. It is therefore important to emphasize how this unit has been grounded in an examination of democracy as an ongoing process. As former federal judge William Hastie said, democracy can "easily be lost, but never is fully won. Its essence is eternal struggle." The goal of studying Reconstruction and assessing the state of our nation today in relation to its goals is not to dishearten students but rather to illuminate for them the continuous need for constructive participation and engagement to maintain and strengthen our democracy.

Choosing to Participate

We conclude this unit by asking students to consider how they, today, can best help to strengthen our democracy. It is important to leave students with a sense of their own agency and the ways that they can use their voices and their choices to make a positive difference in the world. In the first lesson of this unit, students reflected on the relationship between identity, freedom, and agency. As students finish their study of Reconstruction, it is worth having them consider again their own identities and agency and, in particular, how they might cultivate the identity of an upstander. What values, experiences, and skills are necessary? To help students think about this question, this lesson includes a speech by Bryan Stevenson, a lawyer who founded the Equal Justice Initiative to bring about a fairer criminal justice system in the United States. Stevenson discusses both the difficulty and the importance of addressing the contemporary legacies of slavery, Reconstruction, and segregation, but he also inspires hope that individuals can make a difference. This lesson also includes an excerpt from a speech by Ruth Simmons, the former president of Brown University. Simmons describes how education helped her escape the poverty and discrimination of her youth to become the president of an Ivy League university. Like so many freedpeople during the Reconstruction era, Simmons believes that education not only provides essential tools for personal empowerment but also constitutes a lifeline for democracy.

LEARNING GOALS

Understanding: Students will understand that:

- The work of ensuring a democracy's success is never complete; individuals must constantly choose to act to defend and strengthen it.

- Progress toward justice and equality does not always advance steadily but often experiences great leaps forward and disappointing steps backward.

Knowledge: Students will know that:

- The civil rights movement is the direct historical legacy of Reconstruction, and it brought progress toward realizing the ideals of the Reconstruction laws and amendments.

- Despite the successes of the civil rights movement, many dilemmas and debates about justice and equality in the United States remain unresolved today.

RESOURCE LIST

- "Making Real the Promises of Democracy" (document)

- "We Need to Talk About an Injustice" (document)

- "A Lifeline for Democracy" (document)

ACTIVITY SUGGESTIONS

Consider using the following activity ideas and strategies when you implement this lesson in your classroom.

- Have students reflect in their journals on the following quotation by William H. Hastie: "Democracy is becoming rather than being. It can easily be lost, but never is fully won. Its essence is eternal struggle."

  What do students think Hastie means when he says that democracy's essence is eternal struggle? After students finish writing, follow up with a "Think-Pair-Share" activity. (For more information about this strategy, visit facinghistory.org/reconstruction-era/strategies.)

- Before concluding this unit, it is important to provide students with the opportunity to reflect on some of the debates and realities of contemporary American life that have prompted Eric Foner to refer to Reconstruction as "America's unfinished revolution." You might begin by asking students to review their notes and reflections from Lesson 3, in which they explored the meaning of freedom in the context of the aspirations of freedpeople. They should also review their notes and reflections from Lesson 9, in which they explored the meaning of equality. Then conduct a class discussion that focuses on the following questions:

  - What do individuals need in the twenty-first century in order to be truly free? How can we measure freedom today? To what extent do people in the United States today have what they need in order to be truly free?

  - What does equality mean in the twenty-first century? How do we measure equality? To what extent is equality a reality in the United States today?

  - In what ways has American society made progress toward the ideals of freedom and equality since the Reconstruction era? In what areas does our contemporary society fall short of those ideals?

  - What is relationship between equality and freedom? Is one possible without the other?

  If time permits, the class discussion of these questions can be deepened significantly by giving students the opportunity to conduct research into the state of freedom and equality in a variety of facets of American life. You might ask students to work individually or in groups to research the state of equality in such areas of importance today and during the Reconstruction era as political participation (voting and office holding), education, and economics. In what areas do students find evidence of equality, and in what areas do they find evidence of inequality? In what areas do they see evidence of progress, and in what areas do they see a lack of progress? In order to answer these questions, students will first need to determine how they will measure equality. Will they look for equality of outcomes, or will they look for equality of opportunity? How can they know that either exists?

  While students' research may take them to a variety of resources, you might suggest the following to help them get started:

  - "Timeline: America's Long Civil Rights March" (ProPublica)

    This detailed timeline traces the steps and missteps toward civil rights and equality in the United States from Reconstruction to today.

- "King's Dream Remains an Elusive Goal" (Pew Research)

    This report of an extensive Pew survey conducted in 2013 to examine Americans' experiences with and attitudes toward race includes information about education, voting, opportunity, and incarceration.

- "African Americans' Lives Today" (NPR)

- "Latinos' Lives and Health Today" (NPR)

    These are reports from recent surveys that National Public Radio, the Robert Wood Johnson Foundation, and Harvard University conducted focusing on the experiences and attitudes of African Americans and Latinos in the United States.

    To view the resources and additional reports listed above, visit facinghistory.org/reconstruction-era/links.

- The documents "We Need to Talk About An Injustice" (**Handout 16.2**) and "A Lifeline for Democracy" (**Handout 16.3**) provide students with important examples of participation in democracy. In these speeches, lawyer Bryan Stevenson and educator Ruth Simmons discuss the experiences and beliefs that inspire their work and their ideas about how individuals can make a difference. These documents can help students reflect on the connection between their own identities and their agency in the world. Stevenson's speech is also available to view at facinghistory.org/reconstruction-era/links.

    After reading both documents, you might ask students to create identity charts for Stevenson and Simmons and then engage the class in a "Fishbowl" discussion. (For more information about this strategy, visit facinghistory.org/reconstruction-era/strategies.) Students will present opinions, ask questions, and share information when they sit in the "fishbowl" circle, while students on the outside of the circle listen carefully to the ideas presented and pay attention to process. Then the roles reverse. Structure the discussion around some of the questions below, but also let students' contributions guide the direction of the conversation when appropriate. Ask:

    - What issues have Stevenson and Simmons chosen to champion in their work? Why do you think they picked these issues?

    - What is the relationship between one's identity and one's power to make change in society? How do you think Stevenson would answer that question? How do you think Simmons would answer it?

    - What inspirations do Stevenson and Simmons describe in their lives and in their work? What legacies influence them? What inspires you in your life? What legacies influence you?

    - What do Stevenson's and Simmons's speeches teach us about participating in democracy? What qualities do you think are necessary for individuals to develop in order for them to become upstanders?

    - What issues do you think most need to be championed in your community? In your country? How can you address them? How can you help to create positive change?

MAKING REAL THE PROMISES OF DEMOCRACY

One hundred years after the Emancipation Proclamation, Martin Luther King Jr. delivered his famous "I Have a Dream" speech on the steps of the Lincoln Memorial. The following excerpt is from near the beginning of the speech.

Five score years ago a great American in whose symbolic shadow we stand today signed the Emancipation Proclamation. This momentous decree is a great beacon light of hope to millions of Negro slaves who had been seared in the flames of withering injustice. It came as a joyous daybreak to end the long night of their captivity. But 100 years later the Negro still is not free. One hundred years later the life of the Negro is still sadly crippled by the manacles of segregation and the chains of discrimination. One hundred years later the Negro lives on a lonely island of poverty in the midst of a vast ocean of material prosperity. One hundred years later the Negro is still languishing in the corners of American society and finds himself an exile in his own land. So we have come here today to dramatize a shameful condition.

In a sense we've come to our nation's capital to cash a check. When the architects of our Republic wrote the magnificent words of the Constitution and the Declaration of Independence, they were signing a promissory note to which every American was to fall heir. This note was a promise that all men—yes, black men as well as white men—would be guaranteed the unalienable rights of life, liberty and the pursuit of happiness. It is obvious today that America has defaulted on this promissory note insofar as her citizens of color are concerned. Instead of honoring this sacred obligation, America has given the Negro people a bad check, a check which has come back marked "insufficient funds."

But we refuse to believe that the bank of justice is bankrupt. We refuse to believe that there are insufficient funds in the great vaults of opportunity of this nation. So we've come to cash this check, a check that will give us upon demand the riches of freedom and the security of justice.

We have also come to this hallowed spot to remind America of the fierce urgency of now. This is no time to engage in the luxury of cooling off or to take the tranquilizing drug of gradualism. Now is the time to make real the promises of democracy. Now is the time to rise from the dark and desolate valley of segregation to the sunlit path of racial justice. Now is the time to lift our nation from the quicksands of racial injustice to the solid rock of brotherhood.

Now is the time to make justice a reality for all of God's children . . .[1]

---

1 Martin Luther King Jr., "I Have a Dream . . ." speech, delivered Aug. 28, 1963, available from the US National Archives and Records Administration website, http://www.archives.gov/press/exhibits/dream-speech.pdf.

WE NEED TO TALK ABOUT AN INJUSTICE

Democracy is shaped by individuals who champion issues they believe are important to them and their society. Alabama lawyer Bryan Stevenson has devoted his life to correcting injustices in the American criminal justice system. In his speech at a 2012 TED conference,* Stevenson explained the experiences and beliefs that inspire his work. The following is an excerpt.

I grew up in a house that was the traditional African American home that was dominated by a matriarch, and that matriarch was my grandmother. She was tough, she was strong, she was powerful. She was the end of every argument in our family. She was the beginning of a lot of arguments in our family. She was the daughter of people who were actually enslaved. Her parents were born in slavery in Virginia in the 1840s. She was born in the 1880s and the experience of slavery very much shaped the way she saw the world. . . .

And I remember, when I was about eight or nine years old, waking up one morning, going into the living room, and all of my cousins were running around. And my grandmother was sitting across the room staring at me. And at first I thought we were playing a game. And I would look at her and I'd smile, but she was very serious. And after about 15 or 20 minutes of this, she got up and she came across the room and she took me by the hand and she said, "Come on, Bryan. You and I are going to have a talk." And I remember this just like it happened yesterday. I never will forget it.

She took me out back and she said, "Bryan, I'm going to tell you something, but you don't tell anybody what I tell you." I said, "Okay, Mama." She said, "Now you make sure you don't do that." I said, "Sure." Then she sat me down and she looked at me and she said, "I want you to know I've been watching you." And she said, "I think you're special." She said, "I think you can do anything you want to do." I will never forget it.

And then she said, "I just need you to promise me three things, Bryan." I said, "Okay, Mama." She said, "The first thing I want you to promise me is that you'll always love your mom." She said, "That's my baby girl, and you have to promise me now you'll always take care of her." Well I adored my mom, so I said, "Yes, Mama. I'll do that." Then she said, "The second thing I want you to promise me is that you'll always do the right thing even when the right thing is the hard thing." And I thought about it and I said, "Yes, Mama. I'll do that." Then finally she said, "The third thing I want you to promise me is that you'll never drink alcohol." (Laughter.) Well I was nine years old, so I said, "Yes, Mama. I'll do that."

. . . And I'm going to admit something to you . . . I'm 52 years old, and I'm going to admit to you that I've never had a drop of alcohol. (Applause.) I don't say that because I think that's virtuous; I say that because there is power in identity. When we create the right kind of identity, we can say things to the world around us that they don't actually believe makes sense. We can get them to do things that they don't think they can do. When I thought about my grandmother, of course she would think all her grandkids were special. My grandfather was in prison during prohibition. My male uncles died of alcohol-related diseases. And these were the things she thought we needed to commit to.

Well I've been trying to say something about our criminal justice system. This country is very different today than it was 40 years ago. In 1972, there were 300,000 people in jails and prisons. Today,

---

* TED ("Technology, Entertainment, Design") is a nonprofit organization that sponsors conferences comprised of short talks by leaders and thinkers from a variety of disciplines.

there are 2.3 million. The United States now has the highest rate of incarceration in the world. We have seven million people on probation and parole. And mass incarceration, in my judgment, has fundamentally changed our world. In poor communities, in communities of color there is this despair, there is this hopelessness, that is being shaped by these outcomes. One out of three black men between the ages of 18 and 30 is in jail, in prison, on probation or parole. In urban communities across this country—Los Angeles, Philadelphia, Baltimore, Washington—50 to 60 percent of all young men of color are in jail or prison or on probation or parole.

Our system isn't just being shaped in these ways that seem to be distorting around race, they're also distorted by poverty. We have a system of justice in this country that treats you much better if you're rich and guilty than if you're poor and innocent. Wealth, not culpability, shapes outcomes. And yet, we seem to be very comfortable. The politics of fear and anger have made us believe that these are problems that are not our problems. We've been disconnected.

It's interesting to me. We're looking at some very interesting developments in our work. My state of Alabama, like a number of states, actually permanently disenfranchises you if you have a criminal conviction. Right now in Alabama 34 percent of the black male population has permanently lost the right to vote. We're actually projecting in another 10 years the level of disenfranchisement will be as high as it's been since prior to the passage of the Voting Rights Act. And there is this stunning silence . . .

I talk a lot about these issues . . . And it's interesting, when I teach my students about African American history, I tell them about slavery. I tell them about terrorism, the era that began at the end of Reconstruction that went on to World War II. We don't really know very much about it. But for African Americans in this country, that was an era defined by terror. In many communities, people had to worry about being lynched. They had to worry about being bombed. It was the threat of terror that shaped their lives. And these older people come up to me now and they say, "Mr. Stevenson, you give talks, you make speeches, you tell people to stop saying we're dealing with terrorism for the first time in our nation's history after 9/11." They tell me to say, "No, tell them that we grew up with that." And that era of terrorism, of course, was followed by segregation and decades of racial subordination . . .

And yet, we have in this country this dynamic where we really don't like to talk about our problems. We don't like to talk about our history. And because of that, we really haven't understood what it's meant to do the things we've done historically. We're constantly running into each other. We're constantly creating tensions and conflicts. We have a hard time talking about race, and I believe it's because we are unwilling to commit ourselves to a process of truth and reconciliation. In South Africa, people understood that we couldn't overcome apartheid without a commitment to truth and reconciliation . . .

. . . Well I believe that our identity is at risk. That when we actually don't care about these difficult things, the positive and wonderful things are nonetheless implicated. We love innovation. We love technology. We love creativity. We love entertainment. But ultimately, those realities are shadowed by suffering, abuse, degradation, marginalization. And for me, it becomes necessary to integrate the two. Because ultimately we are talking about a need to be more hopeful, more committed, more dedicated to the basic challenges of living in a complex world. And for me that means spending time thinking and talking about the poor, the disadvantaged . . . But thinking about them in a way that is integrated in our own lives.

You know ultimately, we all have to believe things we haven't seen. We do. As rational as we are, as committed to intellect as we are. Innovation, creativity, development comes not from the ideas in our mind alone. They come from the ideas in our mind that are also fueled by some conviction in our heart. And it's that mind-heart connection that I believe compels us to not just be attentive to all the bright and dazzly things, but also the dark and difficult things. Vaclav Havel, the great Czech leader, talked about this. He said, "When we were in Eastern Europe and dealing with oppression, we wanted all kinds of things, but mostly what we needed was hope, an orientation of the spirit, a willingness to sometimes be in hopeless places and be a witness . . ."

I had the great privilege, when I was a young lawyer, of meeting Rosa Parks. And Ms. Parks used to come back to Montgomery every now and then, and she would get together with two of her dearest friends, these older women, Johnnie Carr who was the organizer of the Montgomery bus boycott—amazing African American woman—and Virginia Durr, a white woman, whose husband, Clifford Durr, represented Dr. King. And these women would get together and just talk.

And every now and then Ms. Carr would call me, and she'd say, "Bryan, Ms. Parks is coming to town. We're going to get together and talk. Do you want to come over and listen?" And I'd say, "Yes, Ma'am, I do." And she'd say, "Well what are you going to do when you get here?" I said, "I'm going to listen." And I'd go over there and I would, I would just listen. It would be so energizing and so empowering.

And one time I was over there listening to these women talk, and after a couple of hours Ms. Parks turned to me and she said, "Now Bryan, tell me what the Equal Justice Initiative is. Tell me what you're trying to do." And I began giving her my rap. I said, "Well we're trying to challenge injustice. We're trying to help people who have been wrongly convicted. We're trying to confront bias and discrimination in the administration of criminal justice. We're trying to end life without parole sentences for children. We're trying to do something about the death penalty. We're trying to reduce the prison population. We're trying to end mass incarceration."

I gave her my whole rap, and when I finished she looked at me and she said, "Mmm mmm mmm." She said, "That's going to make you tired, tired, tired." (Laughter.) And that's when Ms. Carr leaned forward, she put her finger in my face, she said, "That's why you've got to be brave, brave, brave."

. . . We need to find ways to embrace these challenges, these problems, the suffering. Because ultimately, our humanity depends on everyone's humanity. I've learned very simple things doing the work that I do. It's just taught me very simple things. I've come to understand and to believe that each of us is more than the worst thing we've ever done. I believe that for every person on the planet. I think if somebody tells a lie, they're not just a liar. I think if somebody takes something that doesn't belong to them, they're not just a thief. I think even if you kill someone, you're not just a killer. And because of that there's this basic human dignity that must be respected by law. I also believe that in many parts of this country, and certainly in many parts of this globe, that the opposite of poverty is not wealth. I don't believe that. I actually think, in too many places, the opposite of poverty is justice.

And finally, I believe that, despite the fact that it is so dramatic and so beautiful and so inspiring and so stimulating, we will ultimately not be judged by our technology, we won't be judged by our design, we won't be judged by our intellect and reason. Ultimately, you judge the character of a society, not by how they treat their rich and the powerful and the privileged, but by how they treat the poor, the condemned, the incarcerated. Because it's in that nexus that we actually begin to understand truly profound things about who we are.[1]

1 Bryan Stevenson, "We Need to Talk About an Injustice," speech presented at TED Conference, March 2012, available at https://www.ted.com/talks/bryan_stevenson_we_need_to_talk_about_an_injustice/transcript (accessed May 28, 2014).

A LIFELINE FOR DEMOCRACY

Ruth Simmons was born into an East Texas family of sharecroppers in the 1940s. In her 2005 commencement speech at the University of Vermont, excerpted below, she describes experiences that helped her escape the poverty and discrimination of her youth to become the president of Brown University.

In my estimation, there is no greater benefit to a child nor greater boon to any nation than the provision of education to every citizen. Education develops intellectual resources, makes possible the advancement of knowledge helpful to society's well-being, and assures the innovation so necessary to ongoing economic vitality. Education prompts the development of capacities that would often otherwise lie fallow, and nurtures a respect for reason and civility, both important to maintaining peace and stability throughout the world. As a personal benefit, education helps one establish a healthy relationship with the broader world. For me, education has done all of this and so much more. Rescuing me from intellectual hunger and deprivation, it has given me the tools to understand the context into which I was born, and positioned me to surpass the limitations imposed on me by history and circumstance. . . .

In 1951 when I started grade school in rural East Texas, the America that I knew was penuriously exploitative, shockingly bigoted, deeply and hypocritically divided along racial lines, and headed for national disaster. My father and mother were living at the time in a small four-room house atop a knoll overlooking the sprawling, fertile cotton fields where they worked as laborers. Neither of them had been schooled beyond the eighth grade. Eleven children had preceded me in our household, so when I arrived there were naturally expressions of exasperation by the older children who understood the consequences of yet another mouth to feed. I was delivered by Miss Addie Bryant, who, as a midwife, was one of the most respected people in our small community. In a community where no one was well educated, a midwife was considered to be in the upper echelon of society. My older sisters and brothers had only occasional opportunity to attend school; the primary responsibility of everyone in our sharecropping family, including the smallest children, was to harvest cotton so, when there was work to do in the fields, school attendance suffered. As a result, few of us were able to attend school with enough frequency to graduate from high school.

But I was lucky. I began school at a time when the cotton gin was taking hold, causing sharecroppers to seek opportunities for employment in cities. Before my parents would make the move to Houston, where I received most of my schooling, I was introduced to education at W. R. Banks School for Colored Children. That first year was an introduction to a world that I could scarcely believe existed: a world where brawn had little bearing, where winning was encouraged, and where no limitations marred achievement. Little could I have imagined the path that I would take as a result of Miss Ida Mae initiating me into a new and exciting world of learning.

Miss Ida Mae Henderson was renowned for her teaching. I don't know if the principal deliberately chose her for first graders because of her inviting personality but everyone I have heard speak of her lights up when they recall their time in Miss Ida Mae's class. What struck one most about her persona was her extraordinary enthusiasm for her students. I had never met anyone so enthusiastic about learning and so full of fervor for the achievement of children. Imagine a rag tag group of poor country children, dressed in tatters, wearing shoes held together with string and minimally nourished. Now imagine them, too, sitting in a bright, cheerfully decorated classroom with a teacher whose attitude and voice bespoke joy at the presence of these children. If you can imagine this miracle, you can possibly appreciate why the sunshine from Miss Ida Mae's voice and smile transfixed us, making us want to bask in that kind of radiance, hopefulness and confidence forever. That is how I came to love learning, by watching someone else who had been infused with the spirit of learning.

Miss Ida Mae was the first person I met who was college educated and, although I did not understand at the time why she was so different from anything I had ever known, I knew that education had wrought something wondrous in her. That something was a delight in learning and in imparting that knowledge to others. The luminescence that radiated from her respect and enthusiasm for learning drew us in. Absorbing her every instruction, I worked hard to secure abundant praise from her, and was convinced that something momentous was happening to my life now that she was in it. With her as my tour guide, I thought I had been given keys to a magic kingdom long before I heard of Walt Disney's. In this kingdom, I was free to go anywhere without worrying about racial restrictions. All the limitations my parents had known fell away as I grasped the power of my mind to push aside the barriers they had experienced and had anticipated for me.

Arriving in Houston the next year, I discovered miraculously that Miss Ida Mae was not the only teacher who was dedicated, uplifting, forceful and self-confident. There were many others with high standards, excellent skills and charismatic personalities who were every-day models for life. Mrs. Caraway, Mrs. Washington, Mrs. Parish, Mr. Saunders, Mrs. Lillie and so many more like them filled my years of public school with admonitions concerning hard work and high attainment. These teachers, working in the inner city schools, did the work of social workers, philanthropists, mentors, counselors, advocates, civic icons, and moral exemplars. They formed a tightly knit network of care that kept communities going and, most importantly, kept the promise of social change and civil rights alive. Through their efforts, change did come.

I recall this story every day as a reminder of the power of education. . . . Learning makes possible the most daunting and elusive change. If you have not discovered that yet, you will learn it in myriad ways over the coming years. Because you have enlarged your reach through learning, you will have the opportunity to influence others in the way teachers changed my life. The light that shone from Miss Ida Mae has lit my path for over forty years. What is the light that you will shine for others? By the way you respect yourself and others? By the way you care for your family? By the openness you have to difference? By the gratitude and humility you show for what you have been given? By the winning spirit that you bring to everything you do? . . .

Teachers remain at the heart of any education that takes root on the one hand and uplifts on the other. They do not merely provide tools or point out which path to take on this voyage. They pack our bags, set us on our way, and give us maps for the most scenic ride of our lives. Along the way we see the history of the world unfold. We see the beauty of what god and man have produced. We learn the elements of design and harmony that give greater meaning and enjoyment to our lives. We see how problems are solved and conflicts are abated. We see the tragic consequences of bigotry, want, and human degradation. Each of us has had a moment of recognition when we understood the value of learning. To have a guide in that process who not only leads us to shore but repeatedly casts us back upon the sea until we can find our own way back to shore is of defining importance. Teaching, wherever it occurs, is a lifeline for individuals, communities, nations, the world.[1]

---

1 Ruth J. Simmons, speech presented at the University of Vermont (Burlington, VT), May 29, 2005, available at http://www.uvm.edu/~cmncmnt/commencement2005/?Page=simmons_commencementspeech05.htm (accessed Oct. 10, 2014).

Connecting to the Writing Prompt

After completing this unit, students will need time to complete their evidence logs, to continue to develop and refine their thesis, and then to begin the process of organizing their evidence and drafting their essays.

GATHERING EVIDENCE

Give students the opportunity to review the documents they encountered in Lessons 15 and 16. Which events, arguments, and other information in the documents connect to the writing prompt? Give students with the opportunity to continue their evidence logs.

Ask students to reflect on the new evidence they have recorded. Does it confirm or conflict with their thinking about the question posed in the prompt? Has what they have learned about the purpose of history and the legacies of Reconstruction changed their thinking about the prompt? Have students record their thinking in their journals.

CONTINUING THE WRITING PROCESS

The "Writing Strategies" section of our website at facinghistory.org/reconstruction-era provides a variety of activities and strategies to help you guide students in completing the writing process and publishing their essays. We recommend that you consult this resource as students

- craft a thesis and organize their ideas;
- support the thesis with evidence and analysis;
- write an introduction and conclusion
- draft, revise, and edit their essays; and
- publish and share their essays and reflect on the writing process.

APPENDIX

Fostering a Reflective Classroom

We believe that a Facing History and Ourselves classroom is in many ways a microcosm of democracy—a place where explicit rules and implicit norms protect everyone's right to speak; where different perspectives can be heard and valued; where members take responsibility for themselves, each other, and the group as a whole; and where each member has a stake and a voice in collective decisions.

You may have already established rules and guidelines with your students to help bring about these characteristics in your classroom. If not, it is essential at the beginning of your Facing History unit to facilitate the development of a supportive, reflective classroom community. Once this is established, both you and your students will need to nurture the reflective community on an ongoing basis through the ways that you participate and respond to each other.

We believe that a reflective, supportive classroom community is fostered by

- creating a sense of trust and openness;

- encouraging participants to speak and listen to each other;

- making space and time for silent reflection;

- offering multiple avenues for participation and learning; and

- helping students appreciate the points of view, talents, and contributions of less vocal members.

CREATING A CLASSROOM CONTRACT

One way to help classroom communities establish shared norms is by discussing them openly through a process called "contracting." Some teachers already customarily create classroom contracts with their students at the start of each course. If you do not typically do so, we recommend that before beginning your class's journey through this Facing History unit, you engage the students in the process of creating one. Contracts typically include several clearly defined rules or expectations for participation as well as consequences for those who do not fulfill their obligations as members of the learning community. Any contract created collaboratively, by students and the teacher together, should be consistent with the classroom rules already established by the teacher. Many Facing History teachers differentiate their own classroom rules, which are non-negotiable, from the guidelines set forth in the classroom contract, which are negotiated by the students with the teacher's guidance.

Consider the following list of guidelines for your classroom contract:

- Listen with respect. Try to understand what someone is saying before rushing to judgment.

- Make comments using "I" statements. ("I disagree with what you said. Here's what I think . . .")

- If you do not feel safe making a comment or asking a question, write it down. You can ask the teacher after class to help you find a safe way to share the idea.

- If someone says an idea or question that helps your own learning, say "thank you."

- If someone says something that hurts or offends you, do not attack the person. Acknowledge that the comment, not the person, hurt your feelings and explain why.

- Put-downs are never okay.

- If you don't understand something, ask a question.

- Think with your head and your heart.

- Share talking time—provide room for others to speak.

- Do not interrupt others while they are speaking

- Write down thoughts in a journal or notebook if you don't have time to say them during our time together.

We have also found that the classroom environment is enhanced by emphasizing journal writing and employing multiple formats for facilitating large and small group discussions. Throughout this unit, we suggest specific teaching strategies designed to encourage students' critical thinking and encourage each of them to share their ideas. Detailed descriptions and additional examples of these strategies can be found in the "Teaching Strategies" section of our website at facinghistory.org/reconstruction-era/strategies.

Journals in a Facing History Classroom

Keeping a journal is one tool that Facing History and Ourselves has found to be instrumental in helping students develop their ability to critically examine their surroundings from multiple perspectives and to make informed judgments about what they see and hear. Many students find that writing or drawing in a journal helps them process ideas, formulate questions, and retain information. Journals make learning visible by providing a safe, accessible space for students to share thoughts, feelings, and uncertainties. In this way, journals are also an assessment tool—something teachers can review to better understand what their students know, what they are struggling to understand, and how their thinking has changed over time. Journal writing serves other purposes, as well. Journals help to nurture classroom community. Through reading and commenting on journals, teachers build relationships with students. Frequent journal writing also helps students become more fluent in expressing their ideas in writing or speaking.

Students use their journals in different ways. Some students may record ideas throughout class, while others may only use it when there is a particular teacher-driven assignment. Some students need prompts to support their writing, while others feel more comfortable expressing their ideas without any external structure. Just as students vary in how they use their journals, teachers also vary in their approach to journal writing. While there are many effective ways to use a journal as a learning tool in the classroom, below are six questions, drawn from decades of experience working with teachers and students, that we suggest you consider.

1. **What is the teacher's relationship to students' journals?** Students are entitled to know how you plan on reading their journals. Will you read everything they write? If they want to keep something private, is this possible? If so, how do students indicate that they do not want you to read something? Many teachers establish a rule that if students wish to keep information in their journals private, they should fold the page over or remove the page entirely.

   Will their journals be graded? If so, by what criteria? (See more on grading journals below.) For teachers at most schools, it can be impossible to read everything students write in their journals; there just is not enough time in the day. For this reason, some teachers decide that they will collect students' journals once a week and only read a page or two—sometimes a page the student selects and sometimes a page selected by the teacher. Other teachers may never collect students' journals but might glance at them during class time or might ask students to incorporate quotations and ideas from their journals into collected assignments. You can set limits on the degree to which you have access to students' journals.

2. **What is appropriate content for journals?** It is easy for students to confuse a class journal with a diary (or blog) because both of these formats allow for open-ended writing. Teachers should clarify how the audience and purpose for this writing is distinct from the audience and purpose for writing in a personal diary. In most classrooms, the audience for journal writing is the author, the teacher, and, at times, peers. Facing History and Ourselves believes that the purpose of journal writing is to provide a space where students can connect their

personal experiences and opinions to the concepts and events they are studying in the classroom. Therefore, some material that is appropriate to include in their personal diaries may not be appropriate to include in their class journals. To avoid uncomfortable situations, many teachers find it helpful to clarify topics that are not suitable material for journal entries. Also, as mandatory reporters in most school districts, teachers should explain that they are required to take certain steps, such as informing a school official, if students reveal information about possible harm to themselves or another student. Students should be made aware of these rules, as well as other guidelines you might have about appropriate journal writing content.

3. **How will journals be evaluated?** Many students admit that they are less likely to share their true thoughts or express questions when they are worried about a grade based on getting the "right" answer or using proper grammar or spelling. Therefore, we suggest that if you choose to grade students' journals, which many teachers decide to do, you base these grades on criteria such as effort, thoughtfulness, completion, creativity, curiosity, and making connections between the past and the present. Additionally, there are many ways to provide students with feedback on their journals besides traditional grading, such as by writing comments or asking questions. Students can even evaluate their own journals for evidence of intellectual and moral growth. For example, you might have students look through their journals to find evidence of their ability to ask questions or to make connections between what was happening during Reconstruction and events from their own lives.

4. **What forms of expression can be included in a journal?** Students learn and communicate best in different ways. The journal is an appropriate space to respect different learning styles. Some students may wish to draw their ideas rather than record thoughts in words. Other students may feel most comfortable responding in concept webs and lists, as opposed to prose. When you introduce the journal to students, you might brainstorm different ways that they might express their thoughts.

5. **How can journals be used to help students build vocabulary?** Throughout this unit, students will be encountering new vocabulary while they develop a more sophisticated understanding of concepts that might already be familiar to them. The journal can be used as a place to help students build their vocabulary by constructing "working definitions." The phrase "working definition" implies that our understanding of concepts evolves as we are confronted with new information and experiences. Students' definitions of words such as *identity* or *freedom* should be richer at the end of the unit than they are on day one. We suggest that you use perhaps a special section of the journal as a space where students can record, review, and refine their definitions of important terms referred to in this unit.

6. **How should journal content be publicly shared?** Most Facing History teachers have found that students are best able to express themselves when they believe that their journal is a private space. Therefore, we suggest that information in students' journals never be publicly shared without the consent of the writer. At the same time, we encourage you to provide multiple opportunities for students to voluntarily share ideas and questions that they have recorded in their journals. Some students may feel more comfortable reading directly from their journals than speaking "off the cuff" in class discussions.

7. Once you settle on the norms and expectations for journal writing in your class, there are many possible ways that you can have students record ideas in their journals. Here are some examples:

Teacher-selected prompts: One of the most common ways that teachers use journals is by asking students to respond to a particular prompt. This writing often prepares students to participate in a class activity, helps students make connections between the themes of a lesson and their own lives, or provides an opportunity for students to make meaning of ideas in a reading or film.

Dual-entry format: Students draw a line down the center of the journal page or fold the page in half. They write the factual notes ("What the text says" or "What the historians say") on one side and, on the other side, their feelings about the notes ("Reactions").

"Lifted line" responses: One way to have students respond to what they have read is to ask them to "lift a line"—select a particular quotation that strikes them—and then answer questions such as, "What is interesting about this quotation? What ideas does it make you think about? What questions does this line raise for you?"

Brainstorming: The journal is an appropriate place for students to freely list ideas related to a specific word or question. To activate prior knowledge before students learn new material, you might ask students to brainstorm everything they know about a concept or an event. As a strategy for reviewing material, you might ask students to brainstorm ideas they remember about a topic. Moreover, as a pre-writing exercise, students can brainstorm ways of responding to an essay prompt.

Freewriting: Freewriting is open, no-format writing. Freewriting can be an especially effective strategy when you want to help students process particularly sensitive or provocative material. Some students respond extremely well to freewriting, while other students benefit from more structure, even if that means a loosely framed prompt such as, "What are you thinking about after watching/reading/hearing this material? What does this text remind you of?"

Creative writing: Many students enjoy writing poems or short stories that incorporate the themes addressed in a particular lesson. Some students benefit from ideas that structure their writing to stimulate their work, such as a specific poem format or an opening line for a story (for example, "I could not believe my eyes when my friend came running down the street, yelling . . .").

Drawings, charts, and webs: Students do not have to express their ideas in words. At appropriate times, encourage students to draw their feelings or thoughts. They can also use symbols, concept maps, Venn diagrams, and other charts to record information.

Note-taking: To help students retain new information, they can record notes in their journals. Notes might be taken in various formats, such as lists, concept maps, and graphic organizers.

Vocabulary: Students can use their journals as a place to keep their working definitions of terms, noting how those definitions change as they go deeper into the resources. The back section of the journal could be used as a glossary—the place where students record definitions and where they can turn to review and revise their definitions as these terms come up throughout the unit.

CREDITS

Grateful acknowledgment is made for permission to reproduce the following: